River Basins
of the American West

River Basins
of the American West

A *HIGH COUNTRY NEWS* READER

Edited by Char Miller

Oregon State University Press
Corvallis

The paper in this book meets the guidelines for permanence and durability of the Committee on Production Guidelines for Book Longevity of the Council on Library Resources and the minimum requirements of the American National Standard for Permanence of Paper for Printed Library Materials Z39.48-1984.

Library of Congress Cataloging-in-Publication Data
River basins of the American West : a High country news reader / edited by Char Miller.
    p. cm.
 Includes index.
 ISBN 978-0-87071-574-7 (alk. paper)
 1. Watersheds--West (U.S.) 2. Watershed management--West (U.S.)
I. Miller, Char, 1951. II. High country news.
 GB991.W3R58 2009
 333.91'620978--dc22

2009012190

First published in 2009 by Oregon State University Press
Printed in the United States of America

Oregon State University Press
121 The Valley Library
Corvallis OR 97331-4501
541-737-3166 • fax 541-737-3170
http://oregonstate.edu/dept/press

Contents

Continental Divides

Char Miller

When flying over the American West at thirty-five thousand feet, you begin to understand why John Wesley Powell argued that the region's watersheds have had a profound impact on its landscapes, natural and human. "In a group of mountains a small river has its source," he wrote in his landmark *Report on the Lands in the Arid Region of the United States* (1876). "A dozen or a score of creeks unite to form the trunk. The creeks higher up divide into brooks. All these streams combined form the drainage system of the hydrographic basin, a unit of country well defined in nature, for it is bounded above and on each side by heights of land that rise as crests to part the waters. Thus hydraulic basin is segregated by hydraulic basin by nature herself, and the landmarks are practically perpetual." (*Report*, page 113)

That pattern, which Powell, the first head of the U. S. Geological Survey, observed with boots to ground we bear witness to while winging from St. Louis to Denver, San Antonio to Los Angeles, or Seattle to Salt Lake City (or any point in between): the West's iconic mountains—the Rockies and Sierra, Wasatch and Cascades—like its less famous and smaller ranges, over the millennia have shed billions of gallons of water that have carved through hard rock and soft soil to create its remarkable watercourses.

These rivers' names are as storied as their sources are renowned. The Yellowstone River, which rises out of the Absaroka Range in northwestern Wyoming, flows north through the eponymous national park and then turns eastward: it is joined by the Bighorn, Tongue, and Powder before merging with the Missouri, serving as its principal upper tributary. Another major tributary, the slow-moving Platte, links with the wide Missouri near Plattsmouth, Nebraska. In time their combined flow will surge into the Mississippi, emptying into the Gulf of Mexico south of New Orleans, thousands of miles from their manifold sources within the central and northern Rockies.

Another Rockies-based river is the 1,885-mile-long Rio Grande: at the base of southern Colorado's Canaby Mountain, a series of streams converge, cut south through the San Luis Valley, cross into New Mexico, running past

Albuquerque and Las Cruces, swinging south and east at El Paso, Texas. There, the river starts to delineate the 1,254-mile international border between Mexico and the United States and picks up tributary waters from the Rio Conchos on its south and later from the Pecos on the north; most years its sluggish movement has just enough energy to push into the Gulf of Mexico at Boca Chica, east of Brownsville.

The same cannot be said for the Colorado River: it rarely reaches its historic mouth on the Gulf of California. Originating out of La Poudre Pass Lake in the northern Rockies, it carries a staggering volume of water as it angles west and south into Utah, Arizona, and California, where its erosive force has created a stunning series of canyons, grand and small. A network of dams and reservoirs along its upper and lower reaches now controls the Colorado's 1,450-mile run, however, allowing agricultural interests and urban water purveyors to pump out its waters and diminish its flow; even its last major tributary, the Gila, which draws on a watershed that includes the San Pedro (whose headwaters lie in northern Mexico), does little to propel the Colorado: the once-thunderous river slows to a trickle as it enters Mexico, seeping into its desiccated delta.

The Columbia suffers no such fate despite its legendary dam structures. Its headwaters are in southeastern British Columbia and its 1,243-mile course begins in a northwesterly direction, sweeps almost one hundred and eighty degrees around the Selkirk Mountains, heading south along the western slope of the Columbia Mountains; joined by the Kootenay, Canoe, and Pend Orielle (the latter's tributaries include Montana's Clark Fork and Flathead rivers), it enters Washington State on its race to the Pacific. The Columbia's expansive drainage within the United States covers more than 225,000 square miles, sprawls across seven states, and absorbs the discharge from, among many others, the Crab, the Snake and the Yakima, the John Day, Deschutes, and Willamette, before surging into the ocean near Astoria, Oregon.

Smaller systems abound throughout the West. The heavy snow that can create white-out conditions in the Cascades melts come spring to form the 263-mile-long Klamath, which flows south and west from its Oregon headwaters into California, picking up additional water from the

Williamson, Scott, Salmon, and Trinity. Another river with its origins in the Cascades, the 447-mile-long Sacramento, gains its initial impulse from the Mt. Shasta drainage district, runs straight south through the northern stretch of California's Central Valley, and near Antioch meets the San Joaquin, which springs from Sierran snowmelt; their fertile delta has established one of the west coast's largest estuaries. Other more (and less) biologically rich rivers pulse down from the Sierras, Wasatch, and other interior ranges, feeding lakes wet and dry, among them California's Owens, Mono, and Soda; Utah's Great Salt and Bonneville basins; and Nevada's innumerable playa. Whether seen from the stratosphere or from a more down-to-earth vista, it is clear how much water has sculpted the topographical contours of the American West.

That does not mean that the region is uniformly wet, a point Powell hammered home in his report on western aridity. The lack of precipitation, he asserted, would offer the most rigorous challenges to European-Americans expecting to plant communities within this land of little rain. With the exception of migrants who ended up in the Columbia and Central California watersheds, those pressing west in the late nineteenth century and whose experience lay in the humid east were in for a shock, a fraught situation that led Powell to an unusual conclusion: the only settlement pattern that made sense was one framed inside the region's many watersheds. It would be folly, he cautioned, to presume that what had worked in well-watered climes would work beyond the Ninety-eighth meridian; this wet-dry boundary running north-south along the Great Plains instead must mark the western limit of the rigidly rectangular structure of private property that surveyors had laid down across the trans-Appalachian public domain. Arid country could not sustain the classic homesteads situated on one-hundred-sixty-acre sections in Ohio, Minnesota, or Arkansas that could ignore environmental realities because water there was relatively plentiful.

Such ignorance would be deadly in the Utah, Arizona, or New Mexico Territories. In these bone-dry landscapes, communities must adapt themselves to hydraulic realities; individual land-ownership, social development, and political organization must be coterminous with local watersheds. Because each such district "is a commonwealth by itself," Powell asserted, "there is a body of interdependent and unified interests and values, all collected in one hydraulic basin, and all segregated by well-defined boundary lines from the rest of the world." United by "common interests, common rights, and common duties," the residents "would work together for common purposes." Should the "entire arid region be organized into natural hydrographic districts," out of its environmental constraints would emerge a political virtue: democracy would be reborn. (*Report*, page 114)

Few paid heed to his innovative resolution or to the warning it contained. Survey chains were laid down across the Great Plains, up and over mountain ranges, through valleys and deserts, stopping only when they reached the edge of the sea. However mathematically logical this subdivisional impulse may have been, it has been responsible—as Powell predicted—for the subsequent and incessant conflicts over the flow, distribution, and control of the water that has been so central to the history of the modern West. It remains key as well to understanding many of the region's economic dilemmas, environmental conundrums, political dislocations, and social inequities. These disruptions and difficulties are the very subject of *River Basins of the American West*, which, as its title suggests, adopts as its organizing structure Powell's principled argument for how best to understand this contentious terrain.

Everywhere the fights have been intense. For more than a century westerners have resorted to bribery, intimidation, and violence; made ready use of the local, state, and federal judiciary; lobbied in legislative assemblies; formed special-interest committees and grassroots organizations to demand the redress they felt was their due. Whatever the chosen strategy, however complex the end results, regardless of place or time, few have been fully satisfied with the results. Yet as it captures some of the most recent squabbles, this collection of articles that first appeared in *High Country News*, the West's environmental journal of record, also reflects some of the out-of-the-box thinking that has begun to resolve some of the region's most enduring and turbulent water fights.

The struggles over the Colorado are a case in point. From the delta to its source, the river bears the marks of a heavy human hand. Dams and diversions have weakened its pulsing energy; massive structures such as the Hoover and Glen Canyon dams have trapped sediment that used to wash into the Gulf of California and have altered the river's currents and temperature—damaging ecosystems, compromising aquatic life, and challenging the viability of some communities along its course. To resolve any of these complicated upstream-downstream issues requires cooperation between Mexico and the United States; internal policy coordination at the federal and state levels in both countries; and a consensus developed among affected areas, rural and urban, whose interests often seem at odds with one another.

Despite this welter of difference and disagreement, there has been some positive movement: beginning in the Clinton administration and continuing through the Bush years, the Department of the Interior has interceded with states battling over the apportionment of the Colorado's waters, a negotiation process that has resulted in California drawing less from the river and committing to increased conservation measures. Some of the technological fixes have been straightforward: canals have been lined with concrete to reduce seepage, a simple solution that has had the unanticipated result of stopping up leaks that Mexican farmers in northern Baja California had depended on to irrigate their fields. And conservation initiatives will be hard pressed to solve the most recent tension—booming population growth along the borderlands is being confronted with an intensifying drought that will have a deleterious impact on life in Los Angeles, Mexicali, and Phoenix.

The situation in Albuquerque, El Paso and Ciudad Juarez, Los Dos Laredos, and Brownsville is no less precarious. That's because the Rio Grande/Rio Bravo del Norte is also affected by declining snowmelt in the Rockies that must be apportioned among a series of competitive users. Capturing these shrinking waters are dams and reservoirs each nation has constructed; how much they hold and release is determined by international treaty that is observed more often in the breach. Ignored

TECHNOCENTRISM

often are the endangered species—such as the Rio Grande silvery minnow—whose life cycles depend on the river functioning as a river. And then there are issues of water quality: metal-laden tailings have been flushed into one of its northern tributaries, the Red, devastating the health of those whose drinking waters came from its toxic stew; farther downstream, urban effluent and agricultural runoff create an unsavory mix. Meanwhile, the twined river-border cities are scrambling to enact water-efficiency regulations; wetlands-restoration activists are seeking legal redress; social-justice advocates are demanding better sanitation and housing for an impoverished citizenry. Imagining the borderlands as its own community may be the first step to constructing the much-needed cross-border coalitions—and a healthier river and body politic—but it is also a monumentally difficult one.

So the Roman Catholic bishops of British Columbia and the Pacific Northwest states discovered when they anointed the Columbia River a sacramental commons. They hoped that by injecting a spiritual dimension into the decades-long dispute over the relative value of fish, farms, dams that they might help broker a bit of earthly peace. Naturally, they stirred up a hornets' nest, although they were not the first to get stung: the Columbia watershed has been beset with contending forces unable to compromise. That is because the dams that so disrupt salmon's migratory patterns and native peoples' lives are keystone features in the wider region's agricultural development, urban growth, and hydropower production. These conflicts of interest only intensify during periodic droughts—the Cascades, like the Rockies, are experiencing diminished precipitation—and have led to a spike in lawsuits so that one petitioner can secure a perceived advantage over another. Still, there is hope embedded within the bishops' pastoral letter, and the emergence of such groups as the Deschutes River Conservancy, whose board of directors reflects the diversity of people who need and use that Columbian tributary. Creating incentives to produce water-saving actions on farms has freed up water for salmon, an incremental solution that if it successfully reconciles the seemingly irreconcilable, may prove a miracle cure.

More miraculous still would be a plan to smooth out the tensions that for decades have roiled the Klamath basin and Missouri's vast watershed. Here too the tensions revolve around dams, irrigation, and endangered species; here too the oft-cross-cutting purposes of governmental agencies, tribal authorities, irrigation districts, and grassroots entities have strained their collective capacity to develop a working solution to what all concede is a tremendously knotty set of problems. To secure a more hopeful future, one participant in the Klamath negotiations acknowledged, "you gotta let go of some of the past."

Yet one path towards that future might well draw on an older argument. What Dan Luecke, a National Wildlife Federation consultant, said of the Platte holds true for a raft of other western rivers: "We're trying to invent a way of governing ourselves on a different political basis, and that political basis is a watershed." John Wesley Powell could not have said it any better.

Indeed, a Powellian calculation figures in the efforts of those dedicated to restoring the West's many brooks, creeks, and streams. Their efforts to regenerate native fish population in the San Juan River; clean up the channelized Alamosa; revegetate the Clark Fork; rebuild riparian habitat along the Weminuche; undam the Mokelumne; and reforest Seattle's Cedar River watershed are akin to the Hoopa people's campaign to bring back salmon on the Trinity River or to those fighting to reintroduce them to the San Joaquin or Yakima—all want to resuscitate flat-lined western waterways.

Whatever the character of these diverse organizations, the very fact of their existence is striking: each is devoted to a precise bioregion, with a tight focus on a particular place that confirms how vital river basins are to all flora and fauna, not least to the human communities from which these dedicated groups spring. By their actions, which embody the confluence of geographic orientation and communal action, they are laying down the foundation for the watershed commonwealths that John Wesley Powell believed would be the salvation of the American West.

commonwealths
↓
salvation of the
west

The Colorado River

A River Resurrected

Michelle Nijhuis

Ejido Luis Encinas Johnson, Sonora, Mexico—There are plenty of rumors about the last stretch of the Colorado River. Most say it's a trickle, a dead zone, a river no more. A paradise lost for good.

Juan Butron knows it's not quite that simple.

Butron and I are standing next to a line of rusting trucks at the edge of a crumbling riverbank, looking fifteen feet down at the wide, shallow flow of the Colorado River at low tide. On the pale-blue horizon, we can see the mouth of the river draining into the Gulf of California. Upstream, a few members of the Cucapa Tribe fish in the salty waters.

This delta was once covered with millions of acres of lush wetlands formed by the ever-shifting, powerful flow of the Colorado River. But upstream dams and diversions have taken their toll during the last century. Behind us now is nothing but desert—not the towering-cactus kind of desert, but a salt-soaked desert with hardly a plant in sight.

The mouth of the river used to sustain fields of cotton and wheat in nearby Ejido Johnson, the tiny town where Butron and his family have lived for almost thirty years. In the *ejido*, Spanish for a communal farming settlement, only a fraction of the land is still good for agriculture. Each morning before dawn, busloads of people leave the town's dusty main street for jobs at foreign-owned farms or factories near the border.

It doesn't sound like life is getting better in the Colorado River Delta. But there's a slim chance it will. During the past twenty years, Butron and his neighbors have watched flood flows and wastewater rejuvenate a few places in the delta, creating river and wetland habitat nearly unmatched on the stretch of the Colorado in the United States. These signs of life have inspired hope in the small towns here, and they've energized other Mexicans who care about the delta. And for the first time, environmental groups in the United States are leaping over the international border that hides the mouth of the Colorado River from the rest of the basin. They're trying to change the oldest unwritten law of the river: Take all the water you can get, and never let it go.

Few accounts of the glory days of the delta survive, but we do have one star witness. In 1922, conservationist Aldo Leopold spent several weeks paddling a canoe through the delta's wetlands in Mexico.

"The still waters were of a deep and emerald hue, colored by algae, I suppose, but no less green for all that," he wrote. "A verdant wall of mesquite and willow separated the channel from the thorny desert beyond. At each bend we saw egrets standing in the pools ahead, each white statue matched by its white reflection. Fleets of cormorants drove their black prows in quest of skittering mullets; avocets, willets and yellow-legs dozed one-legged on the bars; mallards, widgeons and teal sprang skyward in alarm."

In its prime, the Colorado River dumped about 70 percent of its substantial sediment load near its mouth, at the end of its journey to the sea. Think of the uncountable tons of soil and rock that once filled Glen Canyon, Boulder Canyon, and the Grand Canyon; most of that rode the river current southward for hundreds of miles. Over time, the Colorado deposited a deep wedge of fertile soil stretching from north of what is now Palm Springs, California, to the Gulf of California. The soil was the foundation for the verdant forests Leopold described, and it now supports the produce empire in the Mexicali and Imperial valleys.

Healthy river deltas are restless places. The river was once its own manager, building and demolishing earthen dams of soil, flooding and then abandoning depressions such as the Salton Sink. Wetlands and gallery forests formed and reformed along the river, harboring rich populations of birds, fish, and even bobcats and jaguars, who came down from the nearby Cucapa Mountains to hunt in the delta.

A working delta is also a battleground between river and sea. In November of the same year that Leopold was peacefully paddling through the delta, the little steamboat *Toplobampo* chugged upriver from the Gulf of California. There wasn't anything unusual about that; in the nineteenth century, the delta was navigable, and steamboats traveled frequently between Yuma, Arizona, and the Gulf of California. But this particular steamboat never made it to port. A fifteen-foot-high wall of water knocked it flat in the middle of the night, killing eighty-six of its one hundred and twenty-five passengers and marooning the rest for days on the scorching, mosquito-ridden mud flats.

"There was hardly time for a single cry," wrote Frank Waters in his 1946 book *The Colorado*. "The wave caught the *Toplobampo* squarely abeam, snapped the hawsers like threads, and rolled the ship over like a log."

That wall of water was the Colorado's tidal bore, the dramatic result of the clash between fresh- and saltwater. The Gulf of California is famous for the enormous tides that barrel up through the narrow channel between the Baja Peninsula and mainland Mexico. When those tides funneled into the roaring mouth of the unfettered Colorado, no one wanted to be in the way.

This sometimes violent mix of waters in the delta formed one of the largest and most productive estuaries in the world. Fish such as corvina, mullet, and tilapia were plentiful in the southern delta, and shrimp abounded in the upper gulf. The Cucapa Tribe, the "river people" whose members once lived off the delta's harvest of game and native plants, found their best hunting grounds at the mouth of the river.

But the river people and the delta's wildlife were the last to be considered when the waters of the Colorado were divvied up. The 1922 compact on the river split up all the water among the seven U.S. basin states, and no water was set aside for Mexico until the two countries signed a treaty in 1944. The treaty promised Mexico 1.5 million acre-feet of water every year—about 10 percent of the river's flow—but all of that was quickly diverted for agriculture in the Mexicali Valley in northern Mexico.

During the dam-building era, floods became the lifeblood of the delta. For six years after Hoover Dam was completed in 1936, no water from the Colorado reached the sea. Then, after the reservoir filled, a trickle of floodwater made it past the system of dams and diversions and returned to the delta. In 1964, when Glen Canyon Dam was completed, the cycle began again.

Dams didn't erase the tidal bores, but they did make them a lot more ... boring. A few hours before or after our trip to the mouth of the river, Juan Butron and I would have seen the modern version of the tidal bore, a muddy rush of water filling the river's channel. High tide now overwhelms the paltry flow of the river, and the conditions in and near the river mouth are grimly referred to as a "negative estuary," a flow nearly as salty as the ocean. The salt has poisoned much of the wildlife that used to thrive here, and overfishing has almost finished off several species. The Cucapa dwindled with their livelihood, and only about two hundred still live in Mexico, largely isolated from the more than eight hundred tribal members who live on a reservation in Arizona.

The dams also trapped the rich silt that had once reached the delta, leaving only a colorless stream to cross the border. Now, the soil in the delta is eroding, not accumulating. The deep ditch that Juan Butron and I balanced beside is almost all that's left of the delta.

Almost, but not quite. Though the delta is still a damaged landscape, it's finally getting a few lucky breaks. Three years ago, a University of Arizona professor named Edward Glenn and his colleague, Carlos Valdes-Casillas, flew over the northern end of the Colorado River Delta in Mexico. Glenn had never had a bird's-eye view of the river above its confluence with the Rio Hardy, but he'd been exploring the delta region for more than two decades. He expected little more than a panoramic perspective on tamarisk groves and salt flats.

Instead, he and Valdes-Casillas saw a winding green thread of native cottonwood and willow trees along the river channel. "I said, 'Carlos, those aren't supposed to be there; those were supposed to disappear,' " says Glenn. "That sight revealed the whole story to us."

The story is this. For nearly twenty years after the completion of Glen Canyon Dam, almost no water from the river reached the ocean, and the tail end of the Colorado mostly lived up to its gloomy reputation. In 1968, flow readings at the southernmost measuring station on the Colorado were discontinued, since there was nothing to measure.

But by the early 1980s, all reservoirs on the river were full, and the U.S. Bureau of Reclamation allowed the extra water to occasionally flow across the border. It was too much for the Mexicali farm fields to soak up all at once, and in the flood year of 1983, the river reached the Gulf of California for the first time since Glen Canyon Dam went up. The wet winters of the 1990s continued the sporadic floods. Glenn says fish populations in the Mexican stretch of the river have "exploded," increasing as much as tenfold since the beginning of the floods.

Even though most of that water arrives too early in the year to help the riverside habitat, some of the native vegetation on the northern end of the delta has already sprouted back. When migratory songbirds cross the border, they're now welcomed by a sixty-mile-long corridor of forest, stretching from Morelos Dam to the river's confluence with the Rio Hardy. Because the river on the Mexican side is relatively free of riprap and concrete channels, the flood-fed recovery in Mexico is especially dramatic. Researchers estimate there are 34,500 acres of forest containing cottonwoods and willows along the river in Mexico, about three times more than along the lower Colorado in the United States.

"Like a lot of other people, I had a notion that there's sort of this lifeless sewer down there," says Jan Hart, an ornithologist with the U.S. Geological Survey who visited the river in Mexico for the first time last year. "I'd been hearing there were these stands of cottonwoods there, and it was hard for me to imagine, but there they were. When you work in the desert and you see those stands from a distance, it's like seeing veins of gold. You say, 'Wow, this is good habitat.' "

Yet that good habitat is sustained by chance alone. "Those flood flows are accidental, and they're in no way assured or allocated for the delta," says David Hogan of the Center for Biological Diversity's Southern California office. "Reclamation giveth, and Reclamation taketh away."

Edward Glenn knows all about the accidental generosity of the Bureau of Reclamation, since it's figured large in the delta's recent revival. A little more than a decade ago, he helped to uncover one of the agency's big secrets: its engineering has unintentionally created some of the best wildlife habitat in the delta.

In 1977, the Bureau completed work on the MODE canal, which every year carries thirty-five billion gallons of irrigation runoff southward from

Yuma, Arizona. The runoff dumps out on the eastern edge of the delta in Mexico, just a mile or so from Ejido Johnson.

Two years later, Glenn visited the end of the brand-new canal. "I wanted to see where all that water was going, and I found it had formed a great big lake," he says. "I kind of filed that away in my memory, and about ten years later ... I went down to the end of the canal again, and the lake had become a wetland. I knew it was really something, since that kind of habitat is really rare there."

Glenn thought he was the only person in the scientific world who knew about the fifty-thousand-acre marsh, which is in the delta but isolated from the Colorado River. Yet when he told staffers at the Bureau of Reclamation what he'd seen, they pulled out detailed maps from recent aerial surveys. "They knew everything about it," says Glenn. "They just weren't telling anyone."

The Bureau of Reclamation had its reasons for keeping quiet. The MODE, which stands for Main Outlet Drain Extension, was built to drain irrigation water from agricultural fields in southern Arizona while the agency constructed a $250 million desalting plant in Yuma. When the plant was completed, the agency planned to treat the irrigation water and put it in the Colorado River. That water would satisfy an amendment to the 1944 treaty, one that guarantees Mexico relatively pure water from the Colorado.

Then, the agency intended to use the canal to drain leftover brine into the marsh. The concentrated salt solution would kill the marsh and leave its wildlife with nowhere to go; Reclamation giveth, and Reclamation taketh away.

But the hugely expensive water-treatment project took almost twenty years to finish. During that time, the United States used floodwater to fulfill its obligation to Mexico, and irrigation runoff from the canal kept expanding the marsh, now called the Cienaga de Santa Clara. In 1992, the plant began operating at one-third capacity, but it was shut down less than a year later when a flood damaged the MODE.

In the early 1990s, several Mexican scientists recognized the ecological value of the *cienaga*. They pushed to include the new marsh in a biosphere reserve planned for the upper Gulf of California and the river delta, a designation sanctioned by the United Nations. In 1993, when the marsh was added to the reserve at the last minute, it instantly gained a new status that's hard to argue with.

"If anything happens with that water, if [the Bureau of Reclamation] decides to use it for the desalting plant in Yuma, everybody is going to blame them, because the Cienaga de Santa Clara is a famous place now," says Jose Campoy, the young, enthusiastic director of the 2.3 million-acre Biosphere Reserve of the Upper Gulf of California and Colorado River Delta. "I'm going to complain," he promises, "and the whole of Mexico's going to complain.

"But the sad part is, the water going to the *cienaga* is not ours, it's yours," he adds. "So if you decide you want to take it, it's your choice."

Yuma's colossal desalting plant now stands silently next to the Colorado River, and tourists are allowed to peek in the windows and visit an information center. But even though the river's full reservoirs are expected to satisfy the treaty with Mexico for twenty to twenty-five years, the plant might not stay in mothballs. Plant manager Paul McAleese says a power plant in Mexico is interested in buying desalted water from Yuma, and the plant's full-time staff is looking for other customers. A page on the plant's Web site reads like a classified ad ("If you are interested in purchasing high-quality reverse-osmosis water, call ...").

So the coast isn't clear for the new marsh. But the publicity drummed up by Ed Glenn and others has pushed the agency to study the potential effects of the plant on the *cienaga*, and to find other places to dump its brine.

"We're looking for alternative approaches," says Bob Johnson, the regional director of the Bureau of Reclamation. The plant would cost about $24 million a year to operate, and Johnson says the irrigation water flowing through the MODE canal has "created a significant environmental resource in the *cienaga*."

To Juan Butron, the *cienaga* isn't just a "significant resource"; it's a second chance for his community. It's an overcast early morning on the Cienaga de Santa Clara, and Butron and his son Jose Juan quietly paddle an aluminum canoe through a maze of cattails near the MODE canal. It's not long before we hear the loud, clattering call of a Yuma clapper rail from the thickets that loom over our heads.

This accidental wetland is a windfall for the delta's struggling wildlife. The shy Yuma clapper rails are endangered in the United States and Mexico, but more than six thousand are packed into this marsh. The population is so dense and healthy that some birds might be traveling northward to repopulate former habitats on the other side of the border. The Cienaga de Santa Clara is also a haven for migratory birds and the largest known population of the desert pupfish, listed as endangered by both the United States and Mexico.

When the dams cut off the river's flow in the 1960s, the wetlands in this area all but dried up. During the following years, "we could just walk through here," says Juan Butron in Spanish, gesturing at a huge expanse of open water. "We didn't need boats then." About a decade later, water began pouring out of the MODE canal, and part of the past returned.

More than two hundred thousand people live in the small towns like Ejido Johnson scattered throughout the delta. Until the river started to sputter and choke, many made a good living from agriculture or fishing. Even so, Elena Chavarria of the Mexican environmental group Pronatura Sonora says some didn't believe restoration efforts could help their communities.

"When we started talking to them about restoration of the river, when we said the river had been green and clean less than fifty years ago, most younger people had no idea what we were talking about," she says. "For most of their lives, there's been no water in the river."

For almost ten years, Chavarria has organized outreach programs in agricultural towns, small tourist camps near the border city of Mexicali, and Cucapa tribal communities along the river.

"We try to find out what's important to them about the river," she says. "We don't say, 'You have to care about this because of migratory waterfowl.' Sometimes there's good news, and sometimes it's heartbreaking, because progress is very slow."

The water flowing over the border has done what her work sometimes can't: it's started to remind the communities what they can gain from the river. The Ecological Association of Users of the Hardy and Colorado Rivers, made up of hunters, farmers, and fishers from several delta communities, has begun to participate in city and state planning efforts in the northern delta. It now wants to open an office in the city of Mexicali for easier access to the officials who control water in the region.

The Cienaga de Santa Clara has also brought a spark of hope to Ejido Johnson. *Ejidos* were established by the federal government in the 1930s, and most were partially privatized in the 1990s. Since the river started to shrink, there have been few ways to make a living here, and many people have moved away.

Juan Butron wants to give those remaining a reason to stay. He and a few other people in town have started a fledgling tourism business in the marsh, offering canoe trips for birdwatchers and sportfishers. They've turned a once-abandoned house into a small program office, and they've built a couple of palapas for camping on the edge of the marsh.

The townspeople are getting some help from the biosphere reserve and from La Ruta de Sonora, a nonprofit educational tour group based in Ajo, Arizona. Executive director Isabel Granillo, a Mexican citizen, says some in the delta region are surprised that others come from far away to see what's here. "Then they think, 'OK, I'm protecting these things so I can show them to these other people,'" she says.

Tourism isn't a cure-all. But the ever-growing marsh and its trickle of visitors have kept Butron inspired for more than twenty years. "When that water arrived, I thought it was going to be good for the birds, good for the fish, and good for the *ejido*," he says. "I thought we had a future."

It's not just water that's crossing the border. For years, environmental groups in the United States have concentrated on the upper reaches of the Colorado, dismissing the lower river and the delta as a hopeless catastrophe. But as word of the cottonwood forests and the new marsh spread, some groups took a hard look at their maps and erased the international boundary.

"Before, the delta was just covered with saltcedar, and there was no river at all, just sand," says biosphere reserve director Jose Campoy. "Now, with two El Niño events in the nineties, all that vegetation really grew up. That's when a lot of people opened their eyes and said, 'What! Maybe with just a little water, or some floods every two or three years, we can have the river—alive.'"

The U.S. groups joined with the scientists and Mexican environmentalists who have been working on river and delta restoration since the early 1990s. The speedy revival of the river corridor has given the members of this loose coalition hope, too. They think these remnant habitats could someday be linked with one another, a partial reconstruction of the "hundred green lagoons" that Aldo Leopold saw.

But the first goal is to hang on to the water flowing into the delta, since there's no guarantee from either country that the water will stay in the river.

"We're not talking about bringing the dams down," says Mark Briggs of the Sonoran Institute in Tucson, Arizona. "We're talking about getting some flows, not huge ones, just enough to keep native wetlands alive. That's the start."

Even that is a challenge. The United States uses about nine-tenths of the river's water, and to most of the people who use that share, the delta is an abstraction. So these groups started with publicity, releasing easy-to-read reports on the scientific research in the delta.

"We tried to make it interesting to the world," says Chelsea Congdon, a former staffer for the national group Environmental Defense. "We wanted to capture people's imaginations."

Environmentalists are now starting to wedge the delta into the debate over Colorado River water policy, most of which takes place in offices and conference rooms a world away from Ejido Johnson. In November 1999, the Center for Biological Diversity, Defenders of Wildlife, and thirty-seven other U.S. and Mexican environmental groups sent a letter calling for a formal agreement between the United States and Mexico, a promise of water for both the main stem of the river and the newly established Cienaga de Santa Clara.

The next month, fifteen of those groups sent a notice of intent to sue to nine U.S. agencies, citing agency violations of the Endangered Species Act for endangered fish and birds in the delta and the upper Gulf of California. They were to follow through with a lawsuit at the end of June.

Official response to these efforts has been cool. Bob Johnson of the Bureau of Reclamation, for instance, says his agency isn't responsible for protecting animals that are listed as endangered in the United States but located in Mexico. "We're willing to consider the broad needs of the delta in consultation with the country of Mexico," he says, "but Mexico is another country. The laws of the United States don't apply there."

Environmental groups are also trying to push the delta through another crack in the policy barriers. The U.S. government wants to establish a set of temporary rules for managing the river's flood flows by the end of the year, rules that Interior Secretary Bruce Babbitt says must cause "no net loss" of environmental benefits. Armed with Babbitt's statement, several environmental groups are agitating to get some of those flows guaranteed to the river itself. They eventually want a commitment from both governments to keep water in the river all the way to the Gulf of California.

But the U.S. government is not considering the environmentalists' proposal while it develops the temporary rules for flood flows. Instead, it plans to continue to send nearly half the floodwater to urban California for the time being.

Here's why: Because most of the other basin states don't use their full portions of the Colorado, California has long been able to take more than its share. It now uses up to 5.2 million acre-feet per year, far exceeding the 4.4 million acre-feet allocated to the state by the "Law of the River," the series of agreements and treaties among the basin states and Mexico. But now, the other states are increasing their use of the Colorado and they want California to stop hogging the river.

So the Department of Interior and the seven Colorado Basin states are set to adopt a new water-use plan for California by the end of the year. The plan, a priority for Babbitt, would cut California's use of the Colorado down to size by 2015. Both California and Interior say the flood flows are needed in the short term to ease the thirsty state's gradual transition to the new plan. The other basin states have agreed, but reluctantly, since they'd like California to toe the line as soon as possible. Any serious discussion of flood flows for the delta might throw a wrench into the fragile truce among the states and Interior.

Federal officials also argue that any international agreements on flows have to be negotiated by the International Boundary and Water Commission, overseen by the U.S. State Department and its counterpart in Mexico. The commission is cooperating with Mexico on a study of the delta, and a joint declaration between the United States and Mexico in mid-May emphasized the importance of the project.

Yet the promise of another study isn't good enough for most environmental groups. "They've been saying the same thing for seventy or eighty years—that we'll get to the environment eventually," says Michael Cohen of the Pacific Institute, an environmental policy research center in Oakland, California. "Well, when is eventually?"

Big changes in policy may be some time in coming, but the delta is getting a little help from the powers-that-be in both countries. A letter from Deputy Interior Secretary David Hayes to several U.S. environmentalists in mid-May acknowledged for the first time that 80 percent of the best habitat on the lower Colorado is in Mexico. "Restoring the ecological integrity of the Delta is in the interest of both the U.S. and Mexico," he wrote.

There has also been some motion within the Mexican government. Less than half of the protected areas in Mexico have regular funding, but the biosphere reserve is one of the luckier ones. In 1996, three years after its establishment, the huge reserve got enough money to start paying staff. Its annual budget is still at the shoestring level—about $150,000— but director Jose Campoy says the reserve can now pay for salaries, some equipment, and fuel.

Outgoing Mexican president Ernesto Zedillo is far from an environmental champion, but at the beginning of his administration in 1994, he created the Secretariat of the Environment, Natural Resources, and Fisheries, equivalent to the U.S. Department of the Interior. The agency is headed by prominent Mexican environmentalist Julia Carabias, and it includes Mexico's first central office for protected areas. And in early March, Zedillo bowed to pressure from an international coalition of environmental groups and canceled plans for a gigantic salt factory on the Baja Peninsula. The victory boosted the confidence of a similar coalition—the U.S. and Mexican groups working to protect the delta.

Carlos Valdes-Casillas of the Monterrey Technical Institute in Guaymas, Mexico, says there's limited but growing concern about the delta among Mexican officials, and some support for an environmental amendment to the 1944 treaty between the United States and Mexico. "The treaty used to be almost a taboo subject," he says. "It was assumed that it was never going to change."

Official U.S. interest in the delta still pales in comparison to the support for domestic projects such as the Salton Sea restoration. To many on this side of the border, the Colorado River Delta is still a land of rumor and myth. And to many in Mexico, the delta is still a bitter symbol of the forces that hold sway upstream.

But Edward Glenn says there are signs of life, both in the delta and in the seats of power on both sides of the international boundary. When he first started driving from Tucson to visit the Colorado River Delta more than twenty years ago, allies were hard to come by.

"There was no acknowledgement on the official level that these things were environmental assets," he says. "Now, there's a whole cadre of people working on it. They don't need people like me to run down there and make discoveries anymore."

coming to see it
as an asset

June 3, 2000

Michelle Nijhuis is contributing editor to *High Country News*

Quenching the Big Thirst

Ed Marston

When Bruce Babbitt took over as secretary of the Department of Interior in 1993, he immediately found himself in a face-off with the West's traditional powers.

His early high-profile battles with ranchers and miners over new fees for their use of the public lands gave him instant "whipping boy" status among the region's conservative leaders. And over the next eight years they found plenty of fodder for their claim that Babbitt, in cahoots with environmentalists, was waging a "war against the West."

Yet late in his tenure, in December of 2000, Babbitt stood at a podium in Las Vegas' Caesar's Palace Hotel before some of the most conservative and powerful people in the West—and was treated like a hero.

The occasion was the annual meeting of the Colorado River Water Users Association, which brings together the men and women who run the Colorado River—the "water buffaloes" who wring every drop they can out of the river for agriculture and for urban growth.

In his speech that day, Babbitt announced that the seven states that use the river—Colorado, Utah, Wyoming, New Mexico, Nevada, Arizona and California—had signed a peace treaty in the ongoing war over its water. The conflict centered on the West's reigning water heavyweight, California, and its use of the river that is the liquid heart of the West, starting high in the Colorado Rockies and flowing through the deserts of the Southwest on its way to the Gulf of California in Mexico.

"The Golden State" has long used more water than the 4.4 million acre-feet it is allocated under the Colorado River Compact. But until relatively recently, it didn't matter, because the other states were not using their full allocations. The other states, growing larger and thirstier with each passing year, worried that they would never get to use their full apportionments of the Colorado if California's use became institutionalized.

That was not going to happen now, Babbitt said. California had agreed to go on a water diet over the next fifteen years, in exchange for being allowed to temporarily continue taking more than its annual share.

"Within the last decade of the twentieth century ... we have moved from pouring concrete to building the institutions and partnerships necessary to efficiently manage this great river system," Babbitt intoned.

At the end of his speech, the mainly Republican crowd got to its feet and gave the outgoing Democratic secretary a long ovation. "You might have thought it was the Treaty of Versailles. You'd have thought peace had broken out all over the world," recalls University of Colorado law professor David Getches.

But Getches, for one, was far from convinced that the so-called "4.4 plan" Babbitt laid out that day was a triumph at all.

"I think fifteen years will pass and we won't see anything close to California using 4.4 million acre-feet under any conditions," Getches says. "This is like most multiparty, multifaceted deals. It's produced like a quilt. Everybody puts their pieces into it. It has coherence only in that everyone agrees it's finished."

Whether the 4.4 plan is more than a weakly stitched patchwork remains to be seen. To turn Babbitt's conceptual approach into something real and wet, institutions that traditionally battle each other must sit down at the table and hammer out conservation agreements.

The Colorado River water squeeze has been developing for a long time, but for years "surplus" water in the system has allowed everyone to ignore it. Until the 1990s, California had used eight hundred thousand acre-feet of "surplus" that belongs to its Lower Basin neighbors, Arizona and Nevada. Some five hundred fifty thousand acre-feet of that water flowed to the Metropolitan Water District (hereafter referred to as the Met), which supplies water to 5,200 square miles and sixteen million people living in the Los Angeles and San Diego metropolitan areas. The rest went to the large agricultural irrigation districts, including the Imperial and Coachella in the southwest California desert.

When growth in Arizona and Nevada in the 1990s pinched that surplus off, California started using eight hundred thousand acre-feet that belongs to Colorado, Utah, Wyoming, and New Mexico, the Upper Basin states. But the Upper Basin is also growing, and that water won't be available forever.

California continues to grow, too. Not only has the Golden State's need for residential and urban water increased, but its legendary agricultural thirst—farmers use 80 percent of all waters in the state—has not slacked off a bit.

California has turned to the Colorado River because it lacks alternatives. Southern California has long reached for the abundant waters of the northern half of the state that flow into the San Francisco Bay and its large surrounding delta. In 1933, the federal government built the great Central Valley Project to shunt northern waters down to the San Joaquin Valley and further south. Then, in the 1960s, the state built the California Water Project, which provided even more water for farmers and urban communities in Southern California.

But in recent decades, Northern California has held off attempts by the Met to augment the flow with more water, both out of general anti-Southern California sentiment and out of environmental concerns. Forty percent of the rivers of the state come through the delta, east of San Francisco Bay. But the huge working system of saltwater and freshwater confluence that is referred to as the Bay-Delta is now a sick ecosystem, scientists say. It has been deprived of the freshwater flows that make its marshes and tidewaters so ecologically productive.

In 1982, California voters defeated the "Peripheral Canal" proposition, which would have sent more water destined for the Bay-Delta to Southern California. For several decades now, environmentalists have fought off an effort to construct the Auburn Dam on the American River, which flows out of the Sierra Nevada mountains above Sacramento, and which would have sent more Bay-Delta water south. They triumphed at Mono Lake in 1994, forcing the city of Los Angeles to reduce its diversions from the streams feeding the delicate, saline lake on the east side of the Sierra Nevada. And in the 1990s, Los Angeles agreed to put some water back in dusty Owens Valley, which the city had dewatered earlier in the century.

"After the defeat of the Peripheral Canal and the Mono Lake environmental victory, the [Southern California] water establishment decided they had to shore up their Colorado River water," says Tom Graff, an attorney with Environmental Defense who specializes in California water issues. "Mono Lake didn't involve much water—only about thirty thousand acre-feet per year—but it showed the public's values."

Without access to Northern California waters, the Metropolitan Water District has upped its Colorado River consumption. The sacred Law of the Colorado River has been bent and twisted to enable the Met to use 1.2 million acre-feet, instead of the five hundred fifty thousand it is entitled to.

Theoretically, in a dry year, a secretary of Interior could cut California off from this extra water by simply failing to declare the river to be in surplus. But over the past decade, no one—from Babbitt, the Water Master of the Colorado River, to the Upper Basin states whose water California is using—has wanted to see what would happen if the sixteen million people the Met supplies with water were suddenly put on short rations.

Environmentalists feared that their gains of the past twenty years at Mono Lake and elsewhere could be lost if Californians decided that they wanted lush green lawns more than they wanted Mono Lake or a healthy San Francisco Bay-Delta. And everyone feared that a political war would break out in Washington, D.C., as California's huge congressional delegation attempted to change western water rules to save the state's economy.

Because it seemed impossible to simply shut down California's use of the extra water, the six states that share the Colorado River with California began nagging Babbitt, early in his tenure, to do something. So he, along with deputy secretary and chief Interior negotiator David Hayes, began to hold discussions with the Colorado River water establishment.

Babbitt brought the biggest stick available, says Dennis Underwood, the former head of California's Colorado River Board and the commissioner of the Bureau of Reclamation under former President George Bush. "Babbitt said, 'You have to develop a plan to demonstrate how you're going to live within your normal apportionment. Otherwise, I'm not going to approve surplus water,' " Underwood says.

The threat got California moving: what emerged after six years was the California Colorado River Water Use Plan, in which California and its major water users promise to cut use by eight hundred thousand acre-feet by 2016. The plan describes 459,000 acre-feet of initial reductions, and pledges that the additional reductions will be developed over time. The initial reductions will come from still-to-be-negotiated contracts that will line canals, store water in exhausted underground aquifers, force feuding entities to share a major aqueduct, and leave some fields fallow in drought years.

In return, Babbitt signed the key federal promise: the Interim Surplus Criteria allow California to draw down "surplus waters" from Lake Mead over the next fifteen years. It's a tit-for-tat arrangement: water off the tops of Lake Mead and Lake Powell (by law, the two reservoirs have to be drawn down in lockstep) is to be used to give California fifteen years to figure out how to save eight hundred thousand acre-feet a year.

The decision to allow the drawdown of Lake Mead is not without risk. Under the agreement, the Bureau of Reclamation could potentially lower the twenty-eight million-acre-foot reservoir to within four million acre-feet of the point at which electricity generation begins to falter, and to within six million acre-feet of the point at which Las Vegas would no longer be able to withdraw drinking water.

Years before these problems would develop, the marinas on lakes Mead and Powell would be stranded a long way from the water and the boat ramps would be useful for little except skateboarding. Drinking even treated water from Lake Mead would be problematic, because pollutants would become concentrated in the shrinking reservoir.

These scenarios were unthinkable in the past. Until Babbitt signed the new policy, the U.S. Bureau of Reclamation had operated the Mead and Powell reservoirs cautiously. At the end of a heavy winter, the Bureau would be forced to send some water downstream to make room in the reservoirs for spring's mountain runoff. Both reservoirs were always kept filled to the brim, protection against a possible series of drought years.

And "filled to the brim" means a lot of water: together, Mead and Powell hold almost sixty million acre-feet, four years of normal flow on the Colorado River.

Southern California water agencies hated that policy. They saw it as deliberately wasting water that California could be using. If the reservoirs were routinely kept at lower levels, then floodwaters could be captured, and wasteful springtime releases would no longer occur.

"Wasteful" releases, though, can have value. During the 1990s, the Bureau of Reclamation's flood-control releases in late winter made it past the massive California and Mexican irrigation and urban water intakes, and began to restore life to the desiccated Colorado River Delta—the dying, salt-ridden mouth of what writer Philip Fradkin called "a river no more."

Thanks to these releases, about 5 percent of the delta has come back to life. Now, because of the new reservoir-management policy Babbitt put into effect on January 16, 2001, that 5 percent is likely to die back again, and controlled floods out of Lake Powell through Glen Canyon Dam, intended to rebuild beaches in the Grand Canyon, will take place less often.

Babbitt, then, traded away a cautious drought-protection policy and the possibility of wet-year releases to a reviving Colorado River Delta in order to get the California water establishment to skinny down.

By rights, environmentalists at Babbitt's Las Vegas speech should have been applauding even louder than the water buffaloes. They back reducing California's use to 4.4 million acre-feet. And groups such as Environmental Defense have pushed for years to pry water loose from the old, constricting Law-of-the-River rules, so that water could be moved from places of low economic value, such as alfalfa and cotton fields, to places of high value. Once the old "first in time, first in right" water-allocation structure broke down, environmentalists expected government regulation to ensure that some of the freed water would remain in streams to nurture wildlife and marshes.

But it didn't work out that way when Babbitt, a card-carrying environmentalist, brought change to the Colorado River.

Jennifer Pitt, who works for Environmental Defense in Boulder, Colorado, says, "The goal of 4.4 is laudable. [But] the way it's set up means less water in the lower part of the Colorado River. Less water to be used by riparian vegetation."

The environmentalists worked hard to keep water flowing to the Colorado Delta. About a dozen groups, led by Pacific Institute in Oakland, submitted an alternative to the Bureau of Reclamation that would have sent the delta thirty-two thousand acre-feet a year out of the surplus, with occasional spring floods to spread seeds over the delta. The Bureau had invited the environmentalists' alternative. But when the seven basin states screamed in reaction to it—Colorado, for example, seemed more worried about giving a small amount of water to Mexico than giving a large amount to California—the Bureau and Babbitt backed far away from the alternative.

Instead, the Bureau adopted the consensus proposal submitted at the last minute by the seven basin states, and Babbitt honored his promise to adopt a consensus proposal, even though the consensus didn't include the environmentalists or Mexico.

Nevertheless, Eric Kuhn, a progressive water buffalo who runs the Colorado River Water Conservation District in western Colorado, says, "The environmentalists have won the battle for the [Colorado River] delta. Most in the water community accept that they have to deal with the delta." He says that the environmentalists didn't get what they wanted in this round because they "wanted too big a deal too soon." But even so, "They've won. It's not if. It's how much, and when."

Michael Cohen of the Pacific Institute is more ambivalent. He says the 4.4 plan "makes shortages more likely on the system," which could further damage the delta. But he is pleased by a December 2000 agreement, called Treaty Minute 306, between Mexico and the U.S., in which both countries pledge to work toward restoring the delta. "It's a huge step forward," Cohen says.

More basic than the question of whether the 4.4 plan hurts or helps the environment is whether California can really reduce its consumption. Conceptually, the idea of saving water on farms and sending the saved water to cities is simple. But critics say the 4.4 plan lacks teeth: "The Upper Basin states have grudgingly gone along with this on the basis that it's better to have a promise from California. But it's virtually unenforceable," says the University of Colorado's David Getches.

"For some reason, the other six Colorado River states prefer the appearance that California is going to do it, rather than to actually require California to do it," echoes Environmental Defense's Tom Graff. "There are no real sanctions if California flubs its commitments."

Graff says some of the promised steps outlined in the plan, including the commitment to save water by lining the All-American Canal on the Mexican border, and the plan to store water underground at Cadiz, have already hit snags.

Indeed, with Babbitt offstage and no new leader in sight, the hard work is now up to California's water establishment. A look at the past is not encouraging. The only time recently when California's irrigation districts and coastal cities were not on the verge of war was when they were at war. And it was never a simple city-vs.-country lineup: San Diego and the Met fight far more viciously against each other than against the farmers, and the Coachella and Imperial irrigation districts have been suing each other for decades.

Even the state can be flaky. In 1998, the California Legislature appropriated $235 million to line the All-American Canal and send the water that would be saved to the cities. That appropriation showed a statewide commitment to the goal of 4.4. Then, in early 2001, before construction could begin, Governor Gray Davis spent that money to buy a week's worth of electricity; it was only restored recently.

And then there is the sixty-five-year-long battle between the Imperial and Coachella districts. Four irrigation districts share 3.85 million acre-feet of water out of the Colorado. That's more than one-quarter of the river's average annual flow. Amazingly enough, this huge collective right has never been divided or quantified. Coachella has long felt that Imperial, which has the right to drink first, has taken too much river water, leaving Coachella overly dependent on overdrawn groundwater.

At the moment, Imperial and Coachella appear close to signing a Quantification Settlement Agreement. If nothing happens to derail the signing, Coachella Valley Water District manager Tom Levy says thirty-eight other nuts-and-bolts agreements, describing how water will be saved and who will get that water, will go forward.

The Indian tribes on the Colorado provide an additional complication. Many tribes have claims to Colorado River water that are small but senior to all agricultural and urban claims. Any comprehensive settlement will have to guarantee relatively small amounts of water—a few thousand acre-feet here and a few hundred there—to satisfy the Indian claims. Babbitt, who oversaw the Bureau of Indian Affairs, made that need clear in his annual speeches to the Colorado River Water Users Association.

So it is a mess—a mess rooted in the establishment of farms and cities in a desert dependent on a river whose Rocky Mountain headwaters are far away. The present set of deals are so many and so complex that no one knows whether they can come together to reduce California's water use to 4.4 million acre-feet per year.

Still, Coachella's Tom Levy is optimistic. He thinks Southern California has changed in fundamental ways: it no longer believes it has a right to most of the Colorado River or to drink Northern California dry.

Although the state has only laid out enough savings in the state-sanctioned plan to "get down to 4.7 or 4.8, we've said in the plan that in fifteen years, if we have a normal year, we're at 4.4," says Levy. "I think we'll find the added savings. We've agreed to be at 4.4."

Eric Kuhn lines up with Levy. "I largely think it's a political, feel-good deal. But I also think there will be real progress. I see California getting down to 4.7 or 4.8. It's progress. It's about a broad direction.

"I have seen a shift in California attitudes over the last five or six years. That's what you can give Babbitt the most credit for. He was a peer; they couldn't buffalo him."

Even if California's squabbling water institutions manage to deliver on the 4.4 plan's promise, two potential obstacles remain. The first is drought: a series of dry winters could leave the Bureau of Reclamation, which operates the dams and reservoirs on the Colorado, with the ugly choice of cutting off either Las Vegas or California from its primary water supply.

The other obstacle is the public. Although the creation of the 4.4 plan was an open process, with an environmental impact statement and public hearings and excellent news stories, the public paid virtually no attention. Four regional meetings last August attracted no spoken testimony from the general public. Only six citizens submitted written comments, apart from the seven thousand nearly identical e-mails generated by an Environmental Defense Web site. The six written comments are less than many grazing-allotment studies attract.

So the public is likely to be shocked if a few dry years require that "Lakes" Powell and Mead be drawn sharply down. "How did that happen?" fishermen and houseboat owners will ask. "Why weren't we consulted?"

Water consultant Mike Clinton, the former executive director of the Imperial Irrigation District, argues that the system worked the way it was supposed to, despite citizens' seeming apathy. The public wasn't paying attention "because the public doesn't get involved if there is no crisis. A lot of the things being debated are fifteen to twenty years away from now.

"Even though there was a lot of press, it went into people's background noise. They didn't hear it. So it's left to the appointed and elected officials, whose responsibility it is to husband these resources."

There's a different way to see the lack of public involvement. It can be argued that the public had already done its part, and made the big decisions: when the Peripheral Canal went to a vote; when Mono Lake was close to death due to L.A.'s thirst; when the dust storms blowing across the Owens Valley called out for the dry lake bed to be watered; and when Northern Californians demanded that something be done about the Bay-Delta.

The public, directly in a referendum, or through the courts, or by putting pressure on elected officials, spoke each time. And each decision prevented the water establishment from building dams or canals or continuing to withdraw quite as much water from a river or river delta.

So the public was involved, and did make a decision about the direction it wanted to go. Now it is up to the water establishment to work out the details.

There is one more aspect to the 4.4 plan: it is probably bulletproof, in the sense that no one will want to be held responsible for toppling it. Environmentalists are unlikely to launch a major lawsuit, even though the plan did not give them what they wanted at the Colorado River Delta. And even though the agreements protect major environmental gains at Mono Lake, the Owens Valley, and the Bay-Delta, the Bush administration will probably leave them alone.

This is something new in the West. The sustained policy making that Babbitt, Interior solicitor and now Berkeley Law Professor Joseph Sax, and chief Interior negotiator David Hayes brought to western water is unusual, except when it comes to building dams. John Wesley Powell tried to make policy in the nineteenth century, when he warned that the region didn't have enough water to settle all the land in traditional ways. He was run over, hard, by would-be settlers, speculators, and western legislators and governors.

Babbitt has been both luckier and better situated. He shaped his new policy during a wet decade, when there was no immediate crisis. And he had more clout than Powell, because as Interior secretary, he oversaw the agencies that hold the keys to the river's water. As boss of the Bureau of Reclamation, Babbitt was the Water Master, the person who could turn on and off the dams. As boss of the U.S. Fish and Wildlife Service, he could help those who wanted to change water uses do so without running up too high a bill to mitigate endangered species problems. As boss of the Bureau of Indian Affairs, he had the power to bring water-rights lawsuits on behalf of the Indians against those who weren't cooperative.

He also had the credentials to be a water buffalo. He was governor of Arizona when that state passed a law restricting groundwater pumping. As a water attorney, he had represented some rural Nevadans in their fight against Las Vegas' attempt to drain northern Nevada dry.

And finally, he had the luxury of an eight-year run at Interior.

Will the Bush administration show the same kind of leadership? It will take time for Interior Secretary Gale Norton and her appointees to get involved. Babbitt became secretary in early 1993, but he didn't make his first speech to the Colorado River Water Users until late in 1995.

Moreover, the new federal rules are already in place. They were produced by a seven-state consensus. The feds will continue to play an important role. Many of the agreements to implement the California 4.4 plan will require federal permits, endangered species permissions from the U.S. Fish and Wildlife Service, and even federal money.

But the big federal decision—allowing California to keep using more than its share of Colorado River water for the next fifteen years—has been made; it may be that the leadership now has to emerge from the water buffaloes themselves. In the past, this has always been a man's game. But at the moment, the most prominent member of the group is Patricia Mulroy of the Southern Nevada Water Authority. She speaks loudly, she carries a big stick, and she knows how to implement an agenda.

Back when California was trying to convince the basin states to draw Lake Mead down much farther than Babbitt finally specified, Mulroy said, "This is just not acceptable. Where does the need stop and the greed begin? Using surplus is an integral part of our water-resource picture, but we have to do it in a fashion where we don't destroy our own environment."

At Babbitt's last speech, where the Colorado River Delta was slighted, Mulroy told the utility managers, federal officials, tribal representatives, and others that it was time to get to work.

"We are going to have to tackle the issue of the Mexican delta," she was quoted in the *Las Vegas Review-Journal*.

That led environmentalist David Hogan of the Tucson-based, very tough Center for Biological Diversity to call her statement remarkable for a western water manager, but not unprecedented for Mulroy.

It may be that new basinwide leadership will emerge from within the water buffaloes. It may even be that it's time to retire the term.

May 21, 2001

Ed Marston is former publisher for *High Country News*.

It's Time for a New Law of the River

Hal K. Rothman

On New Year's Eve, the normally placid pumping station of the Metropolitan Water District of Southern California at Lake Havasu felt tense. Armed security guards on the scene since 9/11 seemed grim, and tourists seeking bird-watching information were turned away.

It recalled those old black-and-white pictures from when Owens Valley farmers blew up the original California Aqueduct and forced William Mulholland's men from Los Angeles to guard the city's plunder. Though this was probably business as usual, it reminded me that we'd just seen the collapse of the new Colorado River plan.

When the Imperial Valley Irrigation District voted down the transfer of some of its water to San Diego County in December, it disrupted an important cog in California's economy, the sixth-largest in the world. Even a last-ditch attempt on December 31 to rectify the situation could not repair the damage.

Everyone can now see that the Colorado River Compact, the Law of the River, or what I've long described as the "fiction of the river," is obsolete. A decade-long process of recrafting the agreement into a win-win situation for everyone seemed poised to succeed—until the agricultural district exercised its selfish prerogative and told the state, "This water is ours." All parties agree that reallocation of Colorado River water must occur. The Colorado River Compact dates from the legendary 1922 U.S. Supreme Court case, *Wyoming v. California*, when the court ruled the "first in time, first in right" presumption of priority in western water use applied across state lines as well as within states.

Rebuffed by the court, upper-river states like Wyoming and Colorado tried to reserve water for future growth—then imagined as agriculture—

by letting California take most of the water south of Lee's Ferry, Arizona. They salvaged an equal amount for the states on the upper river.

That deal had all kinds of consequences, but the most important was the creation of an agricultural oligarchy of federally subsidized water that persists until today.

Water is power in the West, and it is badly distributed. Three irrigation districts in California, including the Imperial Valley, hold priority rights to 3.85 million acre-feet of the state's 4.4 million-acre foot allotment from the Colorado River. That leaves six hundred thousand acre-feet for the entire Los Angeles Basin's more than twenty million people.

In every western state, 80 percent of the water goes to agriculture and ranching. Yet in no state, even California, do those activities generate 5 percent of the state economy. In short, every hour of every day, water goes to western agriculture because it always has, not because it produces necessary crops, or creates plentiful jobs, or fills state coffers with the taxes on its profits. Do we really need cotton from Yuma, Arizona, or alfalfa from the Walker River in northern Nevada?

Subsidized agriculture also creates competition for farmers and ranchers elsewhere in the country who are not so fortunate as to receive federal subsidies.

Secretary of the Interior Gale Norton is the rivermaster, and she has lately decided to hold states to the terms of the compact. By her decision, excess river water will no longer flow to California and Nevada. As a result, California will have to replace almost one million acre-feet of water this year if no accommodation is reached, and Nevada will lose thirty thousand acre feet. Because of Imperial Valley's one rural vote, the cities that produce California's greatest wealth will feel pain while the agriculturalists who caused it will continue to drown their fields with impunity.

As direct as the secretary's action was, stopping the excess flow isn't enough. Interior Secretary Norton should scrap the Colorado River Compact and reallocate water to reflect the realities of the New West. This is the time for a bold federal role.

A new compact could take into account urban use, environmental law, new economic activity, fluctuation in water quantity, water quality, and countless other contingencies that didn't exist eighty years ago. It could create a Colorado River for the needs of today and tomorrow, not one beholden to a flawed past. Such a step requires the leadership to exercise federal power, anathema to the Bush administration.

This is a decision about the recovery of one of the world's most productive economies. Even as greater Los Angeles rebounds, carrying the Bay Area and nearby states with it, there now looms the threat of a water shortage that will hurt everyone.

The West deserves a better distribution of its most precious resource. Step up, Secretary Norton, shake off that anti-federal cloak your administration wears, and swing away.

call to action

February 17, 2003

The late *Hal Rothman*, author of *Devil's Bargains: Tourism in the Twentieth-Century American West*, taught at the University of Nevada, Las Vegas.

Colorado River States Reach Landmark Agreement

Matt Jenkins

Water from the Colorado River keeps thirty million people alive, and it sustains a $1.2 trillion regional economy in cities like Los Angeles, Phoenix, Las Vegas, and Denver, and throughout the rural West. In recent years, however, drought and competing urban growth have raised tensions among the seven states that depend on the river. Now, a groundbreaking agreement signals a new level of cooperation between those states, and clears the way for the West's booming cities to buy water from farms—potentially even from farms in other states—to protect themselves in extreme drought.

For the past year, representatives of California, Arizona, Nevada, Colorado, Utah, Wyoming, and New Mexico have been meeting behind closed doors. Officially, they've been deciding what to do if a drought gets so bad that there's not enough water to go around. Unofficially, however, they've been trying to get more water to Las Vegas, in an effort to prevent the Southern Nevada Water Authority from blowing apart the entire Colorado River Compact.

The 1922 Compact gave Nevada a paltry 4 percent of the river's flow, and Patricia Mulroy, the head of the Water Authority, is outspoken about her willingness to try to overturn it in court. "If there is no way that the Compact can accommodate Nevada," she said last fall, "then Nevada has no choice but to consider the Compact broken."

But on February 3, after an intense final round of negotiations, the states announced an agreement that should avert the legal warfare. The proposal, which is still being refined and must be approved by U.S. Interior Secretary Gale Norton, helps all seven states by better coordinating operations at the river's two main reservoirs, Lake Powell and Lake Mead. But it also contains a package of bail-out programs for Las Vegas, which will hit the limit of its existing water supply in just seven years if it continues growing at its current breakneck pace.

Mulroy won a significant concession that will allow Las Vegas to stretch water from its massive proposed Great Basin groundwater-pumping project much further. If that project wins federal and state approval, it will pump between 125,000 and 180,000 acre-feet of groundwater a year (each acre-foot is enough for two homes in Las Vegas). Now, with the six other states' consent, the Southern Nevada Water Authority can reuse the treated wastewater from the project that will flow into Lake Mead, effectively increasing that supply by 70 percent.

But the groundwater project faces numerous challenges and won't be finished until 2018 at the earliest. In the meantime, Las Vegas will pay the federal government $80 million to build a new reservoir along the California-Mexico border. The reservoir will catch overflow that farmers in the region currently can't use; in return for funding the project, Las Vegas can take an equivalent amount of water out of Lake Mead until its groundwater project is in place.

Mulroy has also agreed to abandon a controversial plan to tap the Virgin and Muddy rivers, tributaries of the Colorado. Now, her agency will fund a study of ways to "augment" the flow of the Colorado River over the longer term. One of the most promising options is a swap in which Las Vegas would pay for a seawater-desalination plant in Mexico that would supply water to Tijuana and Mexicali, in exchange for access to part of Mexico's share of the Colorado.

Under the terms of the new agreement, cities in one of the Lower Basin states—Arizona, California, and Nevada—could lease water from farmers in another Lower Basin state, marking a quiet but significant shift. Farms use more than 80 percent of the river's water, and that water is potentially an additional reservoir that cities could use to protect themselves from what Mulroy calls "catastrophic shortage."

Because southern Nevada has very few farms to which Las Vegas can turn, interstate transfers are particularly attractive to the Southern Nevada Water Authority. But such leases, particularly ones that idle farmland to free up water, are controversial. Mulroy has attempted them before, but, she says, "The resistance from the other states is enormous."

During the past year's negotiations, however, Colorado, Wyoming, Utah, and New Mexico have tried to safeguard their shares of the river by encouraging the more heavily developed Lower Basin to find water from farms in central Arizona and in California's Imperial Valley.

"There is plenty of room within the Lower Basin for leasing, marketing, transfers, [or] exchanges, while still protecting what we have in the Upper Basin," Jim Lochhead, one of Colorado's negotiators, said last August.

There is no shortage of water to work with in an emergency: Jennifer Pitt, with the nonprofit group Environmental Defense, estimates that there is a pool of some 2.3 million acre-feet of water, enough for nearly five million homes, that cities could lease from farmers in the Lower Basin for less than $100 an acre-foot.

Realistically, cities would only lease far smaller amounts to cover their shortages in a drought. And officially, at least, water managers are downplaying the interstate leasing option. "We're not there yet," says Bill Hasencamp with the Metropolitan Water District of Southern California, which supplies water to Los Angeles and San Diego. But other sources close to the negotiations say that under the new proposal, which the states hope to finalize this fall, interstate leases are clearly allowable.

Just how far the states will take them remains to be seen. Putting together individual deals, which will most likely be one-year arrangements that pay farmers to fallow their land and transfer water, will still require a tremendous amount of diplomacy to prove that farms won't be dried up permanently.

While "there's a pretty tremendous buffer in all that agricultural water use," says Pitt, individual states will always be hesitant to lease it outside their borders for one very big reason: "They see it as their reserve for future growth," she says, and they're concerned that "once you let it out of the state, you won't get it back."

February 20, 2006

Matt Jenkins is a *High Country News* contributing editor.

The Efficiency Paradox

Matt Jenkins

In 1937, Miguel Hernández Rentería left his hometown in the central
Mexican state of Sinaloa and came to the Mexicali Valley, on the U.S.
border, to grow cotton. The desert here receives less rain than the Sahara,
and carving out a living with a horse-drawn plow was an act of faith
as much as pluck. But Hernández proved tough enough to ultimately
support thirteen children.

Then, in 1946, he was confronted with a preposterous problem. Water
began rising out of the ground and inundating his fields. By 1952, it was
as high as his seven-year-old son Gerónimo's neck.

The water was leaking out of the All-American Canal, just over the
border. The canal carries nearly one-fifth of the water in the Colorado
River to farms in California's Imperial Valley. Because it was simply dug
out of the earth and never lined with concrete, it leaks twenty-two billion
gallons of water a year. That water percolates underground, migrates
south across the border, and re-emerges in the Mexicali Valley.

Farmers here quickly turned the improbable scourge into a windfall.
With the aid of the Mexican government, they built their own canal to
capture much of the leakage, which is now funneled to farms close by.
Private and government pumps also send the leaked water to farms such
as the Hernándezes'.

Today, Gerónimo Hernández, at sixty-one, is a tornado of a man
who seems to have inherited his father's tenaciousness. He also has a
wicked wit, introducing himself with a reference to his namesake—*"el
pistolero de Cochises"*—and a motion for a visitor's scalp. "My father and
the first generation of farmers are dead now," says Hernández. Horse-
drawn plows have given way to mechanized cotton harvesters. But he
and his brother still farm four hundred acres along the border, rich fields

punctuated by date palms that give the area a vaguely Mesopotamian feel. The Hernández brothers are just two of more than fourteen thousand farmers in the Mexicali Valley.

Now, however, San Diego and the Imperial Irrigation District are about to begin a joint effort to remove the All-American Canal from service and replace it with a new one, excavated alongside the existing one and lined with concrete to make it impervious to seepage. Then the conserved water—the windfall that has sustained the farmers here for more than half a century—will be transferred to San Diego.

The Hernándezes and other farmers here stand at the edge of an advancing campaign of water efficiency that reaches across the entire Colorado River Basin. Nearly a century ago, the wild and undammed Colorado was, in the eyes of American engineers, a poster child for inefficiency and waste. In the 1920s, they embarked on a campaign of maximum development and tamed the river with a phalanx of dams to

keep its water from running wasted to the sea. Now, in a world shaped by ever-sharpening competition for water—and nearly eight years into a drought—the promise of efficiency has been resurrected.

Water efficiency bears a patina of environmental respectability, and it is frequently seen as a way to conjure more water out of thin air. But a profound paradox stands at the heart of the logic of efficiency: increased efficiency creates losers as well as winners, and the victims often inhabit places far beyond the public eye. Gerónimo Hernández and his Mexican compatriots will soon find themselves among the losers. But the biggest costs of the new obsession with efficiency could ultimately accrue to the very place that bore the brunt of the first round of development: the foundering ecosystem of the Colorado River Delta.

Environmental groups have helped shape water politics to an extent that often goes unremarked. They have labored to convince the West's traditional water power brokers to include the environment in their calculations. And it is largely due to the efforts of environmentalists that, in the last quarter century, efficiency has become a watchword on the Colorado.

In the early 1980s, water agencies in California were using more Colorado River water than they were entitled to. With urban demand booming in Arizona and Nevada, which also rely on water from the river, the agencies knew that a water crunch was imminent. In 1982, in an effort to assure itself adequate water when it was ultimately forced to reduce its take of the Colorado, the Metropolitan Water District of Southern California set its sights on the Sacramento River in Northern California. The agency, which supplies eighteen million people in Los Angeles and San Diego, proposed building the "Peripheral Canal" to tap the Sacramento before it reached the San Francisco Bay-Delta and to funnel the water south. The plan sent Northern Californians into a paroxysm of rage: not only did it sound like an unvarnished water grab, it sounded like one that would strangle the aquatic ecosystems of the Bay-Delta. In a statewide referendum that summer, voters resoundingly defeated the idea.

But Southern California's water crunch still loomed. So in 1983, Robert Stavins, a Berkeley-based economist with the Environmental Defense Fund (who would go on to become an architect of greenhouse-gas emissions-trading programs) wrote a visionary proposal called Trading Conservation Investments for Water. Why not, Stavins argued, "salvage" water that had already been diverted into California's hydraulic maw, but then had been lost to leakage? The Metropolitan Water District could fund water-efficiency improvements in the Imperial Valley, in exchange for the water saved by those improvements.

Stavins' report was written in the language that water managers speak, and it was politically palatable: rather than suggesting a full-blown transfer of farmers' water, it simply proposed helping them tighten up their water-supply system and resurrect water that seemingly had vanished into the ether. The proposal set off a revolution in California's water affairs. In 1988, Met agreed to spend more than $200 million lining and automating the Imperial Irrigation District's canal system, freeing up enough "new" water to serve more than two hundred thousand homes each year.

In the years since, a raft of efficiency-funding programs has come to stand at the center of California's plan to pare back its Colorado River water use; the Imperial Valley is now a proving ground for the idea of water efficiency. All told, the Imperial Irrigation District will squeeze out 15 percent of its water for transfer to residents of Southern California's cities, without reducing agricultural productivity. Much of that water, including that saved by lining the All-American Canal, will go to the three million people supplied by the San Diego County Water Authority.

The Colorado River drains seven states in the U.S. before it skirts the Mexicali Valley; in the days before dams, it went on to empty into the Sea of Cortez. Yet for the seven U.S. states, the Mexicali Valley might as well be the dark side of the moon.

In its last one hundred miles, the river provides water to some half-million acres of farmland—more land than is farmed in the Imperial Valley—and 3.1 million people, not only in the Mexicali Valley but also in places like Tijuana, which lies on the coast, just across the border from

San Diego, and is the largest city in the Mexican state of Baja California. That water is the last of the river's flow: the 9 percent that Mexico is entitled to under a 1944 treaty with the United States.

The city of Mexicali, the capital of Baja California, has a scruffy air, but it is undeniably booming, thanks in large part to the *maquiladoras* that have risen from the Sonoran Desert scrub to crank out products bound for the U.S. A local business group called the Mexicali Economic Development Council, led by some of the area's leading entrepreneurs and commonly known by its Spanish abbreviation, CDEM, has shouldered the somewhat contradictory task of promoting economic growth and quality of life in the city. And it has spearheaded the fight against the All-American Canal lining project.

Last year, CDEM sued the United States in U.S. court, alleging that the federal government failed to adequately consider potential harm to animals on the U.S. endangered species list that depend on leakage-fed wetlands along the border. It also alleged that the canal lining would deprive people in the Mexicali Valley of water that they had come to depend on and acquired rights to, and would set off a wave of migration by displaced farmers. The federal appeals court in San Francisco has, for now, ordered the lining project stopped until it can untangle the case.

For René Acuña, CDEM's executive director, the United States' outright ignorance of the lining project's impacts is yet one more chapter in the story of its blinkered attitude toward Mexico. "They said, 'OK. South of the border is the end of the world,' " Acuña steams, before he comes back sounding like a copywriter for next year's UNICEF cards. "We don't see the fence that divides the countries. We see a region. We are interrelated. We share roots, families, air, water, everything."

A hundred miles to the west, in the spit-shined dream that is San Diego, Dan Hentschke is not a person whose eyes turn misty at the notion of cross-border fraternity. Hentschke, who looks like a little Mr. Clean with Ben Franklin glasses, is the top lawyer for the San Diego County Water Authority. "Look. The Colorado River is fully appropriated. There is no other water to give around. It's done," he says. "Everybody knows what they have. And Mexico's trying to get more than they have."

Hentschke is fond of invoking the analogy of a leaky, ten-year-old garden hose and an unimaginably tactless neighbor. "When you turn on your faucet, the water leaks out, and trickles down into the ground, and waters your neighbor's orange tree. So you go to Home Depot, and you buy a new hose. And the guy who owns the orange tree says, 'Hey! You've had a leaky hose for years. Take a nail, and put a hole in that hose you just got, because I have a right to your water.' "

Even with the seepage from the United States' leaky hose, Baja California is facing a looming water crunch. In downtown Mexicali, the local branch of the National Water Commission is housed behind a whitewashed cinderblock wall that local children have painted with water-themed murals. There, a man named Julio Navarro oversees the valley's massive irrigation district, and it feels as if he is barricaded inside his report-stuffed office. "Managing water," he says, with a quietly exasperated laugh, "is managing conflict."

A new study funded by the North American Development Bank occupies a prominent place on his desk and hints at the shape of the future. Almost all the water currently available for farms and cities in the Mexicali Valley is already being used. Farmers are also pumping out almost 25 percent more groundwater than is naturally recharged into the ground each year, running up a significant debt against the future. Cities—most prominently Mexicali, where a new wave of *maquiladoras* is buying up land on the outskirts, and Tijuana, on the coast—now use about 12 percent of the valley's water, but they are expected to need twice as much by 2030.

The growing urban demand for water here is a mirror image of the water-strapped world north of the line, and the way out, Navarro says, is clear: tightening the system to recover the lost water. In fact, the Water Commission is already four decades into a water-efficiency improvement program, a program that, viewed one way, is essentially a perpetual effort to stay ahead of the coming conflict.

First, the government lined the main canals in the valley with concrete. Then it turned its attention to the secondary canals. Now, says Navarro, "we are working on the small ditches that deliver water directly to the fields" and even on farmers' fields themselves, footing half the cost of ominously named devices called laser levelers. These dust-billowing, laser-guided scrapers are hitched behind tractors and grade fields perfectly level, so water can be more evenly applied, increasing the amount available for consumption by crops and reducing the amount lost to percolation and runoff.

Even after decades of efficiency efforts, however, the district still loses nearly 40 percent of the water in its system every year. Those losses materialize out of the pages of Navarro's report and are tabulated as *pérdidas de agua*: a sort of gold worth chasing after and putting to productive use. And Baja California's booming cities are now exploring an idea lifted straight out of San Diego's book. "If the cities finance efficiency projects," says Navarro, "they can get the saved water." So far, he says, "they're only talking about it. But we think maybe in a year, two years ."

As overlooked as the Mexicali Valley is in the broader affairs of the Colorado River, there is a spot farther down the line that the dealmakers have ignored outright. It is the Colorado River Delta, a netherworld where, before the dams were built, the river created nearly two million acres of lush wetlands as it flowed toward and into the Sea of Cortez. Surrounded by the Sonoran Desert, the Delta was the heart of a complex ecological web that provided crucial habitat for resident populations of wildlife, nourished marine fisheries in the Gulf of California, and formed a critical link in the Pacific Flyway for birds flying north from Central America. And it is only here that the true impacts of the obsession with wringing out every last drop of water all the way down the Colorado River ultimately become visible.

For millions of years, the Delta received the entire flow of the river. As the first round of water conservation began playing out in the 1930s and the phalanx of dams went up, that water disappeared. The graph of the river's annual flow through those years looks like a hospital patient flat-lining.

Ed Glenn is a researcher at the University of Arizona who has extensively studied the Delta. The river ecosystems here, he says, "were shaped by the pulse-flood regime that's common on arid-zone rivers, and especially ones driven by El Niño cycles: in really wet years, pulse floods germinate the trees, and then the water retreats and those trees can live on groundwater." Without the floods that the native cottonwoods need to germinate and reproduce, they were crowded out by invasive tamarisk. By taming the floods—nature's ultimate form of "waste"—the dams undercut the resiliency of the Delta and turned it into a land of cracked mud and impenetrable thickets of salt-sucking tamarisk.

In the early 1980s, however, El Niño provided a brief, brilliant reminder of just what it is that natural "inefficiencies" do, most spectacularly in 1983, when storms stuffed so much snow and rain into the Rockies that the U.S. government was forced to crank wide the spill gates on Glen Canyon Dam as torrents of water charged toward the sea. The downriver surge created a massive, defibrillating spike on the hydrograph that burst Mexican levees and inundated much of the Delta. Like a patient emerging from a coma, the Delta showed signs of renewed life.

In 1999, Environmental Defense and several other conservation groups took up the Colorado River Delta's cause. They suggested that a reliable source of water for a "base flow," backed up with the occasional flood, could probably keep alive the one hundred fifty thousand acres of wetlands that had come back. With the reservoirs upstream brimming with water, holding the line in the Delta did not seem like a preposterous proposition: it would take just two-tenths of 1 percent of the river's long-term annual average flow, boosted by a flood pulse every four years of 1.8 percent of the river's flow.

Almost as soon as the proposal hit the streets, the current drought descended on the Colorado River, and the surplus water evaporated.

The Delta cannot conceivably be restored unless the seven Colorado River states in the U.S., which control 91 percent of the water in the river, lift a finger to help. There is a clear ecological link between the United States and the Delta: the river in Mexico provides crucial habitat both for birds that are federally protected as endangered in the U.S., and for migratory birds that wing their way up the Pacific Flyway into what the farmers along the border refer to as *Gringolandia*.

The U.S. states and the federal government have, however, consistently refused to include the Delta in the equation by which they run the river. They have, in the language of economists, largely externalized the environmental costs of water development from their calculations. In 2005, for example, California, Nevada, and Arizona signed what they hailed as a landmark Multi-Species Conservation Program for the Lower Colorado River, designed to protect endangered species while allowing those states to continue siphoning water out of the river. The Delta is conspicuously absent from the plan.

Now, the drought on the Colorado is dragging into what could be its eighth year. The seven states are urgently finalizing a plan to prepare for the catastrophic shortages that will come with a prolonged megadrought of the sort that climate researchers have found evidence of in the not-so-distant past. From synching up the operation of Hoover and Glen Canyon dams to meet water demands more efficiently, to building a new "Drop 2" reservoir in the Imperial Valley to catch inadvertent "overdeliveries" and flash floods that otherwise would escape down the river to Mexico, the states are turning their collective weight toward ironing out every last inefficiency on the river with an enthusiasm unseen since the original dam-building campaign.

It is hard to believe that there's much left to iron out. Today, about twenty miles below Morelos Dam, where Mexico siphons the majority of its share of Colorado River water to the Mexicali Valley, the river is literally as dry as dust. And yet, further downstream, in an area of marginal farms that the Mexican government ordered depopulated in 1976 and is slowly being reclaimed by the desert, the river, amazingly, re-emerges.

The vast majority of the Mexicali Valley drains to the Colorado River, and, somewhere out on the west edge of the valley, reed-lined drainage canals gather the water that has run off the area's farm fields. Like some mystical essence of the universe revealing itself, this is Julio Navarro's pérdidas de agua, water that has leaked from the valley's irrigation network, but has not been truly lost. The drains merge to form the Rio Hardy, a short tributary that returns water to the very bottom of the Colorado River watershed and the Delta. Much more drainage water remains unseen, in the form of groundwater that lies just below the surface, where plants can tap it with their roots.

By the standard calculations of the Colorado River's water users, the wastewater that makes its way back here is the merest trickle of the river's total flow. But it can be quantified in another extremely important way: it is enough to sustain life. Today, even though they are choked with tamarisk, the Delta's lagoons are secret worlds full of herons, pelicans, and cranes. The place feels like the world after humans are done with it, the world left over. It is filled with the birds, and the sound of the wind, and crowned by an infinite expanse of sky.

Few people know the Delta better than Francisco Zamora, who works for the Tucson, Arizona-based Sonoran Institute and manages its Delta restoration program. Zamora has a habit of making himself look small under his ball cap, but his mind is constantly at work puzzling out the enigmas of the Delta. His group is now partway into a pilot restoration project on the river, an effort largely focused on re-establishing cottonwood, willows, and mesquite in areas overtaken by tamarisk. But the main need now, says Zamora, is water.

The behavior of the entire hydrologic cycle in the Delta—how water is taken out of the Colorado at Morelos Dam, how it flows through the irrigation district, and the ways in which it returns to the Delta—is poorly understood. As a nonprofit, Zamora says, "We haven't been able to get all the resources we need" to tackle those questions. But he is working on it.

Zamora has cajoled numbers from the National Water Commission, sought money to install stream gauges to quantify how much water now makes its way through, and scrounged up $70,000 so scientists at the Autonomous University of Baja California and the University of Arizona can construct a computerized hydrologic model to tease out the intricacies of flow patterns. It is an effort that would normally cost close to a half-million dollars.

Wastewater flows into the Delta are now, at most, two cubic meters per second, less than four-tenths of 1 percent of the river's long-term annual average flow. Zamora is trying to scare up another two cubic meters per second. And he has possibly found it, or at least knows where to start looking.

Zamora is trying to get the city of Mexicali to agree to "donate" the outflow from a new wastewater-treatment plant to the Delta, rather than selling the treated water for re-use in Mexicali. But working closely with Osvel Hinojosa and the Mexican conservation group Pronatura, he has also identified nearly fifteen thousand acres of farmland in the Mexicali Valley that could be bought or leased to free up more water for the Delta. Last year, Hinojosa found the money—in a somewhat promising sign, it came through a grant from the U.S. Fish and Wildlife Service—to buy water rights from one hundred fourteen acres of farmland. He is now using a new provision in Mexican national water law to dedicate that water for the Delta. "We wanted to test the process and show that it can be done," Hinojosa says. "Hopefully, now, other organizations will be interested in providing funds" to expand the effort.

Yet the push for efficiency weighs heavily on his mind. "If we buy two cubic meters per second, but we lose two" because of efficiency improvements elsewhere, says Zamora, "then we go back to the same thing. Or even worse." And so, here, at the end of the line, a somewhat absurd possibility has suggested itself to Zamora and his colleagues: deploying efficiency to fight the environmental impacts of efficiency itself.

The Sonoran Institute and Pronatura are now trying to identify opportunities to fund water-efficiency improvements in the Mexicali Valley and deliver the saved water to the Delta. It may be the only way for the restoration effort to hold the line in a spiraling arms race of efficiency whose costs will otherwise fall entirely on the environment.

Zamora and his colleagues are at a decided fiscal disadvantage, however, when compared with the wherewithal that the seven states and the West's booming metropolitan areas can bring to bear on efficiency. They may be stuck trying to play penny-ante stakes in a game that they cannot afford to win.

Meanwhile, not far north of the Delta—and in several spots throughout the Mexicali Valley—Julio Navarro's plan for staving off a water war is taking shape. The scene is eerily reminiscent of what is planned for the All-American Canal. Alongside an old, unlined canal, a backhoe with a special scoop shaped like the cross-section of a canal is slowly digging a second, parallel trench. Close behind, a dump truck and six men with shovels and trowels are lining the new canal with concrete, to save water for the Mexicali Valley irrigation district.

In the face of the renewed quest for efficiency by the seven basin states and Mexico, the paradoxical need to protect the "waste" that keeps the Delta alive is more important than ever. Jennifer Pitt, a Boulder, Colorado-based analyst with Environmental Defense, says, "I'm in a really awkward position, having to argue against efficiency projects, but we need to get water dedicated to the environment."

Pitt and other environmental advocates have alternately pleaded for and strong-armed access to the world of the water bosses as they make plans to tighten the screws down even further. In an effort to reduce some of the pressure on the river, the Delta advocates have proposed a further expansion of the trading-conservation-investments-for-water idea, in which water users in the U.S. could fund water-efficiency programs in Mexico, in exchange for the conserved water. That could obviate the need for new projects like the Drop 2 reservoir, which will essentially vacuum up any unintentional "slop" that heads down the river toward the Delta. It would also potentially allow U.S. water users to get more bang for their efficiency-improving buck in Mexico.

The seven states are interested in investigating such possibilities—a move, Pitt concedes, that puts the restoration effort on somewhat perilous ground. "If we get everybody playing nice to increase efficiency, and we make no progress on environmental flows," she says, "then we're really screwed."

In the Mexicali Valley, people are contemplating how the cascading impacts of efficiency will change their lives. Not far from Gerónimo Hernández's farm, a farmer named Jesús Figueroa stands on the edge of a field of flood-irrigated alfalfa, his pants rolled to his knees. After twenty-five years in the U.S., Figueroa returned to Mexico in 2001 to help his father run the family's farm. If the All-American Canal seepage dries up, he says, "there are no other options in the valley," and he will likely head back across the line. It would save him a lot of trouble, Figueroa laughs, "if they just move the border line down here"—either way, he'd end up in the U.S.

The problem for the Delta, too, is ultimately less one of technical fixes than of borders and horizons. The contemporary focus on efficiency is a significant shift away from the mindset that tried to outflank the harsh realities of the desert with dams and concrete. It seems to fit the curves of the western landscape far better than a dam. Yet instead of vanquishing the demons of aridity, efficiency has only chased them into the dark. And it has now run up against the quintessential problem of the West.

The entire western pioneering enterprise was, at its core, an effort to push the world's boundaries ever farther. Far horizons offer eternal promise: another river, just over the next ridge, to be tapped for its water; another planet to mine. But we have never expanded our field of vision enough to include all the real costs of being here. We have not civilized the West so much as savaged it, leaving Francisco Zamora and Osvel Hinojosa rattling a tin cup in an effort to pay down the ecological debt run up by every single person who depends on water from the Colorado River.

Untangling the competing demands on the river will be an incremental and possibly perpetual endeavor. It is tempting to argue that the enterprise of developing the Colorado was made feasible in the first place only by writing off the cost of its environmental effects on the Delta. But that simply is not true: those costs are mere fractions of the total amount of water in the river and the money spent to develop that water. They are so small that including them in the dealmakers' calculations from the very beginning would have never come even remotely close to breaking the entire river-development proposition. And so we are now left with a choice: endlessly pursuing yet one more house-of-mirrors fix or, finally, trying to set the equation right.

February 5, 2007

Matt Jenkins is a *High Country News* contributing editor.

Charting the Course of the San Pedro

Michelle Nijhuis

In the hot, dry grasslands of southeastern Arizona, the San Pedro River is an oasis. Unlike many other desert rivers, the shallow San Pedro is free-flowing, and its banks are soil, not concrete. Cottonwood and willow forests line the northward-flowing river, from its origins in Sonora, Mexico, to its confluence with the Gila River, providing a one hundred and forty-five-mile-long haven for migratory songbirds and humans alike.

"It's the best fishing hole, by far the best birdwatching area, and it's the best place to catch some early afternoon shade when it gets really hot," says Paul Hardy, director of The Nature Conservancy's Upper San Pedro River program. "Its health is impaired, but it hasn't been degraded to the point that other Southwestern rivers have."

These days, the San Pedro River Basin is booming. The towns of Sierra Vista and Huachuca City are attracting retirees looking for good weather and a small-town lifestyle. Subdivisions and unplanned "wildcat" developments are on the rise, competing with the river for the basin's limited water.

The fate of the San Pedro has been a hot local issue for years, and its designation as a National Riparian Conservation Area in 1988 helped bring it national attention. Now an international environmental commission has joined the debate, hoping to point the way toward a better future for the desert river and the basin's communities. The next step is up to local residents. If they don't take action, federal regulations could force their hand.

Many conservationists feared the 1993 North American Free Trade Agreement, a treaty intended to reduce trade barriers between Canada, Mexico, and the United States, would allow corporations to evade environmental regulations with a quick and easy border crossing.

In response to these concerns, negotiators created the trinational Commission for Environmental Cooperation. The commission, which has no enforcement power, analyzes environmental problems related to international trade.

Two years ago, the Southwest Center for Biological Diversity and the Denver-based law firm Earthlaw petitioned the commission, asking it to study the effects of residential groundwater use, irrigated agriculture, and cattle grazing on the health of the San Pedro River. Their petition was successful, and in May 1997 the commission began its first investigation in the United States.

Just over a year later, the commission began pumping out reports. First came a draft report from a panel of experts, which described the threats to the San Pedro from increasing groundwater use by residents of the basin. The report was summarized and distributed in southeastern Arizona newspapers. The commission, in cooperation with the Udall Center for Public Policy at the University of Arizona, then held a series of public meetings inside and outside the basin, and the Udall Center released a two-inch-thick collection of public comments in September. A final expert report is expected to be completed in the spring.

This past fall, a thirteen-member advisory panel including local politicians, a rancher from the San Pedro Basin, academics from all three nations, and a former prime minister of Canada—used the draft expert report to come up with some recommendations for the communities of the San Pedro River Basin.

"It's a very eclectic group," says Jack Pfister, a professor at Arizona State University and co-chairman of the advisory panel. "It's made consensus a little more difficult, but it's a strong group."

The panel's report, released in December, addresses problems on both sides of the international border. On the U.S. side, the panel recommends more aggressive growth management in the basin and the retirement of irrigated fields along the San Pedro through easements or buyouts.

"Their call for stronger zoning and control represents great progress," says Robin Silver, conservation chair of the Southwest Center and landowner in the San Pedro basin. "They're admitting that there need to be some changes locally, and we were vigorously attacked for suggesting the same thing just a few years ago. But if there's no enforcement, this means nothing."

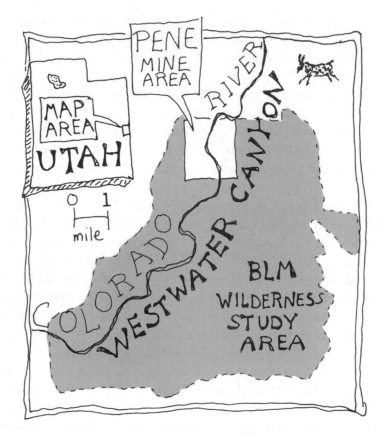

The small towns near the San Pedro must now decide what to do with the panel's recommendations, and it doesn't look like the decisions will come easily.

"Our experience is that these guys [from the commission] are little more than new-age, feel-good thugs," says Harold Vangilder, a Sierra Vista city councilman. "If the San Pedro River is a national treasure, we are an impoverished nation. You can't drown a fish in it."

There is a great deal of local resistance to conservation measures for the San Pedro. Some environmental groups, including the Southwest Center, have long pointed to Fort Huachuca—a military base in Sierra Vista with more than ten thousand employees—as the biggest drain on the river. Although the commission reports have opposed the closure of the fort, citing its importance to the local economy, the commission has still drawn fire from supporters of Fort Huachuca.

"It's made a lot of people feel defensive and a little bit paranoid," says Al Anderson, a Sierra Vista resident and owner of the Gray Hawk Ranch, a guest ranch for birdwatchers located near the San Pedro River. "[The commission] has made it harder for our elected officials to deny and ignore the issue, but it's also made them stonewall."

Other residents are supportive of the recommendations, but wonder where they'll find the money to implement them. "Without somebody coming forth with a grant to set up a central agency—without someone in power to bring these recommendations into actual being—nothing's going to happen," says Jack Ladd, a rancher on the San Pedro and a member of the advisory committee.

"To ask a community of forty thousand people to come up with multiple millions to solve this problem—it just isn't feasible," says Marie Hansen, public information officer for the city of Sierra Vista. "But I think the attention we're getting [because of the commission report] can be positive in terms of securing funding." Private foundations have expressed interest in funding the conservation effort.

Recent rumblings of federal regulation may cast the commission's advice in a new light. At the end of December, in response to a lawsuit from the Southwest Center, the U.S. Fish and Wildlife Service proposed the designation of sections of the San Pedro as critical habitat for the Huachuca water umbel, an endangered semi-aquatic plant. A critical-habitat designation would give the federal agency responsibility for protecting the San Pedro, taking much of the decision making out of the hands of basin residents.

It's a switch that few locals want to see, regardless of their political stripe. "What will get us over the hump? A stick like the [Endangered Species Act] would probably do it," says Hardy. "But none of us wants to see that. It would be our local failing if the [Act] is invoked."

"If the recommendations of our report are totally ignored, the ultimate consequence is going to be a long, protracted battle in court," adds Pfister. "That may still happen, but at least we're pointing the way to an alternative course of action."

April 12, 1999

Michelle Nijhuis is contributing editor to *High Country News*.

A Thirst for Growth

Tony Davis

A small oasis of cattail marshes and ponds thrives amid the paved roads and parking lots in this city of strip malls and car dealers. Though birdwatchers slink along its shores, trying to catch a glimpse of a black-necked stilt or American avocet, this marsh is not natural. Its water comes from the toilets, sinks, and grease traps of the burgeoning Sunbelt city of Sierra Vista.

This is the Environmental Operations Park, a $7.8 million wastewater-recharge project designed to help the city hold onto as much of its precious water as possible. Fifty acres of marshy wetlands take up nitrogen from partially treated sewage. Then, the water is transferred into thirty acres of basins, where it is supposed to settle into an aquifer, replenishing the water that's been pumped out. The recharge project sinks 1,840 acre-feet of water into the ground each year—enough water to cover 1,840 football fields a foot deep. It is the most visible accomplishment of the Upper San Pedro Partnership, a six-year-old consortium that represents government, environmental, and development interests.

The partnership has embraced a very ambitious goal: to balance pumping and recharge, and eventually put more water back into the ground than farmers, businesses, and residents take out. If it succeeds, Sierra Vista will be able to do what virtually no other community that relies on groundwater in the arid West has ever done—live sustainably on a limited water supply. In water lingo, it's called "sustainable yield."

Achieving this would also halt the decline of the Southwest's last undammed and ungrazed river, the San Pedro, which needs ample groundwater to maintain its surface flows. The San Pedro's marshy jungles of cattails and bulrushes and its unmatched stands of cottonwoods and willows support three hundred and fifty to four hundred species of birds. Up to four million visitors come here every year: Sierra Vista has become an internationally known birdwatching destination. But the city's excessive groundwater pumping could dry up the river; studies have been sounding a warning for two decades now.

The sewage-recharge project is just one of one hundred activities the partnership has started to save the San Pedro. Over the past six years, it has raised $46 million to plan and build recharge projects, finance water studies, and carry out conservation projects. It has started a "Waterwise" public education program. And it has won friends in the research community and among many public officials.

The partnership is the most effective watershed-management group in Arizona and perhaps in the West, says Tom Whitmer, a member of the Partnership Advisory Commission and an Arizona Department of Water Resources official. Mark Anderson, a top-level United States Geological Survey official in Tucson who also sits on the twenty-five-member advisory commission, agrees: "They're making things happen," he says. "They're more influential than a lot of organizations at securing money to support science to make management decisions."

Despite the partnership's work, groundwater pumping is still on the rise in Sierra Vista. Critics, including both local and national environmental organizations as well as neighborhood groups, are growing impatient. The Arizona Department of Water Resources estimates that the overdraft has reached about eighty-four hundred acre-feet annually, a 20 percent increase since the partnership was founded. Holly Richter, a Partnership Advisory Commission member and The Nature Conservancy's Upper San Pedro program manager, says that when conservation measures are properly accounted for, the overdraft is more like thirty-five hundred acre-feet. But the Audubon Society, another partnership member, says that number can't be validated without further study.

There are other questions. The U.S. Geological Survey has found layers of clay and silt one to two hundred feet thick, one hundred feet beneath the wastewater-recharge ponds. Clay is far less permeable than sand or gravel, and it could be actually diverting the effluent northward, away from the river. One spring a mile and a half north of the recharge plant seems to be increasing its flow.

The critics say that even if the recharge plan works, it's no more than a Band-Aid slapped on the San Pedro's primary threats: growth and unregulated groundwater pumping. So far, the Upper San Pedro Partnership has been unwilling to confront these issues. Partnership leaders say conservation can't do the job alone, and that growth can't be stopped, although it can be redirected. They warn that Sierra Vista may eventually need to import water.

In an era of drought, the partnership wants it all: growth, a bustling economy—and a healthy San Pedro River. The question arises: is that even possible?

The Upper San Pedro Partnership, like so many of the West's collaborative enterprises, grew out of the muck of past failures and old conflicts. Doubts about Sierra Vista's water use began to surface in the 1980s, when the first of a long list of studies from state and federal agencies and university scientists warned that the San Pedro River was living on borrowed time. Continued overpumping, they said, was to blame.

In 1984, the federal Department of Housing and Urban Development responded, briefly imposing a moratorium on new Federal Housing Administration-approved mortgages in the Sierra Vista area. A hailstorm of developer protests followed, and the moratorium was lifted the same day news of it broke in local papers. Ten years later, as evidence of overpumping mounted, community leaders formed a Water Issues Group. It agreed to push for state legislation to create a locally run groundwater-management area. But that effort imploded, too, after nearly a thousand people turned out at a January 1995 public hearing in Sierra Vista to accuse the group of "jamming it down our throats," according to the *Sierra Vista Herald*.

In 1997, the Commission on Environmental Cooperation—which represents Mexico, the United States, and Canada and enforces environmental rules under the North American Free Trade Agreement—commissioned a team of experts to look at the San Pedro. Its 1999 report advocated "aggressive water conservation and harvesting strategies." It called for a locally approved strategy to limit water pumping, an effort to manage and guide population growth, and the voluntary retirement of irrigated agriculture in the Upper San Pedro River Basin north of Mexico.

Jack Pfister, the retired Phoenix-area utility executive who chaired the commission's San Pedro Advisory Panel, added a postscript to that report. He said that many panel members believe the river will survive "only if the local leaders have the courage and creativity to give protecting the river the same priority and energy as promoting growth."

Today, although little has been done in Sierra Vista to limit urban pumping or manage growth, The Nature Conservancy and Fort Huachuca, a nearby Army base, have bought nine hundred acres of farmland to retire its groundwater pumping. The federal government has reintroduced beaver in the San Pedro, hoping that beaver dams will back up water and help restore century-old marshes. And a key commission recommendation—the formation of a local advisory panel—was realized in 1998. That group became the Upper San Pedro Partnership, which now represents twenty-one interest groups, including eight federal agencies, four state agencies, five local governments, The Nature Conservancy, the Arizona Audubon Society, and Bella Vista Ranches, the area's largest developer.

Four years after its formation, the partnership received an unwitting boost from a federal judge and the Endangered Species Act. For many years, the Tucson-based Center for Biological Diversity had been pressing legal action against Fort Huachuca, accusing it and the U.S. Fish and Wildlife Service of failing to properly account for the fort's impacts on the endangered Southwestern willow flycatcher and the Huachuca water umbel, a semi-aquatic plant. In April 2002, U.S. District Judge Alfredo Marquez in Tucson ruled that the base's operations are in fact likely to jeopardize the continued existence of both species.

The decision sparked fears in Sierra Vista that the military base would be cut back, or shut down altogether. Fort Huachuca has been the area's economic bulwark for more than a century; it employs nine thousand people full-time and pumps up to $600 million a year into the local economy. Intense congressional debate followed, and legislation was introduced that would have absolved the fort of responsibility for all off-post water use. Finally, a rider to the 2003-2004 Defense Authorization bill was passed, limiting Fort Huachuca's liability for actions outside its boundaries.

The compromise legislation, introduced by Senator John McCain, Republican-Arizona, was blasted by some activists as a slow death sentence for the river. Yet it had a silver lining: it ordered the Upper San Pedro Partnership to produce a series of annual reports on how it will end the overpumping of groundwater by 2011. The law does not require that the overpumping actually cease. But the partnership has signed a pledge to stop it, and it has promised annual reports on its progress.

If the partnership succeeds, Fort Huachuca will survive. It may even get larger: officials from Governor Janet Napolitano on down are pushing to add more missions and jobs to the post next year.

To save the river—and still accommodate growth—the partnership has lassoed state and federal dollars to recharge treated sewage and retire farmland. And it plans to spend millions more over the coming decade.

But the group has moved much more slowly when it comes to garden-variety water conservation. Sierra Vista now requires swimming-pool covers to prevent evaporation, and it has subsidized replacement of high-flow with low-flow toilets. Waterless urinals are required in new commercial developments, water misters are banned, car washes must recycle 75 percent of the water they use, and turf use is prohibited in nonresidential development.

But the partnership's 2004 conservation plan concentrates on building new detention basins and recharge plants, instead of telling—or even asking—people to use less water. Ironically, the group believes growth can help reduce the overpumping: it anticipates that rainfall runoff will increase as the desert is paved, and that this extra runoff will dump more water into the washes that help replenish the aquifer. Based on one study, the partnership is using this formula to credit thirty-two hundred acre-feet against an expected thirteen thousand nine hundred acre-feet deficit by 2011.

Judy Gignac, a member of the Partnership Advisory Commission and the general manager of Bella Vista Ranches, says the group plans to introduce a model conservation ordinance next year for local governments. But Sierra Vista officials may be reluctant to embrace it: they say that conservation is expensive and ineffective compared to effluent recharge.

"Our toilet rebate program cost us $100 per toilet, and eight hundred toilets brought us [just] twenty-three acre-feet total savings," says Chuck Potucek, the city manager.

The lack of aggressive conservation measures irks Tricia Gerrodette, a member of the local Audubon Society and an alternate member to the partnership commission. Early this year, she presented the group with a proposal that would ban new residential swimming pools and water-hogging swamp coolers, and require low-water-use home landscaping, among other things. The partnership "flat wouldn't even talk about it," she says.

"There's so little that's real about what is happening here. They are not dealing with growth management, and not much with conservation. There are extremely limited requirements on new housing. We've done almost nothing as far as retrofitting, except for the toilet rebates."

That's not surprising, responds Gignac. "It takes a political will to do [what Gerrodette proposes] and it also takes enforcement," she says. "How you enforce some of those things is tough."

The partnership does have the political will to support continued studies. About $3.5 million has gone into researching river ecology, the feasibility of conservation schemes, a decision-making computer model to understand the effects of water policy changes, and an updated computerized model of the groundwater system's workings. Not everyone is pleased: veteran University of Arizona hydrologist Thomas Maddock, who did some of the early studies more than a decade ago, says, "In essence, if you don't want to do anything on the river, you just keep studying it." He calls the San Pedro "the most studied river in the world."

But all the studies are hobbled by the fact that anywhere from fifteen hundred to eighteen hundred homes near the river get their water from private wells, which by law are exempt from having to tell the government how much they use each year, says Maddock, now head of the university's hydrology department. "We don't know what's causing the stress on our system. If we don't know, how can we make accurate groundwater models?"

Gignac and The Nature Conservancy's Richter maintain that the studies are building a foundation for stronger action in the future. In particular, Richter cites a soon-to-be-finished, $1.5 million study of the river's plant communities as "cutting edge," one of the Southwest's most comprehensive studies of a riparian ecosystem. "Every year, we create an annual conservation plan. All the science that has been accomplished is incorporated into that year's plan, and the plan is updated as new science is available," says Richter.

In the meantime, Sierra Vista's population has grown by 7 percent since 2000. More than forty thousand people live here now, and the metro area could boom to close to a hundred thousand by 2030. Cochise County's population is now one hundred and twenty-four thousand, up from ninety-seven thousand six hundred in 1990. If every square inch of buildable private and state land in the Sierra Vista portion of the basin is developed to the maximum allowed under current zoning, it could theoretically reach about two hundred and ten thousand.

Unplanned subdivisions—often called "wildcat" developments—made up more than 60 percent of the county's building activity in 2000, and they all have unmetered private wells. From 2000 through 2003, the area's private water companies increased pumping by 13 percent, on top of a 40 percent increase between 1990 and 2000.

That's not all: a ten-year-old change in state Water Department policy allows developers to say that Sierra Vista has enough water despite the known threats to the river. Until 1993, Arizona had acknowledged that the area's water supply was inadequate to support new developments for one hundred years. But, under pressure from developers, it reversed that policy, and since 1993, it has given water-adequacy notices to about fifty developments.

Even with inadequacy notices, these fifty developments could still have taken place. The notices are merely disclosure tools for homebuyers. But longtime San Pedro defender Robin Silver believes they can help slow development. He took the policy to court, but lost earlier this year, when a State Appeals Court panel ruled that his group, the Center for Biological Diversity, lacked standing to file the case. Silver is now considering filing a consumer-fraud complaint with the state attorney general's office, after an assistant attorney general said that the case is more of a consumer-disclosure issue.

"It might not stop a development, but imagine if you are trying to get a federal loan or federal project, and the statement says there is an inadequate supply of water," he says.

The Upper San Pedro Partnership has shunned Silver, yet some of its members recognize that the group has not tackled the nine-hundred-pound growth gorilla. "Nobody in rural areas talks about growth publicly. They talk about it behind the scenes," says partnership commission member Whitmer. Even so, he says, Sierra Vista comes closer to doing so than most places.

Recently, the partnership has started to discuss seeking state legislation allowing local governments to transfer development rights. That would allow Sierra Vista to move dense development away from the river to areas where water wells would have less short-term impact.

But the Sierra Vista city government rarely, if ever, turns down a major rezoning. One of its planning commissioners, Robert Caulfield, says the city attorney told commissioners that they lack the legal right to do so, as long as the rezoning matches the city's comprehensive plan and meets all the codes. That's an attitude sharply different from that of neighboring Pima County, home of Tucson, which denies or sharply modifies rezonings all the time.

"It's their property," says Caulfield, a retired Army officer who moved to Sierra Vista in 1997. "As long as it complies with the code, if they want to go from thirty-six thousand square feet per residence to twenty thousand square feet, who are we to say you can't do that?"

But retiree and neighborhood activist Stan Gardner believes the council has been too willing to accommodate developers, and the partnership too slow to take any action.

"I go to some of their meetings. I sit and listen and think, 'Why in the world don't they get something done instead of talking about it?' " says Gardner, who moved here from Ohio two years ago, drawn by the area's birdwatching. "They've been in meetings five years, but as far as I can tell they have accomplished hardly anything."

Sierra Vista could save water, activists say: Gerrodette points to neighboring Fort Huachuca as an example. Since 1989, when legal pressure against the fort increased, its water use has dropped by more than half, to a little more than fifteen hundred acre-feet per year, even though the base's population has stayed roughly the same, according to Gretchen Kent, the post's National Environmental Policy Act coordinator.

Since 1994, post residents have been allowed to use outdoor sprinklers two nights a week, only in May and June. Any family that is cited three times—something that has never happened—may be kicked off the post by the base commander. New homes are equipped with low-flow toilets and refrigerated air conditioners that use less water than swamp coolers. The post has replaced three hundred and fifty top-loading washing machines with water-saving front-loading models, and installed four hundred waterless urinals. When 1.5 million square feet of World War II-era buildings were demolished, their entire water systems were turned off.

The difference between Fort Huachuca and Sierra Vista has not been lost on Army officials. In May 2003, the Army's Washington, D.C., office wrote that "While Fort Huachuca has undertaken aggressive conservation measures, steadily reducing its water consumption since 1988, unrestrained growth in the civilian community has continued to aggravate the water-deficit situation."

City and state water officials respond that they lack the Army's authority, and that they can't control water rates because private water companies provide the water. The state Corporation Commission doesn't allow the companies to raise rates to force conservation. Higher rates could reduce the companies' water sales, the state's Whitmer says. "It's not that private water companies are against conservation. They just can't afford it," he says. The partnership is looking into pushing for legislation to set up a water-pricing scheme to encourage conservation.

Yet many locals seem to favor a tougher approach to water management than the partnership's leaders. The three hundred residents who attended a series of focus-group meetings on water last spring gave their greatest support—by a margin of up to 74 percent—to regulating water use through codes, charging people more for excessive water use, and replacing high-use home fixtures. Importing water ranked last; only 20.8 percent supported it.

"We need to live within our means and not look to outside sources," one respondent said. "Robbing Peter to pay Paul: bad idea," said another. "Why should others make water available for us to waste?" a third wondered.

Whitmer wasn't impressed: "The majority don't understand that water conservation can only get you so far," he says. "You go to talk to people about water, and their general knowledge is that it comes out of a tap." Environmentalists acknowledge that conservation can't do the whole job, but they say Sierra Vista is using that fact as an excuse to do too little. Silver has petitioned the state to impose an active groundwater-management area in Sierra Vista and its vicinity. That would give the state the power to limit pumping if local communities won't do it voluntarily.

Gignac, campaign manager for the re-election effort of the chair of the County Board of Supervisors, says such a management scheme won't work unless it protects the river and not just the aquifer. Most active-management areas are designed to protect only groundwater. But in Santa Cruz County to the west, a state-run active-management area could help protect one of the last remnant wet stretches of the Santa Cruz River.

The Arizona Department of Water Resources will decide whether to propose such a management scheme this fall—four years after Silver filed his petition.

Of course, there is a time-honored western alternative to moratoriums, conservation, effluent ponds, and the like: just buy outside water and pipe it in to save both the residents and the river.

Water importation is not an official partnership policy, but the group is having the U.S. Bureau of Reclamation study it, just in case. Already the idea has produced fireworks.

In July, as a Partnership Advisory Commission meeting wound down, Cochise County Supervisor Les Thompson, a conservative Republican, turned to a volatile subject not on the agenda. It was the partnership's long-term study of importing water from underneath farmland north of Benson, his hometown, twenty-five miles north of Sierra Vista.

Over and over, partnership leaders have said that the study is just a look at the feasibility of bringing in water from Benson, or the neighboring towns of Tombstone and Bisbee, or perhaps even from the Colorado River via the gargantuan Central Arizona Project, whose pipeline now stops just south of Tucson, ninety miles west. The estimated costs of this range from as little as $6.3 million for water from Tombstone (sixteen miles away), to $119 million for the Central Arizona Project. Millions more would be needed just to operate and maintain the systems.

But Thompson was angry because no one from the partnership had told Benson about the study when it began. He wanted the subject taken off the table forever.

"To me, it was like blood. I've been a homeowner twenty-five years. As long as [the threat of taking Benson's water] is there, it [creates] a cloud of distrust. I don't know how to deal with this other than to eliminate the problem," Thompson said.

Gignac quickly told Thompson that she understood his concern. But she added that it made no sense to take any option off the table until it had been fully studied. Sierra Vista Mayor Tom Hessler said he would only kill the idea "with great reluctance."

In the end, no vote was taken. But the incident was just a hint of the increasingly broad, fierce and divisive pressures that are likely to hit the partnership, as growth—and drought—continue, and water becomes more scarce.

"It's going to become more and more contentious," developer Gignac says. "We are going to wait and see if we have the stomach to talk about these things, argue about them, get emotional about them, and see if we can come up with solutions rather than destroying ourselves."

August 30, 2004

Tony Davis is a reporter for the *Arizona Daily Star*.

Of Politics and the River

John Dougherty

A longtime water expert for the U.S. Geological Survey is predicting that the last free-flowing river in the desert Southwest will stop flowing because of excessive groundwater pumping.

"The San Pedro River will run dry, even if they shut off all the pumps tomorrow," says Robert Mac Nish, the former district chief of water resources in Arizona for the USGS. "Nothing is poised to take the necessary steps to save the river. Everyone is standing around and wringing their hands and doing studies. In the meantime, the river is going to go dry."

The San Pedro Watershed includes the nation's first national riparian-conservation area, established by Congress in 1988 to "protect and enhance" habitat for some three hundred bird species. Mac Nish's gloomy assessment comes just weeks after the U.S. Fish and Wildlife Service issued a controversial biological opinion allowing the San Pedro River Valley's primary economic engine—Fort Huachuca and the U.S. Army Intelligence Center located there—to add three thousand personnel to the more than twelve thousand soldiers and family members who live on and off post.

Environmental activists have long argued that Fort Huachuca expansions trigger groundwater-dependent development outside the military installation in areas that threaten the San Pedro. Mac Nish says the June 15 biological opinion "doesn't make sense" and only worsens an already dismal outlook for the river.

The biological opinion is controversial not just for its environmental conclusions, but also for its political dimension, a dimension that includes the federal grand jury investigation of Arizona Congressman Rick Renzi.

The recently completed Endangered Species Act evaluation of Fort Huachuca focused on a plant called the water umbel. The review reached a conclusion that was surprising to many environmentalists: expansion of the fort would have no impact on the water umbel, considered a key indicator of the San Pedro's health.

But the evaluation was conducted under constraints contained in a rider to a Defense Authorization bill that Congress passed in 2003 aimed specifically at Fort Huachuca.

And that rider was no ordinary rider.

It was championed by Renzi, a three-term Flagstaff Republican whose congressional district includes neither Fort Huachuca nor the San Pedro River. And it required the Fish and Wildlife Service to look only at environmental impacts caused directly by federal personnel when it prepared its opinion on Fort Huachuca expansion.

Private economic activities—new domestic wells that only need state and county permits, for instance—would normally be included in the analysis for such an opinion, says Jeff Humphrey, a spokesman for the wildlife agency. But, Humphrey says, "Our ability to do that was removed by that legislation."

It's impossible to say whether the outcome of the biological opinion would have been different if Renzi's rider had not been enacted, Humphrey says: "That would be sheer speculation."

And spokeswoman Tanja Linton says the Army has made no decision on whether or when Fort Huachuca might expand operations.

All the same, Fort Huachuca currently accounts for about two-thirds of all business activity in rapidly growing Sierra Vista and unincorporated Cochise County, injecting $830 million a year into the local economy.

It seems reasonable to wonder whether the potential for an expanding Fort Huachuca could increase the value of nearby private property, such as an irrigated field once owned by one of Congressman Renzi's business partners. That field is now apparently part of a federal grand jury investigation.

In early 2005, Renzi began negotiations with two private groups seeking to exchange environmentally sensitive private land for federally owned land. Though never consummated, those proposed trades have garnered headlines in the national press and attention from the FBI.

In both proposed trades, Renzi asked the private groups, which wanted to acquire the public land for development purposes, to purchase a four hundred and eighty-acre irrigated alfalfa field a half-mile west of the San Pedro River. The field was using up to fifteen hundred-acre feet of water a year, enough to have a direct impact on flows in the nearby river, hydrologists say.

But this field was not just any field. It was owned by James Sandlin, a former business partner of Renzi who'd purchased it for $960,000 in February 2000, property records show.

In May 2005, Sandlin sold the four hundred and eighty acres for $4.5 million to one of the groups seeking to trade for federal land, Preserve Petrified Forest Land Investors LLC, an Arizona partnership that lists former Interior Secretary and Arizona Governor Bruce Babbitt in its management. Preserve Petrified Forest had received Renzi's assurance that he would support a land swap of the San Pedro acreage for federal property in central Arizona the partnership wanted to acquire, the *Wall Street Journal* has reported.

On the day that Sandlin sold the alfalfa field to Preserve Petrified Forest, apparently making a $3.5 million profit, he sent $200,000 to a company owned by his former partner, Renzi.

Soon after the land sale, a lobbyist for the other private group interested in a federal land swap, Resolution Copper Company, complained to Renzi that Preserve Petrified Forest had received preferential treatment. According to the Associated Press, Renzi later dropped support for Preserve Petrified Forest's land swap, and neither of the land swaps has occurred.

Last April, the FBI raided Renzi's business office, which includes a family-owned insurance company. Several news outlets have reported that he is the focus of a Tucson-based federal grand jury investigation. He has temporarily resigned from several House committees, including the committee that oversees land exchanges.

Calls to Renzi's office seeking comment about the San Pedro River and the Sandlin land sale were not returned, and attempts to contact Preserve Petrified Forest's managers, including Babbitt, were unsuccessful.

Former Arizona Attorney General Grant Woods, who represented Renzi last fall, said then that the congressman wanted Sandlin's land to be swapped to the federal government to protect the river and Fort Huachuca operations. Woods said Renzi walked away from the proposed land swap when people questioned his role in the deal, according to the AP.

"He was trying to do the right thing and help a wide variety of constituents out," Woods said. "The minute he heard anyone insinuate there was a problem, he said, 'Fine,' and walked away."

Last October, Guy Inzalaco, a top manager with Preserve Petrified Forest, was quoted in the Washington Post as saying that he hadn't known that Renzi and Sandlin had once been business partners. Inzalaco told the Associated Press he didn't know why Renzi never followed through with the land-swap legislation, leaving his company with four hundred and eighty acres of environmentally sensitive land. "We feel we've been somewhat victimized here," Inzalaco said.

Preserve Petrified Forest is now offering to sell the land for $5.2 million, says Sierra Vista Realtor Beth Wilkerson, the listing agent.

Wilkerson says the land is zoned to build up to one hundred and sixty-one homes and has unlimited water available for development. "The owners are highly motivated to get rid of this parcel," she says.

Proposed land swaps and questionable federal legislation aside, it's clear the San Pedro is in trouble.

Mac Nish's flat declaration that the river will dry up is the starkest warning to date. It's a warning that carries weight, given Mac Nish's thirty-year tenure in Arizona, at USGS and as an adjunct professor at the University of Arizona.

Early this July, the San Pedro River nearly ran dry at a key monitoring station known as the Charleston gauge. The river recorded no flow there in July 2005 and July 2006.

Flows at the Charleston gauge—a location where bedrock forces groundwater to the surface—have been monitored for more than seventy years, and, before 2005, the river had never run dry there. Scientists and environmentalists blame a combination of drought, water absorption by streamside vegetation, and excessive groundwater pumping for the decreased summer flows.

Mac Nish says groundwater withdrawals over the last fifty years have created a deepening and widening "cone of depression" that has now reached the San Pedro and "will continue to deepen at the river even if the pumps are shut off."

The San Pedro, he says, is only beginning to feel the impacts of past groundwater pumping. The city of Sierra Vista, which lies twelve miles west of the river, has been growing at more than 2 percent a year for the last fifteen years, reaching a population of 44,870 in 2006. The city's population is projected to reach fifty-one thousand by 2011, and there are tens of thousands more people living in adjacent unincorporated areas.

That growth rate doesn't bode well for the river. In 2002, groundwater pumped out of the San Pedro River Basin exceeded replenishment by 5,144 acre-feet per year, according to Robin Silver of the Center for Biological Diversity, a Tucson-based environmental group. By 2006, groundwater pumping exceeded replenishment by eleven thousand three hundred acre-feet—or almost 3.7 billion gallons—per year, Silver says.

Despite the clear connection between groundwater withdrawals and the health of the river, Mac Nish says community leaders have avoided taking the necessary steps to save the river.

"I've been working on that basin since the late eighties, and starting in 1990, it became apparent that groundwater pumping was going to have a pretty strong impact on the river," Mac Nish says. "We talked to county officials, city officials, fort officials about the river. But everybody kept looking for other explanations for why the river seemed to be drying up."

The Upper San Pedro Water Partnership, a group of water users authorized by Congress to find ways to save the river, hopes to reduce groundwater pumping immediately adjacent to the river by purchasing property and conservation easements, rather than addressing groundwater depletion caused by water use in Sierra Vista.

"This is such an urgent issue that there is a need to focus on the direct and immediate impacts on this river system, because we are right on the edge," says Holly Richter, chairwoman of the partnership's technical advisory committee. "If we don't solve the short-term impact issues now, there won't be a river to conserve later."

August 6, 2007

John Dougherty is a *High Country News* contributing editor.

The Rio Grande

A Tangled Web of Watersheds

Michelle Nijhuis

The Rio Costilla represents only a tiny part of the overall Rio Grande system, which crosses state and international boundaries, trickles through dams, and loses volume through countless diversions during its two-thousand-mile long journey. The Costilla Creek Compact distinguishes the Rio Costilla, but the river has about fifteen major tributaries, each facing distinct problems, and each struggling with its own complex history.

A sampling of reports, north to south, from the Rio Grande's Colorado and New Mexico tributaries:

- The Alamosa River, not far from the headwaters of the Rio Grande in Creede, Colorado, is still suffering the effects of cyanide pollution from the nearby Summitville gold mine, despite a $120-million federal cleanup effort.

- The Conejos River, originating in the San Juan Mountains of Colorado, has been designated a "Wild Trout Fishery" by the Colorado Division of Wildlife. However, diversion of water from the Platoro Reservoir has drastically reduced the river's flow.

- The Red River, which flows through the ski town of Red River and the Hispanic community of Questa, is considered the most severely polluted stream system in New Mexico. Tailings spills and acid drainage from Molycorp's molybdenum mine waste sites have devastated the river's trout fishery.

- The Rio Hondo sustains Taos Ski Valley and several small agricultural communities. The river's water quality is threatened by resort development at the ski area, including a sewage system that discharges into the river, and by leaking septic systems and livestock grazing in the valley below.

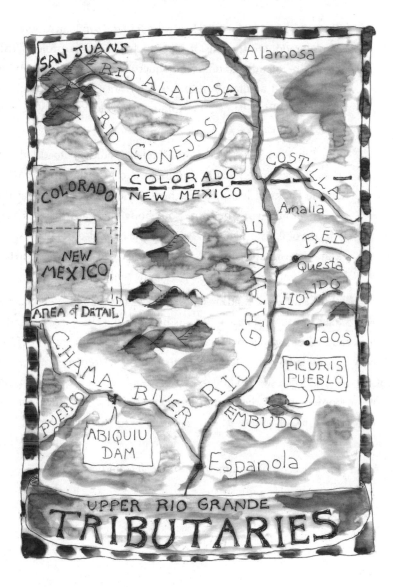

SAN JUANS · Alamosa · RIO ALAMOSA · RIO CONEJOS · COLORADO NEW MEXICO · COSTILLA · COLORADO NEW MEXICO · AREA of DETAIL · Amalia · RED · Questa · HONDO · RIO GRANDE · Taos · PICURIS PUEBLO · CHAMA RIVER · PUERCO · ABIQUIU DAM · EMBUDO · Espanola · UPPER RIO GRANDE TRIBUTARIES

- The watershed of the Rio Embudo, which runs through Picuris Pueblo, has been the site of bitter conflicts over logging in recent years. But Picuris Pueblo activists recently celebrated the ouster of a planned Summo Corporation copper mine, which was set to break ground within the river's watershed.

- The headwaters of the Rio Chama, high in the San Juan Mountains of Colorado, are the site of the San Juan-Chama project. This diversion, intended to offset Albuquerque's drain of its shrinking underground aquifer, transfers water from the Colorado River basin to the Rio Chama. The Abiquiú Dam blocks the river's flow in its lower reaches.

- The Rio Puerco has one of the highest sediment loads of any river in the United States, due in part to historic sheep grazing on the banks of its upper reaches. "When you first look at the sediment numbers, you think somebody made a typo," says New Mexico oral historian Pat D'Andrea. The river also passes through a uranium-mining district, gaining a hefty load of heavy metals and radionuclides as it flows past aging tailings piles.

By the time the Rio Grande reaches El Paso, Texas, and Ciudad Juarez, Mexico, it isn't much of a river. It runs between the cities in a concrete-lined channel, absorbing toxic waste from the increasing number of U.S.-owned maquiladoras in Mexico. From there, what remains of the Rio Grande—known as the Rio Bravo del Norte to those on the Mexican side of the border—traces the international border for 1,250 miles until it drains into the Gulf of Mexico.

October 12, 1998

Michelle Nijhuis is contributing editor to *High Country News*.

A Tiny Fish Cracks New Mexico's Water Establishment

Greg Hanscom

Sitting in his office on the outskirts of this sprawling desert city, Jeff Whitney remembers a poster that hung at an Arizona ranch where he worked as a teenager. A crotchety old cowboy smirked from the wall and the caption read, "There's a lot about this outfit that they didn't tell me."

A native of Wickenburg, Arizona, a small town about an hour's drive north of Phoenix, and a former Hot Shot firefighter, Whitney has a reputation for knowing his way around the Southwest. As a planner on the Prescott National Forest, he worked with a coalition of ranchers, researchers, and agency officials to create a pioneering watershed-management program.

"I've lived and worked with fourth-generation Arizona ranchers. I've been in a lot of these people's shoes," says the burly, mustached biologist. "The only way you're really going to be successful is by finding some kind of consensus."

Talk like this earned Whitney the Forest Service Chief's award in 1993. A year later, the same kind of talk landed him at the bargaining table, struggling for compromise in the middle of an epic tug of war over water on the Rio Grande.

In August of 1994, Whitney was transferred to the Albuquerque office of the U.S. Fish and Wildlife Service. His charge was to lead an ambitious restoration effort on the middle stretch of the Rio Grande, from Cochiti Dam west of Santa Fe down through the wide, sloping Middle Valley to the reservoir at Elephant Butte.

Returning the middle Rio Grande, now more plumbing than river, to something of its former greatness would be a mammoth task. The federal Bureau of Reclamation and Army Corps of Engineers use dams to ration the river's flow, and levees, jetties, and drains to confine it to a narrow strip

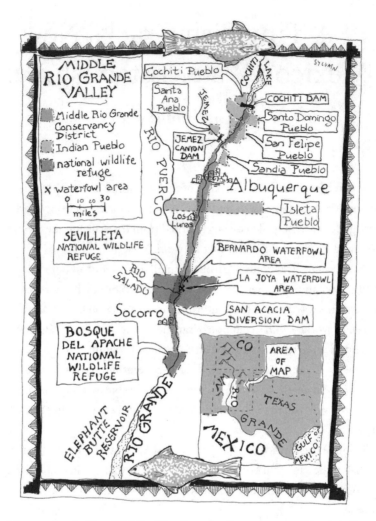

of bottomland. The Middle Rio Grande Conservancy District diverts the river into hundreds of miles of irrigation ditches to feed acequias and backyard farms. Whitney's own agency uses the river to water the engineered fields of the Bosque del Apache National Wildlife Refuge, which attracts hundreds of thousands of migratory birds each winter.

River restoration would be further complicated by New Mexico's status as the only western state without an instream-flow law; if an irrigator or city leaves water in the river, someone else can pull it out. Moreover, none of the water rights on the Rio Grande in New Mexico have been adjudicated, so the conservative approach is to use as much water as you can, to establish a claim.

But by the late 1980s, concern was growing over the decline of the cottonwood forest or bosque and the native fish that depend on a healthy river. In 1993, researchers released a blueprint for restoration that had the support of scientists, the general public, and political leaders. Called the Bosque Biological Management Plan, it outlined Whitney's mission: convince all the players to work together to give the Rio room to be a river again.

"I knew it was serious," recalls Whitney. "But I thought we had a plan and people were committed."

It didn't take long for Whitney to figure out that there was a lot about this new outfit he hadn't been told.

New Mexico water users had signed onto river restoration when relatively high rainfall was keeping water in the river, and Albuquerque thought it had a nearly endless supply of groundwater. But by 1994, Albuquerque, the state's largest city, was eyeing the Rio to satisfy booming growth. People began tripping over each other to get off the restoration boat.

Then, the day before Whitney arrived in Albuquerque, the Fish and Wildlife Service put the three-inch-long Rio Grande silvery minnow on the endangered species list. The minnow, once common throughout the Rio Grande and its tributaries, was now confined to 5 percent of its former habitat, all within the middle Rio Grande. Restoration was no longer voluntary; the hammer of the law now hung over the river.

Over the course of a year, Whitney met with all the water interests. Albuquerque agreed to lease the Bureau of Reclamation up to thirty thousand acre-feet of water it had stored in Abiquin Reservoir. This was "non-native" water that was pumped into the Rio Grande from the Colorado River drainage through the San Juan-Chama project. But the city didn't have the ability to use it yet, so it could be left in the river.

It was a Band-Aid, but it put the state's legion of water lawyers at ease, and bought Whitney time to find a long-term solution.

Then one Friday afternoon in April 1996, he got some very bad news. The Middle Rio Grande Conservancy District had quietly diverted the entire river into its ditches at the San Acacia Diversion Dam outside of Socorro, and minnows were beached.

"We went down to the river Saturday morning," says Whitney, "and discovered a dry river with pools rapidly drying, and dead minnows." When the body count came in, ten thousand minnows were dead, 40 percent of the remaining population.

"It was going to be a long summer," Whitney remembers. "The worst-case scenario had arrived."

Whitney tried to regroup. Bosque del Apache wildlife refuge kept water in the river for the first month by giving up three thousand acre-feet, one quarter of its annual water appropriation. Thunderstorms and dam releases got them through the rest of the summer. "We pieced it together," he says.

Over the next two years, the Bureau of Reclamation leased water for the river, mostly from Albuquerque. The conservancy district pitched in twenty-seven hundred acre-feet in 1997, but never took responsibility for killing the minnows.

Meanwhile, Jeff Whitney canvassed for consensus. In the winter of 1996, Whitney and Gary Rowe, a staffer with the Bureau of Reclamation, called the federal agencies, the state, Albuquerque, and the conservancy district together. The result was a report known as the "white paper" that laid out a plan to keep water in the river for the minnow.

The guts of the white paper called for federal agencies to buy water rights for river flows. During dry years, Albuquerque would pump groundwater, leaving more in the river for fish and farmers. The conservancy district, in turn, would save water by lining canals and developing more efficient irrigation systems. Upstream reservoirs controlled by the federal government would be used to store water during wet years to boost river flows during dry ones. And the state would begin the long-overdue process of measuring diversions from the river and adjudicating water rights, so that users would have certainty.

The white paper won praise from some conservationists, but the drying of the river the previous spring had galvanized most. Already seven of the Rio's native fish species were extirpated or extinct. The minnow was one of nine remaining species, but the environmentalists feared it wouldn't be around for long without more protection. In April of 1997, Forest Guardians and Defenders of Wildlife sued the Interior Department. Fish and Wildlife had put the minnow on the endangered species list in 1994, but missed its 1996 deadline for designating critical habitat.

The lawsuit was aimed at the heart of the issue. Some biologists believed that the only way to protect the minnow was to restore the middle Rio Grande. That would mean keeping water in the river year-round, and allowing it to wash over its banks in spring and meander across its floodplain.

The lawsuit also changed the debate. From that point on, it would be a game of legal strong-arming to force agencies mired in the past to stay at the table.

"Until you force the issue and create a crisis," said John Horning of the Forest Guardians, "we don't deal with the problems."

In October of 1997, Judge John Conway ruled that Interior had violated the Endangered Species Act, but he didn't give the agency a new deadline for critical-habitat designation. Forest Guardians and Defenders appealed, and in December 1998, the Tenth Circuit Court of Appeals in Denver ordered Fish and Wildlife to designate habitat by the end of June 1999.

Water users dug in their heels further, and in May, Senator Pete Domenici (Republican-New Mexico) tried to attach a rider to an emergency spending bill that would have postponed all critical-habitat designations until October 1.

Sam Hitt of Forest Guardians and a pack of volunteers took cell phones to natural food stores in Albuquerque and asked shoppers, "Do you want to talk to Pete Domenici?" They tied up his phone lines for two days. Defenders of Wildlife had members send megabytes of e-mail messages to the senator.

"This is not about the minnow. This is about the Rio Grande, the heart of New Mexico," said Hitt. "We're talking about a major ecological catastrophe. The red light on the dashboard is flashing away. People like Domenici want to speed up. We should be hitting the brakes."

Two days after Domenici introduced the rider, he abandoned it.

On June 29, the day before Fish and Wildlife announced its findings on critical habitat, state Water Engineer Tom Turney was anxious. Before the silvery minnow debacle, Turney had exercised near-total control over the river, mainly on behalf of irrigators. Now, new players were coming to the table. "Tomorrow is the magic day," he said. "It's going to be devastating to New Mexico."

The next morning, Turney's fears were realized. Fish and Wildlife designated the entire 163-mile stretch of the middle Rio Grande, from Cochiti to Elephant Butte, as critical minnow habitat. The agency did not specify how much water would be needed, but it did say that to save the minnow, the reach would have to run as a continuous river, not exist as "isolated pools."

Before the week was over, the conservancy district and the state were suing the Fish and Wildlife Service, demanding a retraction of the critical habitat until the agency had studied its economic impacts.

"Fish need water—that's not enough of an answer," said district biologist Sterling Grogan. "The Rio Grande has been dry as a bone for months at a time since the 1890s. The minnow has developed survival strategies that have allowed it to survive periodic drying of the river channel."

The district estimated that it would take up to one hundred and fifty thousand acre-feet per year to meet Fish and Wildlife's demands. "All of the water users in the middle Rio Grande would be without water in a dry year," said Grogan. "That includes the city of Albuquerque, the pueblos, farmers, and the Bosque del Apache National Wildlife Refuge."

Tom Turney predicted that the effort would cost farmers $200 million to $500 million.

"The water buffaloes are scared to death of the consequences of keeping water in this river," said Sam Hitt. "It's totally overblown. They're like gigantic elephants dancing around a little mouse."

Jeff Whitney sounded harried. "They [the state and conservancy district] think it requires a full, bank-to-bank river year-round," he said. "We're talking about just enough water to keep a trickle going at the bottom extent."

He said it would take fifty thousand acre-feet in a dry year, one third of the conservancy district's estimate. That water could be found relatively painlessly, he said, by following the recommendations laid out three years earlier in the white paper. The 1938 Rio Grande Compact, he said, required New Mexico to deliver 60 to 90 percent of the Rio Grande's water to Texas and Mexico each year. Why not release that water to meet the needs of the minnow, and meet both obligations?

Progress might be easier, Whitney added, if everyone at the bargaining table weren't suing each other. "Nobody sees the irony. Nobody sees the psychosis."

But people were still hoping someone else would pick up the tab for the minnow, and all eyes turned to Albuquerque Mayor Jim Baca, an outspoken conservationist, and former head of both the federal Bureau of Land Management and the Middle Rio Grande Conservancy District. It was Baca's San Juan-Chama water that had kept the river wet for three years. If he would agree to keep leasing water, the crisis could be put off a little longer.

Baca was in a tight spot. To wean itself from its dwindling groundwater, and prepare for a projected six hundred and fifty thousand people by the year 2050, the city was pouring $180 million into a riverwater-treatment plant. On September 1, Albuquerque took the offensive. It announced it would stop leasing water and sued Interior, claiming the San Juan-Chama water stored in Heron reservoir, near Tierra Amarilla, was the city's savings account for dry years and could not be used for the minnow.

The city said it was trying to force the conservancy district to compromise. "Some people think Albuquerque should be the savior of the river. In fact, we've been the savior for years. We've kept the minnow alive," said Jim Baca, adding that the city has reduced per capita water use by 23 percent in five years. "My premise is, Albuquerque has done its part, where is everybody else? The pueblos, the acequias, the conservancy district need to step up to the plate."

Others said Baca was just kowtowing to thirsty developers, who in 1997 contributed 70 to 89 percent of the city council's campaign money, according to a local watchdog group, the Petroglyph Monument Protection Coalition. "In Albuquerque, the political power is held by developers," explains Pilar river guide and activist Steve Harris, "and nobody wants to piss in their Post Toasties."

The legal struggle over the middle Rio Grande could take years, even lifetimes, to play out, but Jeff Whitney and others still have hopes of finding a solution in real time.

Back in April of 1998, a group of conservationists wrote a response to the white paper. The authors included Steve Harris, head of the consensus-minded group Rio Grande Restoration; attorney Laird Lucas with the Land and Water Fund of the Rockies; Sue George, New Mexico representative for Defenders of Wildlife; and University of New Mexico law professor Denise Fort, who chaired the Western Water Policy Review Commission.

Their "green paper" echoed the recommendations of the white paper, but it also had a structural component. It proposed moving back levees to allow spring floods to cover the floodplain and removing the Low-Flow Conveyance Channel, a ditch parallel to the river that drains up to two-thirds of its water between San Acacia and Elephant Butte. And just as others want to tear out dams to protect salmon in the Northwest, the paper proposed removing diversion dams on the Rio Grande that block the silvery minnow from migrating upstream.

In August 1998, a few months after the green paper was released, the Bureau of Reclamation invited the authors of both the green and white papers to a retreat in Santa Fe. For the first time, a whole spread of conservationists as well as Pueblo and acequia representatives sat at the table with the region's water managers. "It was historic," says Steve Harris.

The group, now called the "Green and White Paper Group," meets once a month, and has had some success. A subset of the group has been trying to hammer out a Habitat Conservation Plan or some other compromise modeled on the Platte or Lower Colorado River agreements.

The lawsuits have tested the group's resilience, says Steve Harris, but so far, "everybody's still here. It's slow and painful, but the value is pulling the players together, so we all know the same things. I think everybody's positions are known; God knows, at this point they're practically locked in concrete."

Exactly, says Santa Fe Public Utilities Department Director Mike Hammon. Most of the players have their backs against the wall and refuse to dance.

Hammon is one of the few to step out onto the floor. Like Albuquerque, Santa Fe is fixing to pump San Juan-Chama water—a relatively small fifty-six hundred acre-feet each year—out of the Rio Grande. But Hammon has offered to pump more groundwater during dry years, and leave some of his imported water in the river.

"If all the cities are doing the same thing, you've got some water to work with," he says. "But the [legal] hammers being held over everybody's heads make people nervous to be first. I'm a small fish, so I can take a step out more easily than an Albuquerque."

Cities can't restore the river without the biggest player on the reach, the conservancy district, which shies away from talk of river restoration. The district has instead proposed trucking minnows around diversion dams to wet spots upstream. "Sometimes it's wise to move the water where the minnows are. Sometimes it's wise to move the minnows where the water is," says District Manager Subhis Shah. "There's no use in looking for the minnows where we know the river is going to dry up."

Talk like this just delays dealing with the real issue, the river, says Jeff Whitney. "It's total denial," he says. "They're hoping against hope that they'll wake up from this bad dream and be able to continue to do things as they've always done."

It's late September, and Whitney is moving out of his office, cleaning out filing cabinets and purging his e-mail account. He's on his way to yet another new outfit across town, this time working with an interagency group called the Southwest Initiative, doing region-wide planning. Rumor has it that Whitney was "bumped upstairs' for taking too strong a stance on river restoration. He denies this, saying he's done his part and it's time to move on.

As Whitney leaves, the news on the river is mixed. This fall, Pete Domenici convinced Congress to appropriate $2 million to help fund silvery minnow recovery. In Washington, the Interior Department is watching the Rio Grande more closely than ever, and more money may be on the way.

Late snows and summer rain kept the river wet this year, but they also gave people a false sense of security. "There's enough water in the system, and I'm afraid people are just going to coast," says Whitney. "There's every opportunity to turn things around, but there needs to be a larger will."

The extra water also seems to have washed silvery minnows and their progeny downstream of San Acacia Diversion Dam. A recent survey found that 90 percent of the minnows are now trapped in the section of the river that dried up in 1996. One dry year could wipe out the minnow completely.

The result could be another lawsuit. A coalition of environmental groups represented by the Land and Water Fund is considering filing suit. "We're having these great meetings and talking about long-term solutions," says Sue George with Defenders of Wildlife. "But it's not happening fast enough. We've got to get in there with some litigation and light some fires."

The lawsuit also targets irrigators. The conservancy district, it says, does not have the water rights it claims. The district signed them over to the Bureau of Reclamation in the 1940s, when the federal government bailed out the nearly bankrupt agency. "We're not trying to take any water rights away from anyone. We're saying the federal government owns this water, and has the responsibility to keep some of it in the river," says lead attorney Laird Lucas. "This is the dirty hidden secret in New Mexico water law that nobody wants to talk about."

Ironically, environmentalists and the conservancy district are allies on another legal front. Both are likely to intervene in Albuquerque's lawsuit claiming ownership of San Juan-Chama water in Heron Reservoir. Both groups argue that Interior, not Albuquerque, owns the water in Heron, and is obligated to use it to protect the minnow.

"It's by far the strangest situation I've ever been in. It's out of some of the weirdest science fiction," says Jeff Whitney. "I've taken a very long, hard, focused look at this, and I believe that everyone can get what they require if people stay flexible. We're not on the road to nowhere."

"One thing's for sure," he adds, "2000 is going to be a very exciting year on the Rio Grande."

October 11, 1999

Greg Hanscom is a *High Country News* associate editor.

The Mine That Turned the Red River Blue

Ernest Atencio

Roger Herrera sits in his tidy living room, chain-smoking Pall Malls and telling the story of how a mining company changed his life and Questa, his hometown of twenty-two hundred people. For nearly four decades, the Molycorp molybdenum mine has loomed over this mountain village near the confluence of the Rio Grande and the Red River. Its waste literally towers over Herrera's house; just a couple of hundred yards away, an earthen dam holds back one hundred million tons of mine tailings.

Herrera, sixty-three, says he can't talk much about his relationship with Molycorp because of a 1980s settlement following a civil lawsuit against the mine. But what he can tell is startling.

"I found out from the [state environment department] that a black calf will turn white from mine wastes," he says. "I didn't believe it, but I believe it now. Over here," he points toward the river, "their hair was falling off and they were drying up."

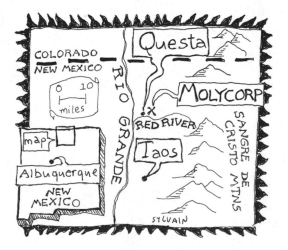

Herrera doesn't talk about the effects the mine had on his family, which for years pumped drinking water from a well near here. He only asks, "So if livestock and wild game can get those metals and elements, what about people?"

Village councilman Malaquias Raél fills in some of Herrera's story the next day. "His kids were getting white hair and white stripes on their nails when they were teenagers," says Raél. "That's supposed to be signs of metal contamination."

A few miles up the Red River Canyon from the Herrera home in the Sangre de Cristo mountains, the mine that generated those metal-laden tailings sits amid the wreckage of thirty-six years of molybdenum mining: 328 million tons of waste rock, a fifteen-hundred-foot-deep open pit, collapse zones from underground tunneling, and gargantuan machinery and milling buildings. A nine-mile-long pipeline carries tailings slurry from the mill to lagoons, a pleasant name for lakes of acidic waste, located on the other side of Questa.

A few Questenos commute to tourism-based jobs in Taos, or at the Red River Ski Area just up the valley. Fewer still scratch out a living as local shopkeepers or small-time contractors, and a handful still work small farms or ranches.

The mine is the boom-and-bust economic engine of Questa. Molycorp has at times been the largest single employer in impoverished Taos County, employing more than six hundred at its peak. But employment has fluctuated wildly, the mine shutting down completely during two extreme slumps.

All told, miners have pulled out of the ground approximately a hundred million tons of molybdenum ore—a grayish metal used in high-strength, light-weight alloys found in mountain bikes and wheelchairs.

Today, a skeleton crew of one hundred fifty people is busy developing a new ore body, running a load through the mill only every few months. Management still hopes to resume full-scale mining of some of the estimated seventy million tons of remaining ore, if the market ever rebounds.

While molybdenum has been the lifeblood of Questa, disputes over the mine have also run toxic through the town's veins. For thirty years, citizens such as Roger Herrera have fought to force Molycorp to take responsibility for the damage it has caused the landscape and the health of the people who live here. For three decades, the company has stubbornly denied any adverse impacts. Attempts to negotiate with mine officials have fallen flat.

In response, community and environmental activists have taken a hard line. And as the mining operation has atrophied, their opposition has grown stronger. They've sued the company and appealed its permits, gumming up the regulatory process at every opportunity. It has turned into a contest of bureaucratic filibustering from both sides.

Now, with a federal Superfund listing looming over Molycorp, activists may have won the battle over Questa and the Red River. But the victory brings with it many new questions, and no one is sure whether this torn community can come together to chart a new course.

Molybdenum has been mined in the Red River Canyon since 1921. The mine was a small operation until Molycorp, a wholly owned subsidiary of the multibillion-dollar Unocal (Union Oil of California) Corporation, developed the open pit in 1964. Since then, the mine has become the single greatest influence on the lower Red River watershed and the community of Questa.

Mining's presence is everywhere in Questa. Pieces of heavy machinery lie around yards and old slurry pipe has been recycled into fence posts and hay barn frames. On a high ridge of the Sangre de Cristos to the east, a stretch of waste rock spills over from the mine. To the west lies the six hundred and forty-acre expanse of tailings lagoons.

Molycorp has, at times, contributed well over $30 million a year to the local economy. With an average Taos County wage of less than $10,000 a year, families have come to rely on mine jobs paying $40,000 to $60,000.

As one local put it, "The mine is everything, really, because it's given us everything. I think it'd be like a ghost town without the mine."

This financial power has also given Molycorp significant political weight, which some say the company has used to push aside citizen concerns and environmental laws.

"Molycorp set out to control the political machine, and that's how they've been able to get away with making a huge amount of profit by not taking care of their impacts," says Roberto Vigil, a fifth-generation Questeno woodworker and longtime community activist. As a result, he says, "Questa has been plagued with corporate abuse and official neglect."

That the mine was careless was common knowledge in the community, even in the early years. Hundreds of spills from shoddy tailings pipelines poured into the Red River, and sometimes directly into *acequias*, local irrigation ditches.

Then came the most glaring sign of industrial arrogance. In the early 1980s, the Red River began to turn a cloudy blue, a symptom of acid drainage and high metal content.

Until then, the Red had been known as one of the best trout streams in the West. Suddenly, the fish were gone. The impact was so pronounced, says professional fishing guide Taylor Streit, that in his *No-Nonsense Guide to Fly Fishing in New Mexico* he divided the Rio Grande into different sections above and below the Red River, because he no longer found the big fish of the old days below the confluence.

During those years, dust from the tailings had also been accumulating until, just west of town, blinding storms had become common. Analysis of the dust showed lead, zinc, cadmium, arsenic, and mercury. Questa High School sat right next door.

"I went with Little Joe to pick up his kids at the high school, and it was engulfed in dust. Kids were running around," says Vigil. "For the next couple of days, my own eyes and throat were burning. I thought about what we were putting these kids through."

More than once, dust storms were so severe that the school shut down and sent students home. In 1980, the state championship baseball game at Questa High had to be canceled because of a dust storm.

"*Es una verguenza* [It's an embarrassment]," village attorney Eliu Romero told the *Taos News*.

While Molycorp is the largest hardrock mine in the Rio Grande watershed, an area of one hundred eighty thousand square miles stretching from Colorado to the Gulf of Mexico, it took a long time for news of its activities to reach the outside world.

In the 1970s, local residents formed Concerned Citizens of Questa to tackle Molycorp issues, ranging from unfair hiring practices to tailings spills, contaminated groundwater, and toxic dust. In a story familiar to activists all over the West, the Questa group in the largely low-income Hispanic community lacked the money and technical and legal resources to take on a multibillion-dollar corporation.

Local government officials, who were often mine employees, offered no help. State and federal agencies frequently looked the other way, allowing Molycorp to operate with lax regulation. With neighbors and relatives in this small town relying on mine paychecks, opposition was frowned upon as disloyal.

That changed in the 1990s. Local activists reached out beyond the town to allies in environmental groups such as the Sierra Club, New Mexico Citizens for Clean Air and Water, Western Environmental Law Center, New Mexico Environmental Law Center, and Amigos Bravos of Taos. The groups brought new resources to bear on the mine.

Not surprisingly, mine supporters resented "outsiders' elbowing their way in, and even some mine opponents were angry about environmentalists taking over what was seen as a local issue. As local activist Joe Cisneros puts it, "We paved the way, we fought this tooth and nail, then Amigos Bravos came and took it."

But the rift between local activists and Amigos Bravos has all but disappeared since the group, founded in 1988 around a Molycorp tailings issue, joined the cause. In 1995, Amigos Bravos filed its first lawsuit against the mine under the Clean Water Act, dogging every step of the regulatory process. Six years, two lawsuits, and dozens of public hearings later, says the group's director, Brian Shields, "It's amazing how many resources you have to put together to fight something like this. It's hard for communities to do that."

The lawsuits and growing public awareness have helped put Molycorp under the regulatory microscope. In 1994, the New Mexico Water Quality Control Commission reported that the mine "has rendered [the Red River] dead for at least eight miles." In 1996, a New Mexico Environment Department report documented pollution from the mine's waste rock.

A 1998 Environmental Protection Agency report again implicated the mine's waste rock as a significant source of river pollution.

In 1999, the New Mexico Natural Resources Trustee, responsible for collecting compensation for natural-resource damage, released the most comprehensive report yet. It documented increased pollution of the Red River since the 1960s, when the open-pit operations began. Later the same year, Molycorp landed on the Washington, D.C.-based Mineral Policy Center's list of the six most poorly regulated mines in the country, and Corporate Crime Reporter put the mine's parent company, Unocal, on its list of the "Top 100" corporate criminals of the 1990s.

Things came to a head last winter, when Molycorp started preparing for a slew of regulatory permits that will all come due at the same time. By the end of 2001, the company must complete state groundwater permits, a state closeout and reclamation plan, and two federal water permits governing discharges into the Red River.

With state and environmental laws staring it in the face, the company will have to clean up its act, or so activists hope.

The stakes are high for Molycorp. Molybdenum prices are rock bottom—$2.55 a pound, compared to $16 a pound only five years ago. Unocal now subsidizes Molycorp to the tune of $14 million a year, of which $2 million goes to environmental remediation in Questa. Yet these numbers pale in comparison to cleanup and reclamation that could cost up to $382 million, according to environmentalists, not to mention the potential of civil actions against the mine.

Meanwhile, Molycorp representatives continue to deny responsibility for any pollution. A 1998 application to renew an EPA permit claimed that "the Questa mine has not harmed, and may have improved, the condition of the Red River."

That assertion is based on a Molycorp-commissioned study that concluded that there are more fish in the stretch of river directly below the mine than above it. The study blames natural erosional scars upstream for the elevated levels of aluminum, cadmium, copper, chromium, cobalt, iron, molybdenum, manganese, nickel, lead, and zinc detected in the river. It also says that the mine's groundwater pumping intercepts any contamination before it gets to the river and runs it through the mill to the tailings. The same study says that, despite the fish stories of yore, the Red River was never a hardy trout stream.

"Looking at the net impact over time, we feel we have information that we don't have any impact," says mine manager David Shoemaker. "If there is a problem, we'll certainly go after it and correct it," he adds, "but I'd say the jury's still out." Others agree with that assessment.

"From the standpoint of an employee, I may be prejudiced in favor of the mine, but they have come up with very convincing arguments," says Carlos Cisneros, who is a state senator, secretary of the local union, and a Molycorp welder. "Just from my layman's viewpoint, it's been polluted pretty much for the last twenty years, but is it caused by mining?"

Molycorp officials add that they are busy planning to clean up the tailings piles and open pit. Under the 1993 New Mexico Mining Act, the company must complete a comprehensive reclamation plan by the end of 2001. That means it must return over thirteen hundred acres of open pit, waste rock, and tailings to a "self-sustaining ecosystem" once the mine closes. The company's draft reclamation plan calls for covering the mine tailings near the mill with nine inches of soil and planting grasses directly in the waste rock everywhere else. The company has offered to put up a $60 million bond to insure the cleanup.

Environmentalists and state agencies say that the company's plan falls far short. The state is calling for more stringent clean-up guidelines and a $130 million bond. Amigos Bravos, which has just released a reclamation plan of its own, says cleanup will cost $378 million. Their plan calls for covering the entire waste-rock area with three-and-a-half feet of cap material and soil, as well as perpetual water treatment and other measures.

"Molycorp is not willing to do what 99 percent of other mines are doing," says Jim Kuipers, a Boulder, Montana-based mining engineer who left the industry five years ago to work as a consultant for public-interest groups. Kuipers, who wrote Amigos Bravos' reclamation plan, says that Molycorp is behind the times.

"Their reclamation proposal is like an Edsel without an engine," he says, "while some other companies are proposing Cadillacs."

Overlooking the open pit from a high ridge, a genuinely perplexed Shoemaker says, "I don't know what everyone's so upset about." Pointing to seedling pines and cottonwoods planted directly into the waste rock, he explains, "We've spent a lot of money on 'reveg' work—at least a million—and we believe this will lead to a self-sustaining ecosystem. We've got twenty-five years of "reveg" to base it on."

Then he adds, "We're going to plant some bigger trees so people can see the damn things."

In a state that has seen little of the nationwide economic boom, officials have done their best to work with Molycorp. Last winter, the state environment department spent six months negotiating with mine officials over a cleanup plan.

In the end, Molycorp's legendary obstinacy held true. After several ultimatums and missed deadlines, says New Mexico Secretary of Environment Pete Maggiore, "We couldn't come up with anything. We had made some concessions to show we were willing to go the extra mile, but were frustrated to find that the ball had been moved.

"Molycorp put themselves in this position," continues Maggiore. "I would suggest that it is not a matter of [the state being] pro-business or anti-business, but it's a matter of business being responsible and being good stewards."

Even New Mexico's staunchly pro-business Governor Gary Johnson finally lost his patience, and on April 1, he recommended federal Superfund designation for the mine. On May 11, the EPA followed with a draft Superfund listing in the federal register. A final decision is expected this fall.

Shoemaker says Molycorp will appeal a Superfund listing. For if the mine lands on the list, the EPA will take over the clean-up process, completing the necessary studies and dictating what work needs to be done. EPA officials will then send Molycorp the bill.

If the company goes bankrupt in the meantime, as the owner of the Summitville Mine in Colorado did in 1992, the taxpayers will be left with the tab.

People on all sides of the issue agree that a Superfund-directed cleanup is cumbersome and weak in public participation. A look at Summitville shows that a Superfund cleanup can also be slow, frustrating, and expensive.

Still, activists such as Amigos Bravos welcome the draft listing. "There are some [Superfund] sites that have worked, others that have become nightmares," says Amigos Bravos' Shields, "but I'm willing to try anything at this point."

Locals ponder what Molycorp will look like under federal supervision.

Steady and good-paying cleanup jobs could keep locals employed for at least as long as mining has, says David Douglas, who owns a cabin on the Red River next door to the mine. "Superfund could bring a new economic boom to Questa, well into the middle of the century," he says "The potential is there for Questa to reinvent itself as a showcase of environmental cleanup."

Pete Maggiore is anxious to help with the transition. "EPA has opportunities for retraining displaced workers," he says. "If we could be of any help in that regard, we'd like to."

Shutting down and cleaning up mines reinvigorates local economies, according to University of Montana economist Tom Power. He says these post-extractive economies attract a new rural type—telecommuters and other well-heeled residents who come for the amenities of open space, clean air, and recreation—who breathe new life into the economy.

Not everyone thinks that's the right direction for Questa.

"Will we turn into another [touristy] Taos?" wonders Councilman Raél. "How do we preserve what we have here and have some economic development?"

For better or worse, tourism remains the bread and butter of northern New Mexico. In the mid-eighties, Roberto Vigil and several others founded the Artesanos de Questa Cultural Center to encourage local artistic traditions and offer an economic alternative to the mine. Several small studios and antique shops have popped up in recent years, marketing local arts and crafts.

Others in Questa would like to see a return to agriculture, once irrigation waters are again safe. An organic-wheat cooperative up the road in Costilla, New Mexico, has been remarkably successful, and local organic produce is finding a larger market.

Questions about Questa's future remain unanswered for now, but almost everyone except Molycorp concedes that the future is Superfund and there's no turning back. The mine may sputter along for a few more years, but will never again bring genuine prosperity to the area. It's up to the community to come together to develop a new economy that suits its unique history and character.

"I think for the future of the next generation, like my grandchildren," offers Roger Herrera, "I want to see that they grow up in a clean, safe environment, instead of having their pockets filled with money with an unhealthy environment."

August 28, 2000

Ernest Atencio lives down the road from Molycorp in Arroyo Hondo, New Mexico. He is former Projects Director for Amigos Bravos and a former *High Country News* intern.

Divided Waters

Megan Lardner

Rocky Dailey sells homes on the outskirts of El Paso, out where the highway disappears into creosote bush and "for sale" signs dot the land. Billboards welcome residents home to desert communities with names like "Las Palmas" and "Oasis Ranch."

"It's the friendliest city in Texas," Dailey tells prospective buyers in his real estate office at Desert View Homes. Out here, the eastern frontier sparkles like gold for developers. El Paso's population is expected to double within twenty years. Its sister city, Mexico's Ciudad Juarez, is expected to double as well, as the burgeoning *maquiladora* industry, ignited by the 1994 North American Free Trade Agreement (NAFTA), draws thousands of new workers every year. By 2020, the population of this sprawling border metropolis could hit 4.5 million.

"There's no way you can stop a city from growing," says Dailey, glancing out the window over an army of lawns and rooftops to the jagged, golden-brown mountains beyond. This is truly a "desert view"; just seven inches of rain fall here each year. But ask this native El Pasoan if he worries about providing water to his new suburbs and he's nonchalant. "We'll have as much water as we can, until it runs out."

The water is running out. Here, where the Rio Grande first enters Texas from New Mexico and its calm flow becomes the turbulent international divide, a water crisis is brewing.

More than two million thirsty urban residents, along with industry and agriculture, are sucking dry their main water source, an underground aquifer called the Hueco Bolson, which stretches beneath the border. Some experts predict El Paso will deplete its fresh groundwater by 2025. Juarez could hit the bottom of the *bolson* even sooner.

"We're starting to bump up against the ceiling," says Ed Hamlyn, with the Center for Environmental Resource Management at the University of Texas at El Paso (UTEP).

The obvious alternative to groundwater meanders right past the two cities' front stoops: the Rio Grande. Yet the river is already stretched thin.

The Rio Grande rises in Colorado's San Juan Mountains, where it is immediately plumbed and put to work, watering fields of hay and potatoes in the San Luis Valley. In northern New Mexico, its water feeds into *acequias*, irrigation ditches built by early Spanish settlers. And south of Albuquerque, in the Middle Valley, the river irrigates chilies, cotton, alfalfa, and pecans, even as environmentalists fight to save some of its water for the endangered silvery minnow and the riverside forest, or *bosque*.

By the time it reaches southern New Mexico, the Rio Grande has been so pinched and drained that it has almost ceased to be a river. In the Hatch and Mesilla valleys, people call it a canal. The *bosque* has been clear-cut and the river straightened and hemmed in between levees. Each winter, it is turned off like a garden hose. Any attempt to save some water for wildlife, or for the river's sake, is seen as an attempt to steal water that belongs to American farmers and cities or to Mexico.

On the border, the river provides nearly half of El Paso's municipal water and irrigates fields on the outskirts of Juarez. The little water that makes it past El Paso and Juarez goes to farmers, who usually divert the last drops at Fort Quitman, Texas. Below Fort Quitman, the Rio Grande runs virtually dry for two hundred miles, until it is met and replenished by Mexico's Rio Conchos.

So the overtaxed Rio Grande provides no easy solution to the water needs of El Paso, Juarez, and the millions of people who live along the border. This isolated stretch of land is turning into a nation of sorts, strongly attached to neither Mexico nor the U.S., existing under laws of its own. So far, those laws have not come to bear on the border's booming cities. The multinational corporations that profit from the *maquiladoras* invest little in the local communities.

But now, there's a glimmer of hope, both for border residents and the river that runs between them. On the El Paso side, the demand for more domestic water may break the farmers' hold on it, and actually return some water year-round to a dead stretch of the river. While Juarez has been reluctant to deal with its own looming water crisis, there, too, officials are waking up to the needs of the masses now living without running water or sewers.

Is the border beginning to mature at last? Will its growing pains and the human misery that has attended them lead to investment in community, and care for the river that gave rise to it?

The border cities' dilemma becomes starkly clear as you follow Interstate 25 south across the desert from New Mexico. One of the first signs that you're getting close to El Paso is a water slide perched atop a hill by the highway. Like the oceans of lawns that surround El Paso's homes, it raises the question: why such lavish use of water in a desert?

El Paso sits on the banks of the Rio Grande, but the city's real water wealth has been underground. Until roughly two million years ago, the Rio Grande ended here, emptying into a huge inland lake not unlike today's Great Salt Lake in Utah. The water evaporated or seeped into the sandy ground, creating the Hueco Bolson.

In the 1950s, when drought hit the Southwest, rivers dropped and farmers in New Mexico and Texas watched their crops wither and die. But El Paso, which pulled most of its water from the ground, boomed along with Sunbelt cities such as Phoenix, Arizona, and Albuquerque, New Mexico. Green lawns spread across the desert and water-hungry garment factories set up shop.

As early as the 1970s, however, El Paso realized the *bolson* wasn't bottomless. By 1980, the city was exploring other water sources. And in 1990, U.S. Geological Survey scientists added to the urgency when they predicted that, at the rate El Paso was going, it would tap all its fresh water within twenty-five years.

In the decade that followed, El Paso began to wean itself from the Hueco Bolson. It turned to the Rio Grande, and the farmers that control it. The city began buying up farmland and convincing farmers to lease their water. Ten years ago, El Paso pulled 85 percent of its municipal water from the Hueco Bolson. Today, the city gets 40 percent of its water from the Hueco Bolson and 45 percent from the Rio Grande. The remaining 15 percent comes from wells northwest of town that tap another aquifer, the Mesilla Bolson.

El Paso also got aggressive about conservation, with some dramatic success, says David Brosman, chief operations officer with El Paso Water Utilities. It revised its rate system, so that the more water residents use, the more they pay. It instigated new rules on when people could water lawns, asked that they wash cars with buckets rather than hoses, and issued tickets to water wasters. It gave rebates for low-flush toilets and handed out 147,000 free low-flow shower heads. The city now pays people by the square foot to dig up their lawns and replace them with drought-tolerant desert plants. An ordinance requiring developers to landscape with desert plants, however, is meeting resistance.

In ten years, El Paso has knocked down its per capita water use almost 21 percent, to 159 gallons per day, compared to 229 gallons a day in Phoenix and 209 in Albuquerque. Today, despite population growth, the city uses about the same amount of water that it did a decade ago, says Brosman. But, he adds, "We're running out of conservation."

What are El Paso's options? Officials have considered building a desalination plant, to clean salty water from deep in the aquifer, or perhaps the first-of-its-kind "toilet-to-tap" water-treatment plant. Both options are expensive, however, and Brosman notes that "a lot of people are pretty skittish" about drinking treated sewer water.

So all eyes are on the Rio Grande, and the river water still used to irrigate fields outside the city. "We need to rely more on the river," says Brosman. "Agriculture brings in only $60 million a year in El Paso County. When you look at the highest and best use of the water, municipal and industrial use is many times greater."

Across the Rio Grande in Juarez, the problem is even more acute. Every year, Juarez's pumps plunge deeper into the Hueco Bolson. Mexico's entire allotment of Rio Grande water goes to farmers, so the city pumps groundwater year-round at full force. At that rate, U.S. experts warn, Juarez will exhaust its fresh groundwater within just five years. Already, several pumps have begun to pull up water too salty to drink.

Meanwhile, the demand for drinking water is only increasing. NAFTA sent many American corporations across the border to Juarez, where they enjoy tax breaks and less stringent environmental regulations and labor laws. Juarez now houses three to four hundred *maquiladoras*, factories owned by companies such as Delphi, General Electric, RCA, and Sony.

The *maquiladoras* have sparked a population boom in Juarez, where workers can earn $5 to $7 a day, twice what they could make elsewhere in Mexico. Some sixty thousand new people arrive each year. But critics say the city has sold itself to industry without adequate infrastructure for industry's lifeblood: the workers.

Estolia Villareal is among hundreds of thousands of Juarez residents living without water. Villareal arrived in Juarez ten years ago from farther south, in the state of Durango, and set up home on a hill that doubles as the city garbage dump. The air there is sour; in the summer, steam rises from the debris. Villareal's days start at 3 a.m. A blue plastic bucket in hand, she steps through the front door of the cramped concrete house where she lives with her husband, three of her children, and several grandkids. Opening a faucet in the yard, she waits. Soon a light stream of water flows, tipping her bucket.

Two years ago, desperate for water, Villareal and her neighbors hooked up this hidden hose to the city water system. The system is unreliable, however; the tap produces water just a few hours a day. The only other water they receive comes every eight days, when city water trucks labor up the hill to fill fifty-five-gallon drums. That water, though precious for washing, is not safe to drink.

Industry recruiters "come to the south promising paradise, work, a good life here," says Villareal. "We don't know what it's like until we get here."

Nor do they know about the endangered aquifer, or that their ever-growing population on the hills exacerbates Juarez's water crisis, says Humberto Uranga, spokesman for the Juarez Water Commission.

"Half the city grew by unregulated invasion," he says. "That is what the *maquila* brought here. The promoters of the *maquiladora* industry don't take water into account."

Maquiladora officials reply that their plants use just 10 to 15 percent of the city's water. But that figure doesn't include the water consumed by their workers. Experts say Juarez's *maquiladora* industry will employ 251,740 people by 2002, nearly double the number before NAFTA.

Future plans to quench their thirst are hazy in a city that only last year installed its second wastewater-treatment plant. More than two hundred thousand residents still lack sewer-line hookups. What's more, Juarez water officials disagree with the U.S. studies that predict their water will run out within five years, a fundamental difference that has kept the two sides from collaborating more closely.

"The life of the aquifer can't be measured. It can only be speculated," says Edmundo Urrutia, a water specialist at the Juarez Water Commission. "Our goal is that the Hueco Bolson lasts as long as possible."

In recent months, however, Juarez officials have started to show signs of concern. There's talk of tapping Mexico's side of the Mesilla Bolson as well as more distant aquifers. But piping in water and repairing the existing water system could cost $800 million over a twenty-year period. NAFTA actually set up a bank to fund projects such as these. Together, the U.S. and Mexico have put $450 million into the North American Development Bank, or NADBank. The money is meant to protect the border environment and workers by funding water and sewer lines and solid-waste projects. But to date, NADBank has loaned out only a fraction of that money, so Uranga is looking to the World Bank, the Mexican government, and private investors. Even in the best-case scenario, he says, the new projects won't get off the ground for five years.

So Juarez, too, is turning to the Rio Grande. Under a 1906 treaty with the U.S., says Uranga, Mexico is guaranteed sixty thousand acre-feet of river water, enough to supply Juarez's present population for half the year.

Taking more water from the Rio Grande will not be easy for either Juarez or El Paso.

In the coming weeks, Juarez officials will release a plan to use more river water. "What the city wants is to take the river water and use it for residents," says Uranga, "and then give the farmers back treated water from the treatment plants."

On the surface, it looks like Mexican water law will make that plan easy. The Mexican Constitution declares that water belongs to the people; water rights are not the property of farmers or irrigation districts, as they are in the U.S.

"In theory, officials in Mexico City, with a stroke of a pen, could take that [water] away" and give it to Juarez, says UTEP's Ed Hamlyn. "In practice, though, farmers control the water. Water is not something you can buy or sell, so they resist anything that could take it out of their hands. It creates a lot of inertia."

The city's plan is sure to meet resistance from farmers like Lorenzo Gutierrez, who once grew melons and corn in Saragoza, a valley southeast of Juarez. When Juarez's second wastewater-treatment plant opened last year, just a few miles from Gutierrez's home, city officials promised farmers treated wastewater from the maquiladoras. Farmers say the treated water hurts more than it helps.

"The water used to be good," Gutierrez says, a Nike USA baseball cap tucked down to shield his eyes from the sun. "Now it burns the earth and the crops with oil and chemicals."

Gutierrez says the chemical-laden water forced his family out of agriculture. They sold the farm piece by piece to developers. Gutierrez now works in construction and his brother drives a taxi.

On the United States side, farmers also stand in the way of urban water plans, and here, they hold the trump card. This section of the Rio Grande, like most, is plumbed for irrigation. One hundred miles north of El Paso in southern New Mexico, irrigators use the Elephant Butte and Caballo dams as giant spigots. Each winter, they turn the river off completely, storing water in reservoirs behind the dams. Come spring, they open the floodgates, pouring 759,000 acre-feet of Rio Grande water each year into the agricultural valleys of southern New Mexico and west Texas.

El Paso owns rights to some of that water and leases another slug of it from farmers. But irrigators still control the dam, so El Paso can only get river water from mid-February to October. Now, the city wants river water year-round, and relations between the city and irrigators are notoriously tense.

In mid-January, it looked like a truce was possible: working under the Texas-New Mexico Water Commission, irrigators agreed to give water year-round to El Paso. The $350 million El Paso-Las Cruces Regional Sustainable Water Project would send water to a new treatment plant, and from there, through a thirty-two-mile aqueduct to El Paso.

But before the ink had even dried on the plan, the city sued El Paso Irrigation District #1. The suit said the district had failed to deliver El Paso's current allotment of river water, which the district sells at the low rate of $15 per acre-foot. The irrigation district countersued, accusing El Paso of planning to drill shallow wells along the river to steal water that belongs to the farmers.

The lawsuits have since been dropped, but the regional water project is in limbo. There are thirty-five thousand landowners in the El Paso #1 district, thirty thousand of whom irrigate less than two acres; they are protective of their dab of water, and the green surroundings it provides them in the desert.

"There may be a time when agriculture does fizzle out, and at that point maybe the water should be committed for municipal use," says Lisa Power, an attorney for El Paso #1. "But as a resident here, there's a beauty to having the river there and farmland. It adds to quality of life."

Those who are willing to let their fields lie fallow and lease water to El Paso want to wring out every drop of money they can. The irrigation district is now asking El Paso to pay $193 per acre-foot of additional water next year, an amount that would rise to $260 by 2020.

Many farmers are holding out for even more, says Power. "Who knows how much water will be worth in a number of years?"

Frustrated by this attitude, the price hikes, and political scuffles, El Paso is looking at its other options, including cleaning deep aquifer water with a desalination plant.

Ironically, the transfer of water from farmers to Juarez and El Paso holds a seed of ecological hope for the Rio Grande. As long as most of the river's water is in the hands of farmers, the Rio Grande will be turned off like a tap each winter, says Kevin Bixby, executive director of the Southwest Environmental Center in Las Cruces, New Mexico. But if the cities can buy water year-round, the river between Elephant Butte Dam and El Paso will have water twelve months a year for the first time since 1916, when the dam was finished.

"People who grew up around here remember the Rio Grande having trees along its banks," says Bixby, who has been fighting for six years to restore this stretch of the river. "[Spanish explorer Juan de] Onate spent the first Thanksgiving in the New World on the river near Juarez. He described the river as an oasis of ducks, fish, trees, geese ..."

Now, between Elephant Butte Dam and El Paso, the river is more canal than river. The International Boundary and Water Commission, which manages the river here, calls it the "Canalization Project," not the Rio Grande. The commission has gone so far as to clear-cut the riverside *bosque*, mowing plants to no higher than a foot in the name of flood prevention; it argues that flood debris caught in vegetation could create temporary dams, flooding fields and homes and taking out bridges.

Convincing water users of the value of river restoration has been difficult, says Bixby. Farther up the Rio Grande, environmentalists and wildlife managers have used endangered species such as the silvery minnow to force farmers and federal agencies to keep water in the river. But here, where the river runs nearly dry for three months of the year, no endangered fish survive.

"We're the fly on the back of the elephant," says Bixby, "but we don't have the mahout stick to make the elephant move—we don't have the Endangered Species Act."

The Sustainable Water Project, however, offers a different hook. The Fish and Wildlife Coordination Act requires federal agencies to consult with the U.S. Fish and Wildlife Service when embarking on a project of this scale. Agencies must not only avoid further damaging wildlife resources, but also pay as much attention to wildlife as to development.

In a lengthy analysis, the Fish and Wildlife Service asked the New Mexico-Texas Water Commission to restore portions of the Rio Grande to a more natural state. While the commission balked at some of the recommendations, it has agreed to restore fish habitat and wetlands, retire farmland and replant it with native plants, and even allow the cottonwood *bosque* to grow back in places.

"It's a modest step forward," says Bixby, who is concerned that the project could still leave portions of the river dry. "The only way to get water [for the Rio Grande] is to buy it, and that's going to cost a fortune. If we can piggyback on El Paso's water, that's a good thing."

Another good thing is in the works, Bixby says: for the first time, the International Boundary and Water Commission is doing a full environmental impact statement on the canalization project.

Doug Echlin, Environmental Protection Specialist for the commission, says the agency is looking at the possibility of restoring natural meanders and flooding, and has already begun replanting the native *bosque* in places. "For many years, it was pretty much, 'mow everything in sight' out there," he says. "Now we're planting cottonwoods and willows in the floodway."

Not everyone welcomes the changes, he adds. "Whenever we plant, we get questions from farmers. 'Whose water are you going to be using? You know those trees will be drinking water that belongs to the district?' "

Bixby acknowledges that any progress for the river will be hard fought. "This is a classic case study of the challenge of environmental restoration in the modern world," he says. "You have a huge human population, a rising demand for resources, and a degraded ecosystem. How can you accomplish restoration in this context?"

The answer depends on cooperation between two states, two countries, two booming border cities, several thousand farmers, and more water lawyers than you could pack into the El Paso County courthouse. Still, there are signs that these people are beginning to work together.

"We can't think about water issues in El Paso without thinking about Ciudad Juarez," says Doug Echlin. "There's just a sliver of river between us and them."

March 12, 2001

Megan Lardner is a graduate student in journalism at the University of California, Berkeley. *High Country News* associate editor *Greg Hanscom* contributed to this report.

A River on the Line

Greg Hanscom

From the front porch of the Terlingua Trading Co., you can see clear to Mexico. Beyond the nearby mounds of mercury-mine tailings and crumbling adobe shacks, the Chisos Mountains jut from the west Texas desert. Beyond the Chisos, cobalt blue against the cloudless sky, stand the Mule Ear Peaks and Bee Mountain, marking the northern fringe of the Mexican state of Chihuahua.

Somewhere south of us, between the layered, dogtooth ridgelines, the Rio Grande slides silently below the steep canyon walls of Big Bend National Park and Mexico's Cañon Santa Elena Protected National Area.

But from here, the river seems an impossibility. The air is stale with cigarette butts and spilled beer, the residue of last night's revelry at the Starlight Theater Restaurant and Bar. The local pirate radio station spills Texas roadhouse out the front door of the Trading Co. The only water here comes in bottles and costs a buck fifty at the counter.

Terlingua, once the center of Texas' mercury-mining industry, is a haven for recluses and river rats— folks who make their living rowing rafts, talking river ecology, cooking in cast-iron Dutch ovens. They live here in the "Ghost Town," paying $65 a month to rent renovated miners' shacks. One guide lives in a cave, an old dynamite cache from the Mexican War.

It's a strange place for river culture. It's a strange place for a river. It's not just that we're sitting in the heart of the Chihuahuan Desert, a place bristling with barrel cacti, cholla, and prickly pear. It's also the fact that the Rio Grande dried up about one hundred and fifty miles upstream.

We watched it waste away two days ago, from the riverfront in El Paso. Photographer J. T. Thomas and I had spent a week traveling down the river from near its headwaters in Colorado to get to El Paso. Over the course of about six hundred miles, the Rio Grande had transformed from a lively trout stream to a sluggish irrigation ditch tapped by farms in the San Luis Valley, New Mexico, and far west Texas. By the time it hit El Paso, it was ankle-deep and heavily guarded.

One of its guardians—a U.S. Border Patrol agent—didn't seem to notice it at all. He was focused on the far bank. "See that orange and green house on the hill? That's a coyote house," he said, pointing through the smoggy sunrise toward El Paso's sprawling twin, Ciudad Juarez. "They're probably watching us right now." Mexicans will pay coyotes, smugglers, $200 for an escort to the U.S. side of the border, he told us. Most are quickly rounded up and bused back to Mexico.

Just below El Paso and Juarez, at Fort Quitman, Texas, not even halfway through its eighteen-hundred-mile trip toward the sea, the Rio Grande disappears. What follows is a "no-man's land," in the words of Bureau of Reclamation planning engineer Mike Landis, who is finishing a master's thesis on the area. "Cattle and horses wander from one country to another [across the dry riverbed] and nobody cares, nobody counts."

Those who know the place call it the "Forgotten River."

Yet here we are, one hundred and fifty miles downstream of the spot where the Rio Grande dies in the desert, and they tell us there's a river out there, beyond the tailings piles and terra-cotta mesas. Like that Texas cowboy in the old Marty Robbins song, "El Paso," the Rio Grande is drawn inexorably south "just to die in the El Paso sand." And like Robbins' cowboy, the great river has managed to "disappear from life and live another time."

But the Rio Grande's second life plays out the same way its first incarnation does. Downstream of Big Bend, the U.S.-Mexico borderlands are booming. As the Rio Grande flows slowly southeast, it is once again called on to water an agricultural valley and growing urban centers. Just a few hundred feet from the Gulf of Mexico, the Rio Grande dries up a second time.

In this in-between border world which, in many ways, has become a nation all its own, things don't look good for the great river. We're here to see what's left of it and ask if there's any hope for reviving one of the West's most hammered waterways.

Our exploration starts here, outside of Terlingua, with some of the many people who depend on a healthy river for their livelihood. It's late afternoon when we slide our rafts into water that is roiling brown, like coffee hit with a slug of cream. Piled high with rubberized dry bags and waterproof ammunition boxes, the rafts slowly loft into the current.

Behind us, a man in a small metal rowboat shuttles a group of children across to the U.S. side of the river, which is perhaps a hundred feet wide. No Border Patrol in sight.

"It's a Class B crossing," explains Darren Wallis, one of our sturdy, suntanned guides. A trip across the river costs a dollar. Americans catch a ride south to grab dinner in Lajitas, Mexico, while Mexican kids cross to school each day in Lajitas, Texas. The Border Patrol doesn't bother them.

We drift into Big Bend between walls of giant river cane and saltcedar. Great blue herons stalk the shallows. Black phoebes snatch insects mid-air. The river carries us through, but in spots it's barely deep enough to float our rafts.

Most of the water here comes from a tributary, the Rio Conchos, which rolls down from Mexico's Sierra Madre, cutting northeast across the state of Chihuahua and joining the Rio Grande near Presidio, Texas, just fifty miles upstream of our put-in. Under a 1944 treaty, Mexico must deliver at least three hundred and fifty thousand acre-feet on average to the Rio Grande each year from the Conchos and several smaller tributaries. In return, the U.S. delivers to Mexico 1.5 million acre-feet annually from the Colorado River.

But since 1992, Chihuahua has been in a drought. Mexican farmers have used much of the Conchos' water for crops, and watched their reservoirs drop precipitously. The old treaty allows Mexican water managers to hold back deliveries to the U.S. during drought years—a stipulation they've used to amass a debt of 1.4 million acre-feet. The Rio Grande has not seen its share.

Yet even with little water from the Conchos, the Rio Grande maintains a steady, if meager, flow here. "The dynamic that puts water in this river is hard to pin down," says river guide and water expert Mike Davidson, co-founder of Far Flung Adventures, a rafting company with a penchant for breeding environmental activists. "We're talking about how a whole part of this continent drains."

One piece of the dynamic becomes quite clear that night as we're finishing our dinner under the stars, rafts parked on a sandbar on the Mexican side of the river. Slowly, without our really noticing it, it becomes really dark. Fat raindrops thwack against our faces and the tents. In moments, it's dumping rain, and headlamps are bobbing wildly about camp. We clean the dishes, pack the food, and dive into our tents, soaked.

It's been raining for maybe fifteen minutes, and already we can hear waterfalls roaring over the canyon rims. In the glow of his flashlight, J. T. watches water seep in through the floor of his tent. He grabs his camera equipment and sleeping bag in time to scramble for high ground as a six-inch tide washes over his bedroll. Darren slogs through the mud and dark to check the rafts. I fall asleep in a puddle to the roar of water on the tent, wondering if I should have pitched it higher on the riverbank.

The next morning, the only signs of the deluge are a high-water mark about three feet above the river, and flowers everywhere. Darren says these plants have adapted to bloom whenever the conditions are right, and they're right today—warm and wet. We spend the day floating through Santa Elena Canyon, between vertical, fifteen-hundred-foot limestone walls. Canyon wrens scold and trill. A peregrine falcon perches high on a cliff, waiting for a duck or a pigeon to make a move.

"Our river has had its roots chopped off," says Davidson. "It doesn't stretch up into Colorado [anymore]. It doesn't stretch up into the Sierra Madre. But it's a wonderful little river."

Davidson believes the Rio Grande in Big Bend holds a secret: upstream, the Forgotten River isn't dead, he says, it's just invisible. Each year, roughly two hundred thousand acre-feet of agricultural runoff makes it past Fort Quitman, he says. What doesn't evaporate joins water from springs and arroyos, and runs through the Forgotten River underground, beneath an impenetrable forest of saltcedar.

"It's really an anomaly," he says. "It's like there's a huge sponge, eighty miles long and two miles wide. It'll hold storm runoff for thirty days, and it keeps these nice moderate water flows in the park."

Davidson needs to be attuned to the river for his business. It's also his passion. He is one of a handful of visionaries along the Rio Grande who understand that this was once a true river, traveled by eels and shovel-nosed sturgeon, and lined in places with wetlands and woodlands. He dreams of someday reconnecting the great river with its roots, allowing it room to flood and meander, its native fish species to spawn and thrive.

He's also a realist. He knows that it will be politics that decides whether the Rio Grande survives here. While the Middle Rio Grande in New Mexico hosts the endangered silvery minnow, those who want to see the Forgotten River revived have no endangered species hook. And downstream of the Forgotten River, where the flow has long been in the hands of agriculture and cities, most native fish species are long gone.

"If the problem is going to be solved, there's going to be beds full of unlikely bedfellows," Davidson tells J. T. and me after two days on the river, as we prepare to leave Terlingua for points east.

Some of the unlikely bedfellows came together in 1998 and formed the Forgotten River Action Committee. Made up of river guides, scientists, and agency officials, the committee in the summer of 2000 helped convene a meeting of then-Interior Secretary Bruce Babbitt and his Mexican counterpart, Julia Carabias Lillo, head of the Secretariat of Environment and Natural Resources. The duo signed a joint declaration of international cooperation, saying they would look into restoring the stretch.

But both Babbitt and Carabias were lame ducks, and their successors, Gale Norton and Victor Lichtinger, have not yet shown any interest in river restoration. Even if they were interested, says Mike Davidson, the drought stands in the way of any short-term progress. "We can get as smart as we possibly can about water management, and sing 'Kumbaya' together at some border conference," he says, "but unless we get some rain, it's all a pretty moot point." So for the time being, the Forgotten River will remain, for most people, just that.

If the river between Fort Quitman and Presidio, upstream of Big Bend, is forgotten, the rest of its length has exactly the opposite problem. Joined by the Pecos River, the Devils River, and a few other tributaries, the Rio Grande fuels the agricultural engine of the Lower Rio Grande Valley, where farmers on both sides of the border grow vegetables, cotton, and sugar cane. Farming here is made possible by a pair of international reservoirs, Falcon and Amistad.

J. T. and I arrive at Amistad after a long drive southeastward across the Texas desert from Big Bend. This is a place built on hope. Amistad is Spanish for "friendship," and in the center of the dam, directly atop the U.S.-Mexico border, stands a pair of giant bronze eagles flanked by U.S. and Mexican flags. The cover of a visitor's map shows four women waterskiing behind a single speedboat. Each carries a flag: perhaps the state flags of Coahuila and Texas, and the national flags of Mexico and the U.S.

At first glance, "Amistad" seems a fitting name, but a visit to the Mexican side of the reservoir shows it's a paradoxical spot. Near the dam is La Playa Tlaloc, the Tlaloc Beach, named for the Aztec god of rain. A thicket of brightly colored picnic pavilions lines a hillside above bar and restaurant. The area is empty except for a young couple sitting at a picnic table with small children in their laps. The reservoir, at fifty feet below capacity, has receded a mile from the "beach."

Out at the water's edge, a fisherman hauls a load of catfish, bass, and a huge carp out of his fiberglass skiff. He's a member of a local fishing co-op, he says, that sells its catch to restaurants and markets in nearby Ciudad Acuna. But because of the drought, he says, for seven years the reservoir has been down—*abajo*. The catch has been down—*abajo*.

Following one of the driest summers on record, Amistad is down to 30 percent of capacity, while Falcon has hit 15 percent. The drop hasn't gone unnoticed. In 2000, suspicious that Mexico had been hoarding water, Texas farmers commissioned a study of the Chihuahuan drought. The study was a bombshell, claiming that rainfall in Chihuahua had actually been 80 percent of normal. Some farmers suggested that the U.S. stop delivering Colorado River water to Mexico until Mexico paid up.

Mexicans, however, pointed to cattle dying of thirst, parched, unplanted fields, and water restrictions in Chihuahua City. There was certainly a drought in progress, but the two countries quarreled over its severity, and whether it was serious enough to justify Mexico's water debt.

Hope for a compromise appeared during President George W. Bush's first visit with Mexican President Vicente Fox last February. Following the meeting, the countries signed an agreement called Minute 307. Mexico agreed to deliver six hundred thousand acre-feet of water to the U.S. before July. The deadline came and went, as did two subsequent deadlines, but the drought has only deepened and only half of the promised water has materialized.

"They have never intended to meet the obligations of the treaty," says Gordon Hill, general manager of the Bayview Irrigation District in Los Fresnos, Texas. "They're running us out of business."

Emotions are high on the Mexican side as well. Farmers on the Rio Conchos in Chihuahua have taken over the local offices of the National Water Commission and blocked reservoir gates to protest delivering water to the U.S. But even Mexican farmers are divided over the issue: recently, farmers in the Gulf state of Tamaulipas, who, along with Texas farmers, depend on Chihuahua to release water into the Rio Grande, joined U.S. efforts to force a payback.

Now, the issue seems to be stalled. The U.S. branch of the International Boundary and Water Commission, the entity charged with mediating such disputes, has asked its Mexican counterpart to ante up by October 2. "In a nutshell," says agency spokeswoman Sally Spener, "the U.S. thinks Mexico should be meeting its treaty obligations."

To date, however, there has been no response, and Mary Kelly, executive director of the Texas Center for Policy Studies in Austin, says it's doubtful that Mexico will be able to pay off its debt any time soon. "U.S. farmers can scream all they want. The fact is that there's not much water there," says Kelly. Time would be better spent, she says, re-examining compacts and treaties that were negotiated sixty years ago, and creating a long-term sustainable water plan for the entire Rio Grande Basin.

Farmers aren't the only ones watching the river. The Lower Rio Grande Valley is also home to a string of cities that have grown like gangbusters in recent years, including Laredo and Nuevo Laredo, McAllen, Reynosa, Brownsville, and Matamoros. Most of these cities get their drinking water from one source: the Rio Grande.

Just below Amistad Dam, the twin cities of Del Rio, Texas, and Ciudad Acuna, Coahuila, offer a stark look at life on the border. It's Halloween night, and J. T. and I walk south across the river to Ciudad Acuna in search of food and drink. The narrow streets, lit by a few dangling streetlights, are filled with people. Kids in store-bought costumes poke into restaurants and bars and yell, "Halloween!" J. T. and I consider teaching a pack of them to say "trick or treat," but decide that they know better than we do what produces booty here.

"The border is like a third country," Ciudad Acuna Mayor Jose Eduardo Ramon tells me later. "It's like one community. There's a river between us, but it's the same community."

It's a community in the throes of enormous change. Ciudad Acuna's population doubled during the 1990s to 108,159 (2000 Census), as people flocked here from the interior to work at the city's sixty-three *maquiladoras,* manufacturing plants owned by corporations such as Alcoa, Bendix, and GE. In Mexico, only the tourist center of Cancun has outpaced Ciudad Acuna's rate of population growth.

"We can't keep up with demand for utilities, schools, paved streets, you name it," says Ramon. Until recently, the city's sewage sat in antiquated lagoons and spilled into the Rio Grande. In the middle of town, sewage ran into a creek once frequented by children. "When I was a kid, we used to fish there," says Ramon. "The last few years, you couldn't stand the stench. It permeated the downtown area."

Ciudad Acuna just finished building a $22 million wastewater plant, and is in the process of replacing miles of sewer lines. Ramon hopes someday to clean up the creek and turn it into a park. But even now, only 60 to 65 percent of households have sewer lines. The city has also recently completed a water-treatment plant, but one in every ten households still has no running water.

It's a snapshot of what's happening all along the Lower Rio Grande. The population of the Lower Rio Grande Valley almost doubled between 1980 and 2000. Analysts predict it will double again by 2020.

Keeping basic infrastructure and environmental protection in step with this surging population growth is a challenge—and the health effects of pollution just make it worse. "Short of a general policy on population—and there's never been the political will on either side of the border for that—you're going to have growth, you're going to have conflicts," says Fernando Macias, general manager of the Border Environment Cooperation Commission, or BECC, based in Juarez.

BECC was set up in 1993, under a side agreement to the North American Free Trade Agreement, as a concession to the environmental community, which was concerned that free trade would spread growth, development, and pollution across the already-stressed border landscape. The sister agency of the North American Development Bank, BECC's task was to funnel money from the U.S. and Mexican governments into sewage treatment, drinking water, and solid-waste facilities for poor border towns.

The program got off to a slow start, however. At the end of 2001, NADBank had loaned only $15 million of the $304 million it had received from the U.S. and Mexico. In response, the NADBank board proposed eliminating BECC, which acts as an intermediary while also ensuring that projects are built with community support and an open public process. The board wanted to free up the NADBank funds for use in Mexico's impoverished interior, despite the fact that BECC estimates that the border will require far more in infrastructure than NADBank alone can fund.

The governors of Texas, New Mexico, Arizona, and California, backed by environmental groups, beat back the proposal, and BECC now has ninety new projects in the pipeline. But Bush and Fox are scheduled to meet again in March, and sources say BECC could once again be on the chopping block.

"If [federal officials] continue to pursue this, they have gone against what everyone along the border has said," says Andrea Abel, a policy analyst with the National Wildlife Federation in Austin. NADBank had set its interest rates so high that poor border communities couldn't afford to take out loans, she says. But BECC and NADBank have recently come up with some innovative solutions, such as low-interest loans and a broader range of environmental projects, including air quality and toxic waste.

"These institutions are headed in the right direction," Abel says.

The fight to save BECC illustrates what a difficult task lies ahead for environmental advocates along the Rio Grande.

Historically, the International Boundary and Water Commission, split into U.S. and Mexican sections, had a monopoly on water issues on the border. For years, however, the agency was more concerned about dividing the water between the two countries than it was with the quality of that water, or the health of the river. That has changed, thanks in part to BECC, the U.S. Environmental Protection Agency, and the Mexican Secretariat of Environment and Natural Resources, which have become more involved in border issues in recent years. The EPA has brought $238 million in grants to bear on wastewater-treatment plants and other border infrastructure. And the U.S. Fish and Wildlife Service has been a leader in conservation and restoration of the river corridor in the Lower Rio Grande Valley.

But building a constituency for these agencies has been difficult because the environmental community along the Rio Grande has been as fractured and stretched thin as the river itself. Local groups often fight isolated battles for slices of the river without any overarching vision or cohesive strategy.

In El Paso, J. T. and I had met with Bess Metcalf, the U.S. director of the Rio Grande/Rio Bravo Basin Coalition. We'd wolfed down green chili while Metcalf described her efforts to pull together river activists on both sides of the border.

In Mexico, a few nascent grassroots groups had popped up, and larger groups such as Ducks Unlimited and World Wildlife Fund were at work on the national level, she'd said. But there was no solid middle-class environmental movement. It was quite the opposite on the U.S.

side, where dozens of small groups worked independently. "There were personal animosities. Environmentalists kept tripping over each other. It was so chaotic."

There are still dozens of conservation groups at work along the Rio Grande—a fact evident on October 20, dubbed *Dia del Rio*, or Day of the River. From Alamosa, Colorado, to Ciudad Acuna, people gathered to celebrate the river, known as the Rio Grande stateside, the Rio Bravo in Mexico. Riverside residents planted trees, cleaned up trash, read poetry. Kids painted pictures of the river and tromped through the riparian forest. In Norogachi, Chihuahua, the community held an all-night ritual of prayers and dancing, asking for protection of the river. In Las Cruces, New Mexico, residents built boats out of everything imaginable and "raced" them down the Rio.

Dia del Rio, organized by Metcalf's Rio Grande Rio Bravo Basin Coalition, is a sign that these groups are starting to come together. "People realize that we're never going to solve the problems on the U.S. side if we ignore what's happening in Mexico," she said. "People realize that we need to speak really with one voice. We need a unified restoration vision."

To that end, the coalition has been working with grassroots groups, from the San Luis Valley in Colorado down to El Paso. Together with the Alliance for the Rio Grande Heritage, they're creating a river-restoration vision for the Upper Rio Grande on the scale of the restoration now under way in the Florida Everglades. "I have to say, I think it's going to bear fruit in the next few years," said Metcalf.

Other groups are tackling the entire cross-border Rio Grande watershed. The Natural Heritage Institute in Berkeley, California, is working with agencies and academics in the U.S. and Mexico to conduct a massive "physical assessment" of the river. When they're finished, they will have a sophisticated computer model of the Rio Grande that should help river managers understand the system as a whole, rather than as a series of rivulets.

But as J. T. and I drive north from Ciudad Acuna and Del Rio, across the west Texas scrub, we can only think that building support for environmental protection in a region with such desperate human needs will be a Herculean task. The task is made more difficult by the fact that the leaders of both the U.S. and Mexico continue to view the borderlands as peripheral. Bush is busy with his international war on terrorism, while Fox has bigger problems in the interior of Mexico.

But through the mayhem of the U.S.-Mexico borderlands, quietly, even invisibly, a river still runs. North of us, past many miles of desert, painted purple by flowering Texas ranger, past Fort Stockton, Roswell, and Santa Fe, a snowstorm is brewing over the San Juan Mountains, seeding another season for the beleaguered Rio Grande.

February 18, 2002

Greg Hanscom is a contributing editor to *High Country News*.

Peace Breaks out on
the Rio Grande

Laura Paskus

This winter, something strange happened on the Middle Rio Grande in New Mexico, where farmers, cities, federal agencies, and environmentalists have been battling for years. As record rainfall graced the river basin, a rare moment of peace also descended upon the river. At the end of February, environmentalists and the city of Albuquerque agreed to bury the legal hatchet over a dispute concerning endangered species— and to work together to keep water in the river.

Major water users on that stretch of the river include about twelve thousand farmers, six tribes, and a handful of cities. The Middle Rio Grande Conservancy District supplies farmers with about three hundred and fifty thousand acre-feet of the Rio Grande's water each year, mostly for irrigating alfalfa. Cities such as Albuquerque, Santa Fe, and Taos also have rights to water in the river, although some, like Albuquerque, have yet to draw on those rights.

Even so, over the last seven irrigation seasons the Rio Grande has been drying up in progressively longer reaches, for longer periods. Last summer, sixty-eight miles of riverbed dried up south of Albuquerque, stranding the endangered silvery minnow at the brink of extinction.

Throughout the drought, the Middle Rio Grande Conservancy District has refused to ante up any water for the minnow. In 2000, farmers even seized control of floodgates when the U.S. Bureau of Reclamation tried to release irrigation water into the dry river channel. And although Albuquerque has leased water to the Bureau since 1996, once the city finishes its new drinking-water project next year—and can finally use the 48,200 acre-feet of river water it has rights to—that water will no longer be available to the river during dry times.

Fearing for the fish, environmentalists sued the Bureau under the Endangered Species Act. Two years ago, a federal judge ruled that the Bureau has the right to withhold water from both farmers and cities to keep enough in the river for the minnow to survive. But Albuquerque Mayor Martin Chavez and Governor Bill Richardson, both Democrats, objected to using municipal water to protect endangered species. Within weeks, Senator Pete Domenici, Republican, convinced Congress to reverse the court decision. Now, that municipal water has been placed forever off-limits for any endangered species.

Rather than addressing river flow, the U.S. Fish and Wildlife Service, the agency charged with protecting endangered species, has scrambled to find other ways to help the minnow: biologists release captive-bred fish into the river twice a year, and the New Mexico Interstate Stream Commission and the City of Albuquerque built a fifty-thousand-gallon artificial "refugium" for the minnow.

But now, an environmental coalition is trying a new strategy: in an attempt to reach the valley's farmers, it is making nice with the city. The coalition—which includes Forest Guardians, the National Audubon Society, Defenders of Wildlife, Sierra Club, New Mexico Audubon Council, and the Southwest Environmental Center—has agreed to drop lawsuits challenging the city's use of the water and its congressional exemption from the Endangered Species Act. In return, the city will usethirty thousand acre-feet of its storage space in Abiquiu Reservoir on the Chama River as a "conservation pool" for dry times. Environmentalists have promised $25,000, and the city $225,000, toward a pilot program to lease water for the pool from farmers. And a new "check-off" option will allow Albuquerque water users to donate $1 to the conservation program in their monthly water bills.

"Our goal is to have farmers come to us and say, 'Yes, I want to do this. I've wanted to do this for a long time,' " says John Horning, executive director of Forest Guardians. "Our broader objective is if we can get farmers interested, that will force [the conservancy district's] hand." By giving individual farmers a financial incentive to curb their water use so that they can lease water to the conservation pool, Horning hopes the district will rethink wasteful flood-irrigation practices.

"We're still shining the light on agriculture," says Horning. "But [the settlement] does it in a way that lets it be known that ag is also the solution."

The details of the agricultural leasing program are not final, and the check-off option won't appear on water bills until at least 2006, after the city's new drinking-water facility is up and running. For now, environmentalists plan to talk with individual farmers about leasing possibilities, and they're encouraging cities such as Santa Fe to start their own check-off programs.

Meanwhile, the conservancy district is studying the feasibility of agricultural leasing, says Subhas Shah, the district's chief engineer. But, he says, if everyone is serious about protecting the silvery minnow, cities should be willing to cede their water, too: "Everyone should help."

March 21, 2005

Laura Paskus is a freelance writer who splits her time between Albuquerque, New Mexico and rural Colorado.

Too Much Can Be Asked of a River

Laura Paskus

What do China's Yangtze, India's Ganges, and America's Rio Grande have in common? All share the dubious distinction of making a "Top Ten" list compiled by the World Wildlife Fund of rivers in trouble. On the lower Rio Grande, where the river forms the border between the United States and Mexico, the challenges include widespread diversion to farms, dams, high rates of evaporation, invasive species, and of course, prolonged drought.

Two days after the World Wildlife Fund released its report in mid-March, I walk to the Rio Grande, a mile and half west of my house, as the grackle flies. A bank of dark clouds squats atop the mesa framing Albuquerque's west side, and the wind is blowing sand and last year's brittle leaves. Looking down, I can see plants greening from their roots; looking up, I find that the branches of the Siberian elms are all tipped with green. Green buds on trees are a call for springtime celebration, but I'm struck by the fact that these invasive elms seem to outnumber cottonwoods along the river. I remember what an outspoken former Forest Service employee, Doug Parker, told me last year: that Russian olive trees were invading the West more aggressively than saltcedar or tamarisk, and Siberian elms were moving in right behind.

I can hear a woodpecker drumming a hollow note, and the chorus of ducks coming in for a landing. Reaching the river, I'm surprised to see it lapping at its banks this early in the spring. But then, warm temperatures arrived in New Mexico in early March and wiped out much of the decent snowpack we'd acquired this winter. The National Weather Service, Army Corps of Engineers, and Agriculture Department were all thrown off this year: they'd predicted snowmelt would occur the second week in April.

Probably no one should be surprised. Climatologists have been warning that the Southwest is in for a warmer future, which means that the snowpack will melt earlier, causing peak runoff to occur before irrigation season even begins. Warmer temperatures also cause greater evaporation from reservoirs and irrigated fields (and off the snowpack itself), as well as longer growing seasons. In other words, the Southwest can expect less water and greater demand for it, unless we start getting smarter about how we treat our rivers.

Here on the middle Rio Grande, the river has dried up in stretches each summer since the 1990s, stranding endangered fish, angering farmers who say they don't receive full allotments of water, and worrying state officials who must ensure that New Mexico shares the river's waters with Texas. And the system is bound to become even more complicated. Since the 1950s, cities along the river have relied exclusively on groundwater pumping, and they are only now accepting the signs that mining groundwater isn't a sustainable way to live. But cities aren't trying to solve the problem by managing rampant development. Instead, they want to pump water from the river.

For its part, Albuquerque will continue pumping groundwater, but beginning next summer, the city will also divert forty-eight thousand two hundred acre-feet of water that flows into the Rio Grande via pipes and tunnels from the San Juan River. Since the 1960s, when the U.S. Bureau of Reclamation built its San Juan-Chama diversion project, some hundred and ten thousand acre-feet have supplemented the Rio Grande's native waters. It's hard not to wonder what will happen to the already stressed river once Albuquerque and fourteen other users start diverting this San Juan-Chama water.

The river flows through this urban stretch today in near silence. The occasional sound of water changing its course against a root is more akin to a flicker than a splash. Even the ducks hush as the wind picks up and the skies darken; tonight, the clouds will drop rain. The river seems more like a flow of red-brown mud than water, and I'm drawn to place my hands under the surface, despite the floating shampoo bottle and some flotsam that resembles the filthy head of a shaggy dog. The water is cold to the touch, and I can almost forget that all of it is spoken for.

April 2, 2007

Laura Paskus is a freelance writer who splits her time between Albuquerque, New Mexico, and rural Colorado.

The Columbia River

Holy Water

Jim Robbins

Beneath nickel-gray clouds that hang heavily over the hills of downtown Seattle, Archbishop Alex Brunett enters towering St. James Cathedral, his footfalls breaking the spell of a quiet afternoon. A handful of parishioners kneeling or sitting quietly in the pews glance up at their spiritual leader, who is talking in an animated fashion about a baptismal font on the floor of the church. We have walked over from his chancery office across from the cathedral because he wants to make a point about the role of water in Catholic theology.

"The water isn't just sitting there," says the archbishop, gesturing toward the small pool, the water in it circulated by a pump. "We don't baptize people in stagnant water, but flowing water. Water that is alive."

That belief in living water is the reason, he says, that he and seven fellow Roman Catholic bishops from Montana, Idaho, Washington, Oregon, and British Columbia have spent the past three years traveling the Columbia River Basin and listening to hundreds of parishioners talk about the river, its salmon, and the economy it has created.

The result of those trips and hearings will be a rarely issued document called a pastoral letter, to be released late this year or early next. Drafts have been circulating for over a year. The latest version of *The Columbia River Watershed: Realities and Possibilities—A Reflection in Preparation of a Pastoral Letter* calls on Catholics and others to forge a new environmental and spiritual awareness about the Columbia River watershed.

Catholic leaders say the letter came about because the river is in desperate straits from a century of logging, mining, grazing, and dam building. Sixteen million salmon once migrated from the Pacific each year to spawn in one of the twenty-eight tributaries along the twelve-hundred-mile-long Columbia; now seven hundred thousand make the journey.

"It is a gift of Creation," Brunett says of the river. "We have to use this gift, but in a way that we don't destroy it. In sermons we urge people to step up and be counted for what they believe. If we believe the river is sacred, we need to say so."

Here is what the two archbishops and six bishops who direct the church in the five states and one Canadian province stand up and say about the Columbia River in the latest sixty-five-page draft:

> *There are problems and injustices in the watershed. Salmon,*
>
> *the indicator species of the life community, are becoming*
>
> *extinct, endangered, or threatened. Greed, ignorance,*
>
> *irresponsibility, and abuse of economic and political power*
>
> *cause problems and injustices.*

And that's just on the second page.

The eight Catholic prelates in the Pacific Northwest lead 1.2 million Catholic parishioners spread over two hundred and sixty thousand square miles in two countries. Catholics are 25 percent of the region's total population and make up the region's largest single church.

The Catholic presence goes back to the mid-nineteenth century, when missions were among the first European settlements Catholicism cuts across all boundaries—Indians, miners, businesspeople, Sierra Club members, loggers, irrigators, fishermen, and insurance salesmen.

No one has taken a poll, but it is possible that Native Americans are paying the most attention to the evolution of the pastoral letter.

"Some switch has gone on; maybe God has spoken to them," jokes Donald Sampson, executive director of the Columbia River Inter-Tribal Fish Commission, a Yakama Indian, and a fisheries biologist. "I hope the pope gets on board."

Then Sampson grows serious. "They came into our country, and the Church was the stronghold for civilization and spreading the gospel and eliminating native religious practices and belief." Sampson's grandmother, he says, told him what happened to her in a Catholic boarding school.

"If she spoke her language she was beaten. They cut her hair and made her march in line. The priests didn't want the Indian people digging roots and following fish.

"Now they're saying, 'We screwed up.' The church is being up-front and dispelling the myth of Manifest Destiny and dominion over the earth. That's refreshing and welcome. But I'd like to see them call for action rather than just reflect."

Sampson would especially like to see the document call for the breaching of the four Snake River dams—a position the letter does not take.

If the final version of the letter in November does call for breaching, it will probably be because of Spokane Bishop William Skylstad, whom many describe as most responsible for moving the letter forward.

Skylstad was asked to lead the effort by a group of lay Catholics, who in 1995 chose the Columbia River as the river most in need of attention. He thinks they came to him "because I grew up on a tributary of the Columbia. I grew up in an apple orchard" along the Methow River in western Washington.

"As a child and youth, I remember the constant roaring of the rapidly flowing river as the waters made their way to the sea." He speaks of "a sense of awe and appreciation for this wonderful gift and treasure in our midst, the flowing waters of life."

But lofty religious agendas need to thread their way through the mundane politics of a bureaucracy, especially one as large and multidimensional as the Roman Catholic Church. Sklystad has had to deal with the arrival of four new bishops in the region who were not originally part of the project, and not all of whom were comfortable with it. Then there is the task of pleasing people united by Catholicism but divided in every other conceivable way.

"He is skilled politically in the best sense of the word," says John Hart, a professor of theology and the environment at Carroll College, in Helena, Montana. "He's well-respected, sincere, and not manipulative. And when he runs a meeting he is very open to the ideas of others."

Yet firm. Kirwin Werner, a Catholic who teaches science at the Salish Kootenai College in Montana, attended a meeting on the letter during which a logger harangued Skylstad at length. "Skylstad stood up to him," Werner recalls, impressed. "And when he [the logger] was done, Skylstad told him, "Well, times have changed."

No one knows those changes better than the steering committee that has guided the letter's progress for the last three years. Headed by Skylstad, it is composed of representatives appointed by each bishop, as well as representatives of the region's Catholic colleges. The committee began its work, in Catholic parlance, with "a reading of the Signs of the Times." (If it had been a federal agency, it would have been called "scoping.") Skylstad and the rest of the committee traveled to eight meetings—one per diocese—between November 1997 and February 1999.

When they met at the federal research facility at the Hanford Nuclear Reservation, "We told them we didn't just want a tour, we wanted to know what was really going on," says John Reid, a leadership and organizational consultant in Seattle, who is also director of the Columbia River Pastoral Letter Project. "We learned that millions of gallons of radioactive water was stored in tanks with twenty-year life spans in the 1940s, and is now leaking into the groundwater," and may spill into the river at one of its wildest places—Hanford Reach.

The committee also visited Castlegar, British Columbia, where Canadian farmers were forced to sell their land decades ago to make way for the reservoirs behind U.S. dams. Now they want their land back or more compensation. And they met in Hermiston, Washington, with Indians who are for breaching the dams and farmers who are against it. They talked with migrant workers, Native American leaders, wheat farmers, and aluminum smelter workers whose jobs depend on cheap hydropower.

The hearings, says steering committee member J. L. Drouhard, who works for the Justice and Peace Office in the Seattle Diocese, were instructive.

"None of the bishops would have been described as an environmentalist walking into it," he says. "All of them are coming to be more environmentalist."

Skylstad says he was pleased with the dialogue. "We never had any great anger," he says. "We're looking at complex decisions that have to be made. There might be sacrifices made; somehow we will do that in a collaborative way that will respect people and traditions. While there were clear and strong viewpoints, everything was done in a respectful dialogue."

The meetings may have been mostly civil, but some of the behind-the-scenes politicking has been less so. Skylstad plays down the controversies, but it is clear that there were objections.

"People said it was too much of a blaming document" in early drafts, Skylstad says. "Given our knowledge and expertise now, we might have made a lot of different decisions about things that were done years ago. But we tried to steer clear about taking off after certain people."

After the hearings, Hart wrote a draft—the one that Skylstad says might have been too blaming—and sent it to the steering committee and to consultants in areas such as the natural sciences. Then Hart wrote another draft. This one was posted on the Web site and comments were invited, making it the first pastoral letter to use the Internet. Then a third draft was written and given to the bishops, who will revise and then release the final version this fall.

Both the deliberate pace and the outreach have helped mute some opposition and have drawn others into the process. Dave Zepponi is a Catholic and director of environmental affairs for the Northwest Food Processors, a coalition of fruit, vegetable, dairy, and bakery processors in the region.

"I still don't know what the letter is going to look like, but it's been a useful exercise to help people focus on the deeper sense of perspective on the river system," he says.

But after the second draft was posted on a church Web site, Hart received a flurry of angry e-mails and calls that accused him of "hiding behind the skirts of the bishop." And members of wise-use groups have shown up at some of the meetings, including one in Helena, Montana, and made their point—loudly.

Another time, a local mining engineer came to Hart's office with his two children. For two hours he tried to convince Hart that mining was not the demon it was made out to be, pointing out that "the cathedral in Helena was built with mining money."

"I told him that just because mining was beneficial to the church in the past, mining techniques are different today, and that while the church used to use asbestos to fireproof Catholic schools, it was found harmful to children and isn't used today," recalls Hart. Indeed, in the penultimate draft of the letter—A Reflection in Preparation for a Pastoral Letter—the bishops vow to reduce the use of gold in churches.

The response to the letter from Catholics in the region has been mostly positive, according to project consultant Reid. "Seventy-five percent are in favor, and people are saying things like, 'I am proud to be a Catholic' and 'My God, the Catholics are dealing with the real world', says Reid. But "20 to 25 percent are saying: 'How dare you,' 'You're being duped,' or 'You've been co-opted by the eco terrorists.'"

Some environmentalists and Indians say just the opposite. They speculate that the letter's failure to call for a breaching of four dams on the Snake River means the bishops were co-opted by their more conservative parishioners.

Sklystad says the letter is as strong as it can be, given the science. "We're not technical experts. We can offer spiritual reflection and offer guiding principles. We call people to good stewardship, to a sense of justice, and a vision for the future. But to come down one way or the other in a technically complex area would overextend our expertise. We don't want to do something in the letter that would look silly three, four, and five years down the road."

Those who want the church to take a position on certain technical issues miss the point, says Frank Fromherz of the Portland Diocese's Office of Justice and Peace. "It's not a giant anvil dropped into your garden with a thud. It's an invitation to think more deeply."

Supporters of the letter say that those who focus on the bishops' failure to call for dam removal miss the letter's important message: that the entire river is sacred. It calls the river and the watershed part of a "sacramental commons," and a sacrament in the Catholic definition is something that allows humans to connect with the divine. It is "a visible sign of an inward grace" according to one dictionary. Hart calls it "a moment of encounter with God."

"To say the river is a sacramental commons means people can experience the Creator in creation, outside the formal church settings," he continues.

It's also an important departure for the church, because it implies that a sacrament does not need to be mediated by a priest. It moves the church closer to the beliefs Native Americans in the West practiced until the Europeans—with the help of the Catholic Church—outlawed them.

The tribes' religious views are an integral part of the mix of politics, science, law, and faith that come together in the debate over the river. To the Umatilla, Yakama, Nez Perce, and Warm Springs tribes, known as the River People, salmon have always been a sacrament, in the same way that the bread and wine of the Catholic eucharist are a sacrament.

The salmon were once human, according to Indian beliefs, "and they created a place for the human beings and turned themselves into fish to provide food," says Sampson of the Inter-Tribal Fish Commission. Each year when the first fish is caught, it is still divided among everyone in the community in the First Salmon ceremony.

The tribes also believe that the treaties they signed in 1855 were a sacred guarantee. If the salmon are wiped out, the tribes claim those treaties would be violated. So they have turned to science and politics to battle for their sacred beliefs. The Columbia River Inter-Tribal Fish Commission is composed of tribal representatives who advocate the protection of estuary habitat, in-stream flows, reintroduction of salmon, and other protection and reclamation measures, "to slowly reverse the problems that got us here," Sampson says. As part of the fight for the sacred, Sampson would like to see the church support the breaching of four dams along the Snake.

Although the draft fails to take a position on the dams or on dredging the mouth of the Columbia River to create a shipping channel, the bishops ask logging companies to remove timber in a sustainable manner, and support an end to logging subsidized by taxpayers. They also ask that off-road vehicles and snowmobiles, which are "disruptive of forest creatures' need for habitat and humans' need for places to encounter the Presence of God in pristine creation, be confined to limited and legally constructed roads."

The letter ranges beyond habitat and salmon and trees to espouse a kind of eco-friendly utopia with sustainable jobs, protection of Native American treaty rights, and the fostering of viable, family-owned farms in Canada as well as in the United States.

"Evils present in the watershed include racism, sexism, classism, and speciesism," says the draft. "These evils are expressed in individual sin when particular persons express these evils; communal sin when a community is permeated by them; and structural sin when social systems and institutions—political, economic, educational or religious—embody them."

Such shifts in church teachings will not be easy for everyone. "It's more difficult for some than others, more difficult for people oriented toward what the church has said in the past," says Hart. "It's probably easier for people who look at the social context and apply tradition, rather than people who take tradition and apply it to social context."

It's often said that the devil is in the details. In this case, it may be God who is—or isn't—in the details. Has the church really gotten religion about the environment? What will the church do to make sure the letter doesn't end up in a file drawer somewhere, ignored by priests and parishioners?

"That the bishops are willing to do this is a significant development," says Dieter Hessel, director of the Program on Ecology, Justice and Faith, an interdenominational nonprofit group in Princeton, New Jersey. "How it's followed up—how rank-and-file Catholics respond—is a real question."

Though Native Americans may want the pastoral letter to go further and to call for breaching the dams, they also know that a theological shift is important if it takes hold among the region's Catholics.

"It's easy to marginalize Native American religion," says Jeremy FiveCrows, a member of the Umatilla tribe and a public affairs specialist at the Inter-Tribal Fish Commission. "It's a lot harder to marginalize your own religion."

The bishops are considering a committee to implement the letter at a parish level once it is completed. The church plans to create teaching documents, videos, and palm cards to be handed out at church and available elsewhere, and it plans to encourage sermons at Mass.

The bishops also hope to work with groups within the watersheds that make up the huge Columbia River Basin. In Montana, the pastoral letter has already inspired a coalition of unions, environmentalists, and church leaders to press for a cleanup of the Clark Fork River, by hiring people to do the cleanup work at a living wage.

Some critics, including Catholics, say there's a fundamental problem with the pastoral letter: it and the church refuse to deal with the issue of overpopulation.

"I told the bishop the church had its head in the closet with regard to the need for population control," says Kirwin Werner, who attended a meeting conducted by Helena Bishop Robert Morlino.

"We're going to have to tackle population control or it doesn't matter what kind of ecological measures we take." The bishop, he says, chastised him at the meeting for his comments.

Publicly, most Catholics involved with the letter adhere to the official position: there aren't too many people; there's an unequal distribution of resources. Privately, some involved in the letter think the church's position on birth control undercuts any major environmental statement the church makes.

It remains to be seen if the church's shift on the environment will lead to the much larger shift on population. Yet the environmental shift demonstrated in the latest pastoral letter draft is enormous. Not so long ago, Christianity was targeted as the cause of ecological problems.

The most famous attack came in 1967, when Lynn White Jr., a historian at the University of California at Los Angeles, published "The historical roots of our ecological crisis' in the journal Science. He argued that the dogma and worldview of the Judeo-Christian tradition made humanity arrogant.

"Man named all the animals, thus establishing his dominance over them," White wrote, interpreting the book of Genesis, the first book of the Bible. "God planned all of this explicitly for man's benefit and rule: no item in the physical creation had any purpose save to serve man's purpose ... Christianity is the most anthropocentric religion the world has seen."

This philosophical framework set the needs and wants of humanity above all else and allowed science and technology free rein, which caused great damage to the natural world, White concluded. "Christianity," he wrote, "bears a huge burden of guilt."

Ideas are powerful, and as environmental problems have become more obvious, the environmental movement has gained great influence over the last three decades, just as organized religion was seeing its influence wane. Billed as an effort to reclaim a river, the pastoral letter may also be an effort by the Catholic Church to reclaim its relevance.

"It's not meant to resolve questions, but to point out the importance of this great river," said Archbishop Brunett. "People say, 'Stay in church where you belong,' but that's not what we've been called to be. We're trying to establish a sacredness in the world around us."

September 11, 2000

Freelancer *Jim Robbins* lives in Helena, Montana, where he writes about the West for the *New York Times* and others.

Troubled—and Shallow—
Waters on the
West's Largest River

Michelle Nijhuis

Mountains, it is often said, are the West's water towers. If snowfall fails to fill the towers, or warm temperatures empty them too early in the year, fish, farmers, and other water users face a dry summer. That's especially true for the sprawling Columbia River Basin, the Texas-sized watershed that not only covers large sections of Oregon, Washington, and Idaho, but also drains parts of four other states and British Columbia.

The Columbia River and its largest tributary, the Snake, are constrained by large dams for irrigation, flood control, and power generation, but their reservoirs store relatively little water. While the Colorado River reservoir system can store about 300 percent of that river's annual flow, Columbia reservoirs can hold only about 30 percent, with more than half that capacity in Canada. That makes the basin, with its approximately seven million U.S. residents, roughly seven million irrigated acres, and huge hydropower demands, especially dependent on what's stored in its alpine water towers.

But this spring, the Northern Rockies and the Cascade Range are far from full. Because of low snowfall and early melting of the snowpack, the federal Natural Resources Conservation Service expects streamflow between April and July at the lower end of the Snake River to be just 51 percent of average. And at The Dalles, about eighty miles east of Portland, the projected spring and early-summer streamflow in the main stem of the Columbia is 65 percent of average. Only the basin's northernmost neighborhood, in Canada, can expect anything approaching average flows.

So far, electric utilities in the Columbia Basin expect to be able to meet power demands, but low flows could lead to higher rates this summer or fall. Price hikes would squeeze not only individual consumers, but also industrial customers, such as the region's energy-intensive aluminum smelters.

The dry summer will also add stress to a strained natural system. "Essentially, every year is a drought year for fish in the basin," says Andrew Purkey, director of the Columbia Basin Water Transactions Program. That's because many rivers and streams in the basin are overappropriated, he says, meaning that more water rights have been granted than there is water to meet them. To remedy this situation, Purkey's program uses funding from the Bonneville Power Administration and other groups to lease and purchase water rights for fish. But he expects to have a hard time finding irrigators willing to let go of water this year.

Low summer flows aren't the only problem facing fish, particularly salmon and other anadromous species that migrate between freshwater spawning grounds and the sea. "Different stocks in different rivers have adapted to a particular timing of streamflow," says Patty Glick, climate specialist for the National Wildlife Federation. If warm temperatures cause peak flows to happen significantly earlier than usual, she explains, adults may arrive at the mouth of a stream too late for upstream travel, or juveniles may not be ready to ride downstream.

"In the Columbia and Snake rivers, there are already so many obstacles that have altered the rivers," she says. "If the runoff happens too early, that's just an added whammy."

State officials are hastening to prepare for summer water shortages. In Washington, a statewide drought emergency has freed up funding from the state Drought Emergency Account; it also allows the state Department of Ecology to quickly transfer water rights between water users, and to permit additional use of groundwater. Governor Christine Gregoire, Democrat, recently requested about $12 million in extra drought-response funds from the state legislature, money that could be used to buy water and pay for water-supply projects.

Oregon Governor Ted Kulongoski, Democrat, declared drought emergencies for two counties in early March, and the Oregon Drought Council has recommended that he add six more counties to the list. Kulongoski is also seeking $450,000 from the federal government for a statewide assessment of future water needs.

If climate scientists are correct, long-term planning is not only prudent, but necessary. Alan Hamlet and his colleagues from the Climate Impacts Group at the University of Washington anticipate that by the 2040s, average summer flows in the Columbia at The Dalles will drop by 11 percent—assuming that winter precipitation remains largely unchanged. If winter precipitation declines, summer flows could plummet as much as 25 percent. "The real concern is that we're going to have to choose between hydropower and fish," says Hamlet.

Such difficult choices could cause Northwesterners to cast a covetous eye at the Canadian lobe of the Columbia Basin, which is colder in winter and likely to retain more of its mountain snowpack in the future. Unless the two countries plan ahead, says Hamlet, the potential for a cross-border "train wreck" is high.

How did the basin get into this fix? Even before human-fueled global warming reached its present pace, persistent drought was no stranger to the Columbia. Forest Service research biologist David Peterson and his colleagues recently read the rings of venerable Douglas firs, ponderosa pines, and other trees throughout the basin, and found that six major multi-year droughts have hit the Columbia and its tributaries during the past two hundred and fifty years. One especially severe drought began in the 1840s and lasted twelve years, while another deep dry spell occurred in the 1930s.

But as in the rest of the West, relatively wet conditions during much of the twentieth century lulled Northwesterners into complacency, and led them to develop beyond the Columbia's capacity to provide water in dry times. "Natural systems are adapted to drought," says Peterson. "It's human systems that are not well adapted."

April 18, 2005

Michelle Nijhuis is contributing editor to *High Country News*.

A River Once More

Matt Jenkins

If you're looking for a steelhead trout in Bend, Oregon, head toward the river. Tucked off Brooks Street, downtown, is the Bend Brewing Company, where you can get a steelhead fillet served up between two pieces of focaccia, with a pickle on the side.

On this August afternoon, the deck is crowded with thirty-something women going for the fleece-clad hourglass look, and men who carefully cultivate a style of raffish dishevelment. Their various dogs are leashed to the parking signs outside. Beyond, the river flows wide and languid through town.

The Deschutes River rises near the volcanic crest of the Cascade Mountains, gathering water for the two hundred and fifty-mile journey to its confluence with the Columbia. Upstream from Bend, the river boils silvery green down through ancient lava, charging through craggy chutes resplendent with ponderosa pine and Douglas fir, before it slows and widens, shimmering in frothing cascades like hammered silver.

Even in downtown Bend, the Deschutes has a living energy that helps explain why it's such a popular destination for anglers in search of trout. Sadly, though, the steelhead at the brewing company comes from a Washington fish farm. Steelhead and salmon have been gone from the Upper Deschutes Basin for more than half a century.

Venture a mile downstream, and you'll begin to get a sense why. Here, between two low bluffs of cracked and pockmarked volcanic rock, a ninety-four-year-old dam slows the river and channels it into three canals that water more than seventy-four thousand acres of farmland.

Settlers arrived in the Deschutes around the turn of the last century, fired with zeal to put the land under the plow. Much of the basin lies in the blast zone of the Newberry Volcano, making the pursuit of agriculture in the area akin to farming a giant hibachi. But optimism has never been in short supply here, and the settlers' pioneering spirit, backed by tons of black powder used to blast canals out of the rock, broke the ground for some twenty-two hundred farms and one hundred and eighty thousand acres of irrigated land around the Upper Basin.

The entire enterprise was built atop a fairly simple notion, central to western water law: the only legitimate use of water is human use. And "using water," Wallace Stegner once wrote, "means using it up. You can literally dry up a stream if you have a prior right for a so-called beneficial use." So the story went on the Deschutes, which until recently disappeared at the North Canal Dam.

Today, however, a thin sheet of water, just a couple inches deep, glides over the crest of the dam and continues downstream to boost flows for fish. It doesn't look like much, but it represents a giant step forward in an effort to revive the Deschutes. "You're looking at just short of a hundred cubic-feet per second," says Steve Johnson. A big man with a bad knee who keeps a can of Skoal tucked in his sock, he runs the Central Oregon Irrigation District. Johnson is working with other irrigation districts, the region's fast-growing cities, local Indian tribes, and a river-restoration group called the Deschutes River Conservancy in an ambitious effort to ease back the ratchet of a century's worth of water development.

The effort runs counter to pretty much everything Westerners have done with rivers for a long, long time. But Johnson is convinced that playing by the old rules only creates the kind of news stories that keep irrigation district managers like him up at night. "You read stories about Vegas and L.A. fighting for water," he says. Just five years ago, people here had a front-row seat when, in the throes of a severe drought, federal agents shut down farmers' headgates to protect endangered fish in the Klamath Basin, a hundred and thirty miles south.

"The irrigation districts look out the window, and they see these same issues," says Johnson. "You can't pretend it's all gonna go away. You have to engage the issue."

And the issue here is plain to see. For a quarter of a century, the state watermaster for the Deschutes was a bulldog of a man, now sixty-three years old, named Bob Main. At a certain point, Main says, "Nobody could stand there and see a big river on one side of the dam, and a nothin' on the other side, and not think, 'Gee, maybe we oughta do something about this.' "

At its root, reviving a river that has been strangled for human advantage is an exercise in realigning relationships of power.

Starting with the opening of the frontier, farmers have laid claim to the vast majority of the region's water and have long dominated its water politics. Over the years, cities have slowly built up water for their own needs, sometimes by buying out farms. Federal environmental laws and lawsuits from Indian tribes and environmentalists have also forced farmers to put some water back into rivers. But negotiating a new balance has been a long and tenuous process that has frequently led to water wars and endless court fights.

In the Deschutes, however, things have largely been sorted out outside the courtroom. That's in large part because of the tone set by the tribes of the Warm Springs Reservation, sixty miles downstream from Bend. The tribes, a confederation of Wasco, Warm Springs, and Paiute Indians, have considerable clout: a series of 1970s court decisions affirmed their rights to half of the salmon harvest, and federal law makes Indian water claims paramount to those of all other users.

But the Warm Springs tribes also made a conscious calculation to work as cooperatively as possible with other water users in the basin. "Rarely is the result of a lawsuit the last word: it's just a prelude to congressional action, or further litigation," says Jim Noteboom, the tribes' attorney. "We concluded a long time ago that it's not rational to do that."

Nonetheless, for several decades, the tribes have pushed steadily to revive salmon and steelhead runs, which were cut off by hydropower dams built on the Lower Deschutes in the 1950s. The obvious first step was to get water back into the river in the Upper Basin, where the fish spawn. "If we want to have fish runs all the way to the top end, we've got to have water in those sections up there," says Dee Sehgal, the director of the tribal environmental office. The fish need "a healthy watershed, not just here on the rez, but top to bottom."

In the early 1980s, rather than sue to assert their water rights, the Warm Springs tribes began negotiating a settlement with the state, the federal government, and local irrigation districts. Impressed by this, Zach Willey, an economist with the nonprofit group Environmental Defense, began talking with Jody Calica, the head of the tribes' natural resources department. "The Warm Springs were exceptionally together, and there was some residual goodwill among all the actors," says Willey. "They'd had their run-ins, but the tribes weren't totally on the out-and-outs with the irrigators or anyone else."

Calica and Willey wanted to build on that goodwill and create an institution that could work to restore the river, even in the face of continued water demand from farms and cities. In 1996, they formed a nonprofit group that would later become the Deschutes River Conservancy. The conservancy now has a fourteen-member staff that uses a variety of methods to put water back in the river, relying on a 1987 state law that gives instream flows equal standing to traditional "consumptive" uses like farming.

The conservancy's nineteen-member board of directors is essentially a council of everyone whose lives and livelihoods are tied to the river. It includes representatives from the tribes, cities, the basin's eight irrigation districts, ranchers and farmers, federal agencies like the Forest Service and Bureau of Reclamation, and environmental interests. The idea, says Willey, was to get "all the people who could put roadblocks up inside the process."

The tribes, meanwhile, have gently nudged the quest to bring back salmon and steelhead one step farther. In 2004, they partnered with Portland General Electric to operate its two hydropower dams on the Lower Deschutes. As a condition of the deal, the tribes insisted on a $135-million, fifty-year program to modify the dams to allow fish migration, and to reintroduce summer steelhead—listed as threatened under the Endangered Species Act —as well as spring chinook and sockeye runs above the dams. The first fry will be planted next year, and spawning adults should return in 2011.

If the reintroduction effort succeeds, the conservancy and its partners will have demonstrated that river restoration is possible even in the face of growing competition for water—something that has long been considered impossible in many parts of the West.

Steve Malloch, a Seattle water lawyer and consultant who last year wrote a major assessment of instream flow efforts around the West, says, "Most instream-flow people are looking at a little tiny scale. The conservancy is saying, 'We're going to have growth, we want our agricultural community to survive—so their needs must be met—and we have to make room for the fish. The only way this whole shebang is going to work is by recognizing that it's really tough to make progress working on each individual piece in isolation.' "

The dry run for the Deschutes restoration effort is a small tributary called Whychus Creek, twenty miles northwest of Bend.

Just upstream from the town of Sisters, at a spot fragrant with the scent of ponderosa, there's a small diversion dam with a headgate for an irrigation canal. It looks like the same sort of slightly shabby concrete structure you'd find on practically any stream in the West. And, just as North Canal Dam emptied the Deschutes, the dam here completely drained Whychus Creek, which also happened to be home to some of the best steelhead spawning habitat in the entire basin.

"I took over in '97," says Marc Thalacker, the manager of the Three Sisters Irrigation District. "I had one of the farmers come in to the office and say, 'If there's any water in the creek, you're not doing your job.' At that point, I knew there was a serious problem."

Thalacker has covered the walls of his dusty office with newspaper stories about how the "hammer" of the Endangered Species Act has dropped on farmers in salmon country. Exhibit A is the showdown in the Klamath River Basin, just to the south on the Oregon-California line.

Throughout the 1990s, federal wildlife agencies and Klamath farmers fought a series of legal skirmishes as it became increasingly clear that there was not enough water to fully supply the area's farms and leave enough instream for endangered fish. Then, in 2001, a severe drought forced the government to cut farmers' water by 90 percent to protect the fish. Facing a minor insurrection, the government dispatched federal agents to guard the locked-down irrigation headgates, and farmers' crops withered in the field.

Thalacker has a seemingly manic compulsion to untack the stories, run them through his photocopier, and press them into the hands of visiting reporters. He has used the same technique to convince farmers in his district that they're better off working cooperatively than trying to retain every drop of their water, and risking all-out warfare.

The farmers' cooperation is critical to restoring Whychus Creek, because the obvious place to get water for the creek is from their irrigation ditches. While the local lava is used to fine effect as a landscaping embellishment in some Bend neighborhoods, it is hardly the ideal medium through which to run a canal. In fact, it is so porous that half the water never reaches a farm. Bob Main, the former watermaster, says there are places where "I could just stand next to a canal and hear the water cascading into the lava tubes underneath."

Oregon's 1987 instream-flow law opened new horizons for district managers like Thalacker. It gives irrigation districts a way to reduce their environmental impact—and potential exposure to Endangered Species Act violations—by allowing them to finance irrigation-efficiency improvements with public money, and then permanently dedicate the conserved water instream.

Since 1998, Thalacker has lined twenty miles of ditches—about a third of the district's total—with heavy-duty plastic pipe, which has raised water efficiency from 50 percent to 99 percent. The water that has been saved has been returned to Whychus Creek. In return, the $2 million project has been funded almost entirely with public dollars from the river conservancy, Columbia River hydro dams, a state lottery-funded watershed program, and the federal government.

"I've probably worked with fifty or sixty farmers"—many of whom have volunteered equipment and labor for the projects—"so they all kind of understand what it's about," says Thalacker. The district now takes 30 percent less water from Whychus Creek than it did historically, but actually delivers more water to farmers than before. Some landowners in the district have also used money from the federal Natural Resources Conservation Service to convert from flood irrigation to more-efficient sprinkler irrigation; the water saved through such efforts is also dedicated instream.

John Hicks teamed with four of his neighbors for the first such project. "When you're flood irrigating, your efficiency goes in the toilet," he says. "Since we converted to the sprinkling situation, I use roughly 40 percent of the water that I used to use, and my [hay] yields have gone up dramatically."

In Whychus Creek, those efforts are adding up. This year, the district nearly reached the twenty cubic-feet per second target flow that the Oregon Department of Fish and Wildlife estimates is necessary to support salmon and trout. (One cubic-foot per second, or "second-foot," equals 7.48 gallons per second, or roughly two acre-feet per day.) Even in August, the height of irrigation season, water pours over the district's diversion dam and heads downstream toward the Deschutes and the Columbia. About a third of that water is conserved from canal-piping projects; one-third is temporarily leased from farmers; and one-third has been permanently purchased from farmers and a developer and turned instream.

Next, Thalacker plans to replace another third of his district's canals with pipe. With a $6-to $7-million price tag, this stage is considerably more expensive than the first, but Thalacker has secured public funding for the project in exchange for dedicating the saved water instream. Once the water is back in the creek, it will carry the same 1895 "priority date" as the district's water right, which protects it from being taken by lower-priority water users. Thalacker gets excited when he talks about projects like this, and he also sometimes sounds like a vintner doing things he oughtn't with a particularly fine wine: "When we're done with the new pipeline, there's gonna be six more second-feet of 1895 in Whychus Creek."

Now, the Deschutes River Conservancy is turning to a challenge of an entirely different magnitude: reviving the Deschutes itself.

The natural flow of the mainstem Deschutes is thirteen times that of Whychus Creek. Twelve times more farmland depends on water from the mainstem than from Whychus. And pressures from urban growth are far greater on the mainstem as well: the river-restoration effort will have to compete for water with the booming cities of Bend and Redmond. Thanks in part to their frequent appearance on Top Ten Best Places to Live in the West lists, these cities have been growing at between 6 and 8 percent a year. That's a growth rate that, percentage-wise, rivals Las Vegas and Phoenix.

In the past—and in much of the rest of the West—the cities could simply pull more water from the river, or sink another well. But last year, the state of Oregon, recognizing that water in the Upper Deschutes Basin is over-appropriated, announced that it will not issue any new water rights here. Now, new needs can only be met through a Rubik's Cube-like reshuffling of the existing supply. And while ag-to-urban water transfers are nothing new—farmers and cities on Colorado's Front Range have been cutting deals for decades—working the environment into that relationship is fairly radical.

It also puts considerable pressure on the irrigation districts, which hold most of the water. That led Steve Johnson, the Central Oregon Irrigation District manager, to seek a better sense of what demands his district will face. Using a quarter-million-dollar grant from the U.S. Interior Department's "Water 2025" initiative, Johnson and the conservancy spent the past year estimating future needs for both the cities and the river. They then used that information to create a twenty-year plan for meeting those needs, while still sustaining farming in the Upper Basin. It is, in effect, a blueprint for avoiding a water war.

Bruce Aylward did much of the work on the plan. Before he came to the conservancy in 2002, Aylward worked as a consulting economist to the World Bank, and he prefaces much of what he says by drawing an x and y axis on the nearest whiteboard. He found that, despite the high rates of growth, future urban demands should be relatively small. The real need—nearly three-quarters of total future demand—will be for water to restore the river. He also discovered that an acre of houses uses about a third of the water necessary to irrigate an acre of agricultural land; developing farmland actually frees up water that can go back instream. "In the end," says Aylward, "I had to conclude that sometimes growth is good."

Water does not, however, simply flow from farmland to cities and rivers. Free-market environmental economists have touted water markets as the most efficient way to move water from agriculture to new uses. But unregulated markets are prime habitat for speculators and developers with deep pockets, all of whom can drive water prices sky-high. In Reno, Nevada, another city that has hit the limits of its available water, housing developers were paying a mind-boggling $50,000 an acre-foot for water rights last year. Under those conditions, people of more modest means— and organizations trying to restore river flows—are simply priced out of the market.

In the Deschutes River Conservancy's conference room, Aylward pulls the cap off his dry-erase marker for a quick lesson in how to incorporate social and environmental conscience into a water market. "To have people making a profit off a public resource doesn't really make sense," he says. "But you can design the market to meet societal purposes, rather than just having a market for the sake of having a market."

Earlier this year, Aylward helped create the nonprofit Central Oregon Water Bank, which he now runs out of the conservancy's offices. Rather than trying to turn a profit on water deals, the state-chartered bank buys water from farmers, pools it together, and then permanently "reallocates" it—at cost, plus transaction fees—to cities and the river.

The crux of that effort was getting farmers to give up water. Again, Steve Johnson's Central Oregon Irrigation District took the lead. This summer, his district and another local one agreed to relinquish some of their water for reallocation by the bank. It was a perilous step into the unknown: It requires drying up farmland, which potentially hurts the district as well as the farmer, because irrigation districts raise operating revenues through assessment fees on each acre of irrigated land.

But Johnson thinks he's hit on a way to make it work. When a farmer sells his water, the buyer pays a $1,000-an-acre "exit fee" to the district.

That fee goes into an endowment fund and generates interest to replace the lost assessments.

Johnson's district is starting small: its board of directors has agreed to allow just two hundred and forty acres to go out of production this year. But even that was a huge threshold to cross. "I had to work with my board for six months to show them that, whether we like it or not, the cities are gonna grow," says Johnson. "I had a board member tell me, 'My mind understands and agrees with what you're saying, but my heart's telling me something different.' So there's a cultural shock and a cultural change that's still ongoing."

But Deschutes farmers can always find a powerful example of the perils of being unwilling to yield even a little. All they have to do is look just a hundred and thirty miles down the road. "Unless you want to end up like the Klamath, you have to compromise," Aylward says. "And a compromise where you keep 90 percent of your district intact and your finances look good, as opposed to the wild unknown, with water agents running around and prices going up, isn't bad."

Still, the path that people in the Deschutes has chosen comes with its own price, and difficult choices may lie in the years ahead.

Aylward's twenty-year plan for meeting urban and instream demands looks first to water that will spin off as development spreads across a projected nine thousand acres, some 5 percent of the basin's irrigated land. The remainder of the water, says Aylward, will come from efficiency projects, to avoid taking any more land out of production.

Efficiency, however, is expensive. It can be far cheaper to simply buy or lease a farmer's water right, take that land out of production, and return the water instream. In the Deschutes, buying an acre-foot outright runs from $330 to $550. Leasing an acre-foot for a year costs, on average, less than $4.50. In contrast, Aylward estimates that, in the future, it will take an average of at least $1,000 of canal-piping work to yield an acre-foot of water.

The emphasis on efficiency projects drove the total cost of the twenty-year plan to $135 million. Getting the money needed to make the plan work will be a challenge. Johnson and Aylward have proposed a four-way split between the federal government, the state, nonprofit and quasi-governmental interests including the conservancy and the Bonneville Power Administration, and the irrigation districts.

"I think everybody has to have skin in the game," says Johnson. But he adds that the war in Iraq and Hurricane Katrina have substantially eaten into available federal funding. "The 2007 budget, which Congress is trying to pass right now, is tight. The thinking is that the '08 budget is worse."

That raises the question of whether there is a more cost-effective way to meet the challenge. Nearly three-quarters of the plan's $135 million price tag is for efficiency improvements, but they will yield only about half the total water needed. "You could do the same thing with $50 million less," says Aylward, "if you just took a small percentage [more] land out of production."

Yet taking a mixed approach—call it the middle path—makes it possible to shift water to new uses without completely raiding farms for their water. That's an issue that Marc Thalacker has grappled with on a small scale in the Three Sisters Irrigation District.

"Yeah, we can say we're just gonna cater to growth and dry up farmland. But do you want to dry it all up?" he says. Efficiency projects like pipelines may be more expensive than fallowing land and transferring the water instream. But, Thalacker says, "The pipeline is creating sustainable ag"—that is, allowing farming to continue in the face of urban growth—"so you're still protecting ag, and at the same time creating flows for fish."

And by allowing irrigation districts to let go of their water at a comfortable pace, the process also gives them some control over a potentially scary future. "Buying water and retiring farm land in an ag community risks hollowing out the infrastructure for that community," says Malloch, the Seattle attorney. "Are enough farms left to keep the ditches running and the schools, equipment dealers, and farm-supply companies in business? Dry up enough land and eventually the economics no longer work for that community."

Because the economics of farming are marginal, "That will happen in a lot of places whether the water gets bought or not," Malloch adds. "But

I think the conservancy is working with people to manage that process and keep a core agricultural community going."

The effort is not without critics. One longtime member of the Central Oregon Irrigation District, who recently stepped down, says that the river-restoration effort has been perpetrated by "highly educated, very intelligent people that have never tried to irrigate a garden." Other farmers have likened the steelhead reintroduction to the federal government's reintroduction of wolves into Idaho: once the fish are back, they will likely be protected under the Endangered Species Act and farmers will suddenly be liable for harm to them.

And while few people inside the river-restoration effort are willing to say so out loud, the entire project is something of a calculated gamble. Even if the instream-flow targets can be met, they may not be enough to successfully re-establish steelhead runs in the basin. The federal government could come calling for more water.

Still, if the Klamath provides a cautionary example of what happens when the ratchet is tightened down too far, the Deschutes may be the counterexample: an effort to slowly unwind the water-development ratchet before it breaks and mauls someone. "We can all see the problem, and if we work together, nobody gets anything taken away from them," says Bob Main, the former watermaster. "They may give something up, but they will get something in return."

That something might only be peace of mind, but even that may be worth the price. During his tenure at the state water-resources department, Main oversaw not only the Deschutes but the Klamath, too. There, he witnessed firsthand the carnage as farmers, Indians, and environmentalists threatened each other with the prospect that, as he puts it, they would "legally undo everything you hold dear."

"Here," he says, "nobody feels attacked and destroyed by somebody with a bigger hammer. This is an effort that can go on for another fifty years."

Main is quick to concede that unwinding the ratchet is a perilous process, one that takes patience—and trust—on everyone's part. But people here are committed to playing by the rules they've created for themselves. In the cost-benefit analyses constantly running through Steve Johnson and Marc Thalacker's heads, money spent on lawsuits could be put to far more productive use piping canals.

Each additional cubic-foot per second put in Whychus Creek or the Deschutes is water that will never touch a farmer's fields. But it's also insurance that the federal government won't step in with its own set of rules, as it did in the Klamath.

Thalacker concedes that he sometimes loses sleep worrying about whether, when the fish return in 2011, there won't be enough water to sustain them. "But as we have each success, it moves us up to the next project," he says. "And let's say in 2011, we've got a good steady flow of twenty second-feet in the creek. If someone says, 'Well, you know, we really need twenty-five,' is an environmental group going to come sue us over that? I don't believe so. I think they'll come to us and say, 'How do we get that next five second-feet?' "

If the Deschutes has proved anything so far, it's that incremental efforts—second-foot after second-foot after second-foot—add up. In our determination to turn the West into something it was never meant to be, we unraveled an intricate world. Re-creating that world begins with fussing and obsessing over the tiniest details of every single stretch of screwed-up stream.

Similar efforts are already under way on neighboring Columbia River tributaries like the Umatilla, Walla Walla, John Day, and Yakima rivers. And somewhere far beyond these incremental efforts lies a much bigger possibility: the chance to break out of the cycle of water shortages and water wars, and step into a world where steelhead and salmon can sustain themselves.

That day is a long way off. But more than a century's worth of bad news cannot obscure this fact: nowhere is it written that irrigated agriculture, cities, and fresh, wild-caught steelhead sandwiches are fundamentally irreconcilable phenomena.

October 16, 2006

Matt Jenkins is a *High Country News* contributing editor.

The Klamath River

No Refuge in
the Klamath Basin

Rebecca Clarren

Wildlife biologist Tim Griffiths leans out his truck window, squints at the bright, scorching sun, and shakes his head with wonder. Yellow-headed blackbirds perch on slender cattails, bald eagles swoop through the sky, and white pelicans dunk their tugboat-size beaks in the shallow water.

"This place is pure magic," says Griffiths of the refuge that hosts 80 percent of all wildfowl in the Pacific Flyway and winters the largest concentration of bald eagles in the continental United States.

There are times during the year, he says, when the sky turns black as the sun disappears behind waves of birds that roll overhead. But this fall, when over 1.5 million birds return on their southern migration, the waterfowl had best make reservations at a Holiday Inn. What should be a sea of over twenty-five blue marshes has diminished to three small ponds. Reeds rise out of dry wetland bottoms like a crewcut on a balding man. A sign that cautions "Deep water" sticks out of a barren and cracked mud bank. Surrounding the refuge lie fallow fields where birds once foraged for grain.

A terrible drought and the needs of three species of endangered fish mean that this bleak scene is not about to improve. In early spring, the U.S. Bureau of Reclamation, the agency in charge of water allocation, ordered that the majority of available water remain in the region's waterways. That's good news for fishers and Native American tribes hundreds of miles downstream in the Lower Klamath Basin, who usually see scant salmon runs and dry rivers due to irrigation. But the news has thrown farming towns in the Upper Basin into chaos.

Food bank supplies have been stretched thin to feed families, and social service agencies report that cases of depression and domestic violence have jumped. In towns like Klamath Falls, Oregon, population seventeen thousand, and Tulelake, California, population one thousand, businesses have closed and school enrollments have dropped by as much as 30 percent. Native Americans and agency staffers who support the Bureau of Reclamation's action have been refused restaurant service, and some say they worry about their safety.

The unrest boiled over in early July, when hundreds of farmers and their supporters used torches and crowbars to open the headgates of an irrigation canal four times in one week. Local sheriffs and police stood by, claiming lack of jurisdiction. Now National Park Service police and FBI agents guard the headwaters, but that hasn't deterred the farmers. They are laying a pipeline that will take water from Upper Klamath Lake directly to the irrigation ditches, bypassing the headgates.

Griffiths, twenty-five, who grew up in this basin, is also frustrated. The decision to protect the endangered fish— two species of sucker and the coho salmon—will also limit water to the Klamath refuges and adversely affect four hundred and thirty other species.

"When I was studying conservation management at Oregon State University, they drilled it into my head that you manage for the ecosystem and that if you manage for one species you're in trouble," says Griffiths, who works for the nonprofit hunting group, the California Wildfowl Association. "Why did they teach that in college if it's not being practiced in the real world?"

Griffiths says the recent events in the basin have made him rethink the most important law wildlife advocates have in their toolbox: the Endangered Species Act.

The law should be more flexible, he says, a viewpoint expressed by an array of biologists, community leaders, local politicians, and agency staffers. Even Oregon Governor John Kitzhaber, Democrat, the only governor in the region to support breaching four dams on the Snake River for endangered salmon, wants to overhaul the law.

"The biggest problem with the Endangered Species Act ... is how [it] is implemented," Kitzhaber told a crowd of angry farmers in mid-April.

"I don't intend to stand by and see this community or the children in this community become extinct."

Suddenly, the remote and long-ignored Klamath River Basin has become a flashpoint for the twenty-eight-year-old Act. People throughout the West who have felt the bite of the regulatory law are rallying around the Klamath farmers and calling for reform.

The mainstream media have been quick to frame the conflict as one of farmers vs. fish, but the issue is far more complicated. There is a long history in the Klamath of trying to stretch a finite water supply to meet the needs of farmers, Indians, and wildlife, and for most of the last century the farmers have had priority. Now, three endangered fish have been pushed to the front of the line, and life in the Klamath may never be the same.

From a small airplane flying at one thousand feet, it's hard to believe that the Klamath Basin is short on water. Upper Klamath Lake, Oregon's largest freshwater lake, is the center of a spiderweb of waterways—rivers, canals, sloughs, and the watery wetlands of six Klamath Basin wildlife refuges.

But the luscious display of sparkling waters from this altitude is deceiving. To get a forecast of the valley's moisture, one must fly into the mountains and look for snow. As early as last March, that forecast looked bleak: the mountains surrounding the basin had only 21 percent of normal snowpack, indicating that the area's worst drought in a century was on its way.

Even so, up until the last minute, biologist Griffiths and many locals believed the Bureau would come through for the fourteen hundred farm families just as it always had. Many of these farmers are the descendants of veterans from the First and Second World Wars who were promised land and plenty of water if they would relocate to the Klamath. As participants in the second-oldest Bureau of Reclamation project in the country, Klamath residents took water delivery for granted.

But in March, the U.S. Fish and Wildlife Service released its biological opinion for the endangered shortnose and Lost River suckers, two bottom-feeding fish that live in Upper Klamath Lake. The FWS found that to recover the species, the U.S. Bureau of Reclamation must hold Upper Klamath Lake at a higher level than last year. At the same time, the National Marine Fisheries Service recommended the Bureau spill more water out of the lake to increase flows in the lower Klamath River to protect threatened coho salmon habitat.

As the drought deepened, the two agencies told the Bureau that to maintain the recommended flows, it would have to cut off the water to the farmers and refuges. Still, farmers and refuge managers were optimistic that the Bureau would ignore the other agency's recommendations.

Local politicians did everything in their power to ensure that it did. They tried to force a review of the biological opinions, even appealing to Vice President Dick Cheney, who in turn asked eighty federal biologists to review the decision. Cheney ultimately modified the Bureau's operating plan, thus allowing seventy thousand acre-feet of water to farmers east of Klamath Falls. But the majority of farmers within the federal Klamath Basin project—and the Tule Lake and Lower Klamath Lake wildlife refuges—remained waterless.

When Phil Norton, manager of all six refuges in the Klamath Basin, heard the news, he remembers thinking, "It's going to be a long, hot summer."

The farmers didn't accept the situation. They sued the National Marine Fisheries Service, the Fish and Wildlife Service, and the Bureau of Reclamation, claiming that, by not delivering water, the federal government was breaking its U.S. Reclamation Project trust agreement. But a federal judge refused to override the Bureau of Reclamation decision and on April 4 ruled that if the agency delivered any additional water it would violate the Endangered Species Act.

Two days later, ironically on one of the season's rainiest days, Bureau of Reclamation officials announced that the agency could not supply irrigation water and at the same time meet the overriding needs of threatened fish.

"We've been delivering water in this community for ninety-four years in a row; for this to happen is just tragic," says Jeff McCracken of the Bureau of Reclamation. "Our hands were tied by Mother Nature and the law."

In the past, the Bureau of Reclamation refused to let Mother Nature stand in the way.

When the first white settlers arrived in the late 1800s, the Upper Klamath Basin was covered by approximately 187,000 acres of shallow lakes—collectively bigger than Nevada's Lake Tahoe. Believing that prime farmland lay underneath those wetlands, homesteaders began to drain and dike the land. By 1905, the newly created Bureau of Reclamation began transforming the landscape.

The Bureau drained 80 percent of the wetlands in the southern basin, built seven dams, eighteen canals, forty-five pumping plants, and five hundred sixteen miles of irrigation ditches. Eventually, the Klamath Reclamation Project covered two hundred and thirty thousand acres of the four hundred thousand acres of farmland in the basin.

In this artificial system, the Tule Lake and Lower Klamath wildlife refuges were an afterthought created after the reclamation project, to keep birds away from grainfields. But the refuges had no water rights, and so, by the 1920s, Lower Klamath Lake was bone-dry. It wasn't until the homesteads surrounding Tule Lake were in danger of floods in rainy years that in 1942 the Bureau of Reclamation drilled a tunnel through a ridge and began pumping water back into the Klamath refuge.

"The only reason Lower Klamath came back as a refuge is because the Bureau was worried about its farmers," says Robert Wilson, a Ph.D. candidate whose dissertation is on the history of refuge management along the Pacific Flyway.

William Kittredge, a writer and professor at the University of Montana who grew up in the Klamath Basin, describes the system as "incredibly managed." The water, he says, "goes up and down and all around."

It is not surprising that, by the 1970s, the native fish were having a hard time. Not only had flow regimes been disrupted, but water quality had declined dramatically due to pesticides, fertilizers, and animal waste in the watershed. Extensive clear-cutting along the Klamath River silted the river, causing warm temperatures and low flows. By 1985, commercial fishing was banned from some coastal areas to protect declining coho salmon. Three years later, a coalition of environmentalists and tribes convinced the federal government to list the shortnose and Lost River suckers as endangered.

In the years that followed, as fish runs continued to decline, the U.S. Fish and Wildlife Service and the Bureau of Reclamation failed to enforce federal flow standards or to regulate pesticide use on the leased farmland within the refuges.

Then, in 1991 and 1994, drought hit the basin. Due to the listing of the fish under the Endangered Species Act, for the first time since 1905, the Bureau cut the farmers' water.

"Suddenly, people realized that these water problems were going to come home to roost," says Kittredge. "Nobody had really gotten their head around the idea that they'd have to change."

In response to the 1994 drought, then-Oregon Senator Mark Hatfield, Republican, appointed a twenty-seven person working group to develop ways to restore the ecosystem, maintain the economy, and reduce the impacts of future droughts. The consensus group has created several wetland restoration projects in the Upper Basin and helped to facilitate dialogue between disparate parts of the community. But since Hatfield left office in 1996, the federal agencies haven't given the group enough money to make significant changes, says Alice Kilham, one of the group's original leaders. And still fish runs have declined. In 1997, the government listed the coho salmon as threatened, and between 1995 and 1997, the shortnose and Lost River sucker fish declined by as much as 90 percent.

Now, at long last there is substantive action, but not the type the working group wants, says Kilham.

"It's a tragedy we've come to this," she says. "This is a terrible way to have these things worked out."

"I don't believe we can have consensus and conservation when we have a community in chaos," says refuge manager Phil Norton. "I'll freely admit I think the ESA should be tweaked; everybody's losing under this."

Larry Dunsmore, a biologist for the Klamath tribe, who also served on the Hatfield group, agrees.

"The ESA has totally polarized the situation at a time when what we need is significant restoration that requires buy-in from the private landowners," says Dunsmore. "I can't help but wonder if we'll look back at this time as a step forward or a step back."

Ask most farmers in the Upper Basin, and they'll quickly answer that the recent regulatory action has been a leap away from consensus.

"I've been at the table for ten years, I've put thousands of miles on my pickup, and now they've got all the water and I've got nothing," says Don Russell, director of the Enterprise Irrigation District and the Klamath Basin Water Users Association. "Those enviro groups and those California tribes found a way to use the ESA to hurt farming. We'll never be able to work with those folks anymore."

Russell sits with farmer James L. Moore at his kitchen table, drinking sun tea—"the only thing we have an abundance of," they joke. The two have known each other since high school, and as they stare out the kitchen window at Moore's one hundred and seventy acres of browning alfalfa fields, they fume.

"The Bureau totally betrayed us. The agency could have stood up and said [to the U.S. Fish and Wildlife Service], 'Your science stinks,' but it didn't," says Russell, mopping his brow. "I feel funny putting my hand over my heart and saying 'my land of liberty.' "

Moore nods, sighing deeply. A descendant of one of the original homesteaders in Klamath Falls, he has some of the oldest water rights in the basin. He never expected that the Bureau wouldn't deliver his contracted water, so he didn't drill a well as some farmers have. Without water, Moore says, his land has decreased in value from $2,000 to $20 an acre.

"I've already lost my alfalfa crop; that's about $20,000 down the tubes," says Moore. He grips the contract his grandfather signed with the government, which had promised that his heirs would always have water. "I don't have any reserve kitty, just many hard years in ag. Nobody wants to walk away, but what can I do?"

What some are doing is mounting a campaign to dissolve what they say is the root of all this evil: the Endangered Species Act. Homemade signs line the roads of Klamath Falls, Merrill and Tulelake: "Community destroyed courtesy of the ESA," "Whatever happened to the American Dream?" and "Endangered community, amend the ESA."

"If we don't put the skids on the species act, it will shut this country down," says Russell, who has traveled to Washington, D.C., to garner support for his cause. He and a group of other farmers in the area want Congress to make federal biological opinions subject to independent scientific review, and to make all scientific studies public before listing decisions are made.

Russell thinks the farmers have a chance. They have an ally in Interior Secretary Gale Norton, who has ordered the National Academy of Scientists to review the science behind the agency recommendations to shut off the water this year. And Republican Representatives. Greg Walden of Oregon and Wally Herger of California, and Senator Gordon Smith, Republican-Oregon, have sponsored legislation to amend the ESA. A bipartisan working group in the House of Representatives is currently examining ESA reform.

"I definitely think it will be amended," says Joan Smith, a Siskiyou, California, county commissioner. "I don't think when the ESA was written it was meant to annihilate communities, and that's what is happening here."

But many downriver water users and environmentalists counter that other communities in the basin have been hurt by Upper Basin water use.

"The Endangered Species Act is working exactly like it's supposed to. It's helping us find a balance between the different needs in the basin," says Jan Hasselman of the nonprofit Earthjustice. "The Bureau of Reclamation has given the irrigators every drop of water they've needed since [the agency] opened shop in 1905, but the government has obligations to different people in the basin besides the irrigators."

Troy Fletcher, chairman of the Yurok tribe, says his people's treaty rights to healthy fish populations have long been ignored. Fletcher grew up on the banks of the Klamath River, and it was there that he learned to fish for steelhead and coho salmon, the lifeblood of his impoverished tribe.

"Eighty percent of the reservation is without electricity or phones; the nearest grocery store is two hours away for some tribal members. We subsist on fishing and not much else," says Fletcher. "One of the most offensive things to me is when I hear of the 'poor farmers.' When we get into the poorest of the poor, we're gonna win that fight."

For the last nine years, Fletcher has been working to convince the federal government to put more water in the river to help declining salmon runs. His tribe has studied river flows and fall chinook salmon; developed a watershed-restoration project that decommissions roads; upgraded culverts and planted trees in riparian areas; and closed its fishery up to three days a week. But other basin water users have not reformed, says Fletcher.

"I was far more optimistic early on; I just thought people would want to follow the law and that anyone could understand that pesticides and 80-degree water temperature aren't good for salmon, but I think I've matured now," says Fletcher, thirty-eight. "Every one of those state agencies has tried to lessen the impacts on farmers and hasn't stood up for us."

Fletcher says that, even with the ESA, his tribe has an uphill fight to restore healthy salmon runs. What's needed, he says, is more water, even in a year with normal precipitation.

Low river levels have also changed Paula Yoon's life. A former commercial fisher, Yoon smiles broadly as she talks about the years she and her husband fished for steelhead and coho salmon in Coos Bay.

"My husband's first gift to me was three big fish; they were beautiful," says Yoon, who lives in Bayside, California. "That's the best part, sharing the fish."

But in the late 1980s, the fish runs had declined so drastically that she went back to school, and her husband began spending summers fishing in Alaska. In 1991, he was killed there in an accident while crabbing.

"That made me think a fisherman should never have to leave his shores to provide for his family," says Yoon, who has two children. "We need to learn to live sustainably in our region and feed ourselves."

Yoon agrees with Fletcher that reducing agricultural demand in the Upper Basin will help fish runs in the Lower Basin, but she says that is just a first step. Now that people on both ends of the river have been hurt by the overallocation of water, Yoon hopes all the water users will be motivated to come up with a solution.

"Unfortunately, it takes the ESA and a crisis until we go through the anger and denial phase, and then we realize that's not going to get us anywhere, and we have to work together," says Yoon. "The ESA is not just related to species that are endangered, but it's necessary for helping us as humans who are dependent on those species."

That is the crux of why amending the Act is a bad idea, says Don Berry, former undersecretary of the Interior under Secretary Bruce Babbitt. If it were left to local agency folks, they wouldn't be able to stand up to local pressure and "eat their broccoli," says Berry. "Take the spotted owl or the Northwest salmon—we should not have gotten there on the legs of the ESA." But there is no other mechanism besides the Act to determine when an ecosystem is in trouble, he says.

Other conservationists agree.

"You can gut the ESA, but at the end of the day that doesn't create more water," says Jim Walton of the Wilderness Society.

Environmentalists in the Klamath Basin are looking beyond the Endangered Species Act to on-the-ground solutions.

Wendell Wood of the Oregon Natural Resources Council wants Congress to pay willing sellers $4,000 an acre for their reclaimed land. Currently, land prices have hit rock bottom due to the water shortage, but Wood says that if Congress would buy the land for a price above the market rate, the money could help some farmers to make a transition into new careers.

Many locals say this could be their only option. In the global economy, farmers are having a hard time selling their potatoes, alfalfa, and sugar beets, even when they have the water to raise them.

"A lot of people are right on the edge of bankruptcy," says John Anderson, a Tulelake native who has been raising mint and cattle for thirty-one years. "A lot of us are now saying, let's try and work to come up with something that we can get broad-based support for."

Anderson says selling part of his land and water to the government makes sense, if he is promised that at least a portion of his water will be available, despite drought or endangered fish.

"If I don't have an assurance like this, I won't have any contracts [with people who want to buy my mint] and I don't think I'll be able to recover."

Already, more than two dozen farmers have agreed that they would sell. That means nearly ninety thousand acre-feet of water could be left in the rivers and wetlands. And Anderson says that if the program were in place, more people would negotiate, making more water available for fish.

But many say the potential $200 million program isn't an ideal solution. Alice Kilham worries that it will create a patchwork of wetlands within farmland, which will help neither the farmer nor the wildlife. "We need to plan, so that we know where we want farms and where it makes sense to have refuges."

Tim Griffiths says that the willing-seller program won't increase the amount of water in the basin, because restoring the farms to wetlands will require just as much water as farming.

"You're not going to alleviate the water-storage problem unless you say 'no water on these lands,' " says Griffiths. "But then there's going to be a weed field, and that's very poor-quality habitat."

The only solution, says Griffiths, is for people on both sides of the issue to settle for less. That means farmers will have to accept that they may not always get their full allotment of water, and "extreme environmentalists" will have to realize that even with the willing-seller program, they will not be able to restore the basin to a pre-farming state.

"All I know is, it's a circus here right now," says Griffiths, "and we need people to be willing to compromise."

But that may take some time. So far, no legislators have agreed to carry a bill for the willing-seller program. Farmers still have not received the $20 million of drought relief that was promised to them in late spring. Anti-federal sentiment still pulses through the Upper Klamath Basin, and many locals are wary of a solution backed by federal dollars. While

Secretary of the Interior Gale Norton recently released up to seventy-five thousand acre-feet of water to help farmers feed their livestock and save their crops' root structure, some farmers still weren't satisfied, calling it a "spit in the bucket." And since no water will reach the wildlife refuges, conservationists and federal biologists are disgruntled. For now, many continue to see this conflict as war.

"It's kind of like Pearl Harbor to us," says Don Russell. "We've been attacked; we're sitting in rubble and smoke. But these people are resilient, and they're not going anywhere."

August 13, 2001

Rebecca Clarren lives in Portland, Oregon, and writes about environmental and labor issues.

The Message of Thirty Thousand Dead Salmon

Katherine Vandemoer

Call me a radical, but I think fish need water. I'd hazard a guess that most Americans would agree, since it's just plain common sense.

But when it comes to the over-promised waters of the Klamath Basin in southern Oregon and northern California, common sense often seems to fly out the window. As a scientist, I watched in horror as the latest Klamath train wreck unfolded this summer. You may have seen photos of the rotting corpses of thirty thousand dead salmon floating in the Klamath River.

These fish were not killed by some freak natural disaster or a toxic chemical spill. They died because the Bush administration made a conscious decision to choke off water to the Klamath River this summer, despite repeated warnings about the effects. All summer long, conservation groups, commercial fishermen, Native American tribes, and even the California Department of Fish and Game asked for more water for the river. Their pleas were ignored. Healthy salmon entered the Klamath River to begin their journey upriver to spawn, but water was low, very low, the fish stacked up, disease spread, and the rampant die-off began.

How could this happen? Isn't this the administration that vowed to bring "sound science" to environmental debates?

Apparently, to the Bush administration "sound science" means science that sounds good to the anti-government, anti-endangered species activists now running our natural resource agencies. In the Klamath Basin they have attempted to turn good science on its ear, declaring that fish don't need water, in an effort to maximize deliveries for irrigation in the high desert.

Disputes over the Klamath Basin's scarce water resources are hardly a new phenomenon. State and federal governments have simply promised too much water to too many interests, and the reality is that even in a good year, there just isn't enough to go around.

But in debates over water in the West, reality often takes a back seat to politics. During the summer of 2001, when the Klamath Basin was struck by one of the worst droughts in memory, biological opinions from federal scientists made water flows for threatened fish a priority. Not surprisingly, irrigation interests were outraged, but they didn't blame the government for over-promising scarce resources. They blamed the fish and the laws that protect them.

It didn't take long for the Bush administration to kick the fish back down to the bottom rung of the ladder along with the Native American, commercial, and recreational fishing communities that depend on them. Unhappy with the conclusions of federal biologists, the administration set out to find some science more to its liking. Interior Secretary Gale Norton hired the National Research Council to review the science surrounding water distribution in the basin, essentially asking, "Is it certain more water will restore the fish?"

It was a politically shrewd move, similar to asking, "Is it certain smoking cigarettes will give you cancer?" As any scientist will tell you, nothing is ever certain.

In one bold and cynical move, the Bush administration rewrote the rules in the Klamath Basin, suddenly holding fisheries science to a standard that was impossible to meet. Though the council's interim review concluded more research was needed to form solid conclusions, and the review itself has been harshly criticized by other scientists, irrigation interests and the administration seized on the results.

You can now see and smell the consequences rotting on the banks of the Klamath River. In 2002, river flows were choked down to a sickly trickle. From mid-July until the end of August, more water flowed down the main irrigation canal in Klamath Falls than was being released into the Klamath River at Iron Gate Dam. Endangered fish in Upper Klamath

Lake and the six national wildlife refuges that dot the region didn't fare much better.

But as tragic as the 2002 Klamath River fish kill is, the worst could be yet to come. This is only the first year of the administration's flawed yen-year water-management plan for the basin. Despite the slaughter, agency officials are not backing down on their plans to continue maximizing irrigation deliveries, no matter what the cost. Even worse, the administration has signaled its intent to apply this "sound science" model to other endangered species debates around the West.

Most children, by the time they enter kindergarten, know that fish need water. It is painfully clear that the Bush administration needs remedial education on the subject.

October 28, 2002

Katherine Vandemoer is executive director of WaterWatch in Portland, Oregon.

"Water Bank" Drags Region Deeper into Debt

Rebecca Clarren

From her house near Klamath Falls, Oregon, Kelly Holcomb loves to look out her kitchen window at the juniper-dotted mountains nearby and the vast green fields of the Klamath Valley. But she doesn't like what she sees to the west, where a neighboring farmer installed a large well a few years back. The well taps into the same aquifer where Holcomb's family gets its drinking water.

Not long after the farmer started pumping twenty-four hours a day, seven days a week, Holcomb turned on the kitchen faucet; a tiny trickle dribbled out, then nothing. Her well, dug in the 1930s, was suddenly dry. Holcomb and her husband had to spend over $10,000 to deepen it.

"Listen, lots of our friends are farmers. We have horses; we buy hay," says Holcomb, who owns a western clothing and jewelry store. "I want the ag community to stay in business, but I don't believe it should be to the detriment of everyone around them."

What upsets Holcomb most is that her neighbor isn't even using the water; he's selling it to the federal government in a program that, ironically, was supposed to end the tug of war over limited water supplies in the Klamath Basin. In the past five years, the basin has become a flash point in the regionwide struggle over water between environmental, urban, and agricultural interests.

In 2002, NOAA Fisheries started the "water bank" program to free up water to help threatened coho salmon. The U.S. Bureau of Reclamation manages the project, which is funded for ten years. It pays farmers to stop irrigating altogether, or to use only well water on their fields—or, as in the case of Holcomb's neighbor, to pump their well water into irrigation canals, so the Bureau can leave more water in the river.

The water bank was supposed to keep everyone happy. But four years and $20 million later, a solution to the basin's water problems is as elusive as ever —and the water bank may only be making things worse.

"Ten years of the water bank isn't going to solve the problems down here," says Jim Bryant, who was the Bureau of Reclamation's Klamath director from 1991 to 2003. "It's a pipe dream."

The program appears to be sending more water downstream to help fish. However, the actual results are hard to quantify because the Bureau doesn't monitor the water diversions of the twelve hundred farmers in the Klamath Project, according to a report issued earlier this year by the Government Accountability Office.

In July, low water levels and high temperatures diminished the oxygen in the river water, killing several thousand endangered sucker fish just south of Klamath Falls. Roger Smith, a fisheries biologist with the Oregon Department of Fish and Wildlife, says the water bank isn't helping the ecosystem long-term.

By encouraging groundwater pumping, the water bank has also led to conflicts between farmers and numerous homeowners like Kelly Holcomb, who have seen their well water dwindle. The Klamath Valley and Tule Lake areas have seen an eightfold increase in groundwater pumping since 2000, according to a May 2005 report by the U.S. Geological Survey. In California, an irrigation district along the border owns at least ten new wells that, on average, pump eighty-two hundred gallons per minute.

In fact, the Bureau may be robbing Peter to pay Paul, because the wells most likely draw water away from the springs that feed the region's rivers and lakes. And preliminary findings indicate that the current rate of pumping is not sustainable. In the past five years, the aquifer has sustained a net loss of thirteen feet; in summer months, it's dropped by up to forty feet in some places.

"We've never seen declines like that, not on that scale," says Ned Gates, a hydrogeologist with the Oregon Water Resources Department. "Part of it is it's been a drought, but if this pumping wasn't going on, I think you'd see a lot of recovery."

This summer, a coalition of environmental groups asked the state to place a moratorium on all new water rights, including well-pumping permits, until the U.S. Geological Survey finishes two long-term studies to determine how much water the aquifer holds and the effect of groundwater pumping on rivers and lakes. In August, the state denied that request.

Writing new groundwater permits is "insanity," says Bob Hunter of WaterWatch of Oregon, when the basin's water is already over-allocated among farmers, homeowners, wildlife refuges, and imperiled fish. The state hasn't even determined how much water is due to the Klamath Tribe, which owns the basin's most senior water rights, he adds.

Even some farmers call the water bank shortsighted. Third-generation Klamath Falls farmer Bobby Flowers, a former Farm Bureau president, says the only farmers who support it are those who are selling water to the government

The Bureau acknowledges that the water bank is too expensive to maintain forever, but agency staffers are short on details for other alternatives. Talk of long-term solutions, such as buying out farmers, has hit roadblocks within the Bush administration, which argues that farm buyouts ruin rural communities.

For landowners like Holcomb, the situation is simply not acceptable.

"I don't have any answers, but I know what's wrong," says Holcomb. "My neighbor made $60,000 from the government to pump his well that first year, and he's been pumping two years since. I don't mind pumping water for farming, but when it's bought and just shipped out of here, it isn't right."

October 17, 2005

Rebecca Clarren lives in Portland, Oregon, and writes about environmental and labor issues for several magazines.

Peace on the Klamath

Matt Jenkins

On an April afternoon alive with light, Troy Fletcher—an imposing Yurok Indian who could pass for a bouncer—is knocking together tuna-salad sandwiches in the kitchen of his new house, a doublewide that got trucked in from the coast three days ago. He's wearing Hawaiian shorts and a T-shirt that says "The Future is Ours." A flat-panel TV drones on in the living room, and a hot tub sits out back, waiting to be hooked up. Fletcher, who is forty-six, pads to the fridge for a Budweiser and says: "I've been waiting forever for this." The reference is only partly to the house.

Here, where the lower Klamath River winds down into the gorges of California's North Coast, the river is a world unto itself. This is an isolated and truly wild piece of country, a place that seems to live by its own rules. It is Bigfoot's reputed stomping ground. It is also home to several tribes of coastal Indians whose cultures revolve around the river's salmon and steelhead, and who can smoke a fish into sublimity.

Not just this stretch of the river but the entire basin—which reaches several hundred miles inland into the Oregon high desert and covers an area about the size of Denmark—is known for something else. No other corner of the West has seemed so determined to live up to the maxim, endlessly misattributed to Mark Twain, that "whiskey's for drinkin' and water's for fightin' over." That attitude has attained a triple-distilled kick here, in a running battle between Indians, environmentalists, fishermen, and a notoriously combative band of farmers two hundred miles up the river.

Fletcher has variously served as the Yurok's executive director, fisheries director, and now, policy advisor, and he has been as deep in the fight as anyone. The Klamath River was once home to the third-largest salmon run on the West Coast. But fish populations plunged when dams blocked

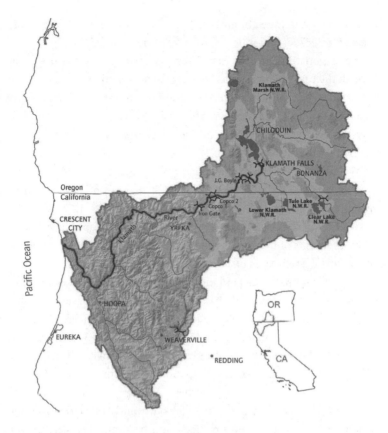

salmon and steelhead from the upper reaches of the river, where they spawn, and irrigation drained off much of the river's water.

For decades, the situation somehow wobbled clear of a full-blown crisis. Then in 2001 a severe drought hit. To save fish protected by the Endangered Species Act, the federal government shut off the farmers' irrigation water—and incited an insurrection that brought death threats, a shooting spree, and the intervention of federal marshals. A year later, the government made sure the farmers got their water—and caused a massive salmon die-off that enraged the river's Indians. From a distance, the situation has seemed irredeemable. But for the past three years, Fletcher and his erstwhile enemies have been trying to negotiate the shape of their future together. They have sought to keep all their communities going, and the effort has forced everyone to tackle the most volatile parts of the river's rip-roarin' politics.

"We've been in the fight for ages," Fletcher says. "But we can't afford to litigate for decades and watch our fish continue to die."

The negotiation process has been as tortuous as the river's run through the canyons, and it has been tightly wrapped in secrecy. But after ninety years, salmon will soon be bound once more for the river's upper reaches. And the long-warring parties say they have laid the groundwork to sustain native fish, farming, and Indian communities, creating a peace on the river that can last.

"We turned the traditional alliances upside-down," Fletcher says. "Now you've got the deck shuffled, and it makes no rhyme or reason who's out or who's in."

Two hundred miles up the river, not far from Mount Shasta's snowy flanks, the farms of the Upper Klamath Basin fit together in an awkward jigsaw with the remnants of Tule Lake and lower Klamath Lake.

This was originally the land of the Klamath and Modoc Indians, who were hunted down, rounded up, and deposited on a reservation that was subsequently dissolved. In their place came Czech and Irish immigrants and, later, veterans returning from the First and Second World Wars, who drew lots for homesteads out of a pickle jar in the town of Tulelake.

The area is unabashed meat-and-potatoes farm country. No frisee gets grown here, and no mache, either. The main crops on the roughly twelve hundred farms here are alfalfa for dairy and beef cattle, wheat, and potatoes, which usually end up sliced and fried and Frito-Lay'd. Some farmers do a middling commerce in things like mint, horseradish, and strawberry seedlings.

Like much of the West's farm country, the Klamath has suffered from a surfeit of optimism running all the way back to the days of Theodore Roosevelt. The crusade to irrigate the desert parceled out too much water to too many people, leaving the region's native fish and wildlife to go, quite literally, belly-up.

Nothing has done more to tilt the scales back toward something like balance than the Endangered Species Act. The 1973 law effectively grants a water right to endangered species like coho salmon, though only enough for minimum "survival" flows, and only when species are in imminent peril of extinction. But many farmers here saw even that as regulatory overkill: flows to preserve endangered species supersede all existing water rights, upending the western water hierarchy in which farmers typically have first place.

The tension between water priorities for farming and those for wildlife had long been growing throughout the region, but it was in 2001 in the Klamath Basin that things finally blew up more spectacularly than anywhere else. That year, the Klamath Basin received just a third of its average annual precipitation. On April 6, the federal government announced that it needed to keep water in the river for coho salmon— which are classified as threatened under the Endangered Species Act —and in Upper Klamath Lake for the endangered Lost River and shortnose sucker fish. The Bureau of Reclamation cranked the headgate on the farmers' canal closed and locked it down.

Many farmers had already planted their crops when the water was shut off; all told, Klamath farmers lost between $27 million and $47 million that year. Some were literally ruined, and the headgate in the town of Klamath Falls quickly became the stage for some hard-core political theater. Farmers organized a protest there that dragged on throughout the summer. Armed with cutting torches and power saws, they reopened the headgate four times.

"You're dealing with farmers: they can handle anything," says Bill Ransom, who helped organize the protest. "[The federal agencies] were gonna have to do a lot more than they did to keep it closed." In between assaults on the headgate, the farmers grilled salmon. The fish weren't from endangered runs, but still, the point was clear.

Finally, in July, the federal government deployed law-enforcement agents from around the region to guard the headgate. The whole affair took on the feel of a tent revival—or, in its own weird way, a civil-rights march. "The day they came, the people there linked arms around the headgate and started singin' hymns," Ransom says. "It kind of dumbfounded them, I think."

The FOX News satellite trucks weren't far behind the marshals ,- and a growing din from the right proclaimed that environmentalists and the federal government were using the Endangered Species Act as a weapon for "rural cleansing." The drama was very consciously stage-managed, but the situation was truly volatile. And emotions eventually came uncorked. In December, three local men in their twenties terrorized the town of Chiloquin, the center of the Klamath Indian tribes, firing a shotgun at buildings and signs and taunting the Indians as "sucker lovers."

The farmers themselves were far more methodical. They hired the most notorious private-property rights lawyer in the country to seek a billion-dollar indemnity from the feds (that case still lingers in the courts, with uncertain prospects). And they begged Karl Rove to get their water back. In 2002, with the help of Dick Cheney, they succeeded —only to cause the die-off of tens of thousands of salmon.

That fish kill seemed a sort of desecration for all the Indian tribes on the Klamath, not to mention the hundreds of commercial fishermen who were shut out by subsequent, last-ditch government fishing bans meant to protect the increasingly beleaguered salmon runs. The entire situation seemed to be wobbling more wildly than ever before.

At the eastern edge of Klamath Falls, not far past the county fairgrounds, the Klamath Water Users Association's office is tucked into a spartan mini-mall that's also home to a custom boot shop and a pizza joint. Greg Addington, a Carhartts-and-Skoal kind of guy, runs the association; essentially, he was deputized by the farmers to defend their water rights. When Addington started in early 2005, he says, "I only knew, 'Troy Fletcher: He's a bad guy.' He was Public Enemy #1 here."

That was before Addington spent three years negotiating with Fletcher.

After 2002, there were several attempts to talk about resolving the problems, but they went nowhere: the wounds were too raw. Sometime in the fall of 2004, however—after the farmers lost several key legal fights—things started to change.

The Bureau of Reclamation had sponsored a series of several-day "listening sessions" meant to initiate some kind of dialogue. It was a woo-woo, pass-the-talking-stick sort of deal that the farmers and Indians normally wouldn't be caught dead at.

"They were really painful," says Troy Fletcher. "It's hard to sit through two days of 'talk about your feelings.' It really sucked." Yet as long as any one of the warring parties attended the sessions and spoke out, none of the others could afford to stay home.

Then, in March 2005, at a listening session in the town of Tulelake, the microphone came around to Fletcher. For reasons he still struggles to fully explain, he took a deep breath and said: "I don't know all the answers here, but I do know that what we've been doing just isn't working. Let's do a ceasefire and start trying to work on some stuff together."

For a lot of veterans of the water fight—even people on Fletcher's side— it sounded like some sort of setup. "This is a very long war. My entire life, all I've known is the fight with the irrigators," says Leaf Hillman, the vice-chairman of the Karuk Tribe, whose members live downstream near the Yurok Reservation.

Hillman, who has a congenital disdain for happy talk, and a thick braided ponytail you could ring a bell with, didn't attend the Tulelake meeting. He sent one of the tribe's biologists instead.

"My guy, as part of reporting back, said, 'You know, Troy stood up and said we need a ceasefire.' He said it was a genuinely moving moment," Hillman recalled. "I looked at him and I laughed. I said, 'You don't know Troy. That sounds like a brilliant damn Troy moment where he's hooked some people into believing that he actually believes this shit.' "

But that moment signaled the first real thaw in relations. "About a week or two later we set a meeting, where we brought Greg and a bunch of people down," says Fletcher. "And that's where I think we really started zeroing in. Us and the Karuk kind of jointly reached out to these guys, and fumbled through a couple meetings."

They met in a room at the back of the Karuk tribal housing office in Yreka and "spent about four hours hashing it out," Hillman says. "We started laying stuff out there honestly, away from any audience, where we didn't have to posture for the media. It was the first attempt to bring the tribes and the irrigators in a room by themselves, away from the spotlight, to say, 'Look, we all are in bad shape here.' "

Imagine that you are a mama coho in ... oh, say, 1918. Halfway around the world, the Great War is winding down. And here you are, chugging in from the sea to lay your eggs, following your nose up the Klamath back to the creek where you were born. *Swim on, old girl, swim home!*

You struggle hard. And then, two hundred and ten miles up the river, in a narrow, rocky gorge where the water comes sluicing down, you wriggle through the rapids and—*bonk!*—smack face-first into the toe of a brand-new dam called Copco 1. Behind it, you smell three hundred and fifty miles of river and streams and creeks beckoning, but they are no longer yours.

That dam was the first of four on the river that now spin out electricity for PacifiCorp, a utility owned by investor Warren Buffet's company Berkshire Hathaway. It is only because of a pair of fish hatcheries that the Klamath salmon runs have persisted into the twenty-first century.

Tribes like the Yurok, not surprisingly, have long thought that the dams need to come down. The farmers, on the other hand, saw PacifiCorp as an ally. For one thing, the company's dams keep salmon—and at least some of the regulatory headaches that trail endangered fish—from making it as far up the river as the irrigation project. It didn't hurt that PacifiCorp kept the irrigators flush in cut-rate power, either.

As it happened, negotiations over the dams' future had just gotten under way at about the same time the Indians and farmers began talking. The operating licenses for the dams, issued by the Federal Energy Regulatory Commission, or FERC, were up for renewal. And PacifiCorp, hoping to head off lawsuits, began gathering practically everyone who had a stake in the river to negotiate the terms and conditions of its new licenses.

Ultimately, that included the Klamath farmers; the Yurok, Karuk, Hoopa, and Klamath tribes; commercial salmon fishermen; several federal agencies; and a number of environmental groups— altogether, some twenty-eight different governments and organizations. Throughout 2005, their representatives holed up in hotels in various towns in northern California and southern Oregon to negotiate.

At first, the talks focused narrowly on the dams' licenses. But in the evenings, after negotiations ended for the day, Addington and Fletcher occasionally shared a beer in hotel bars and had what Addington refers to as "off-line conversations." In the beginning, they stuck to safe subjects, like their kids. But eventually, they edged back toward the conversation that had begun in the back room in Yreka.

In one sense, the early talks were a way to run through some of the rumor and rhetoric that dominated each side's pronouncements in the wake of the water showdown. "I got to a point where I just trusted Troy, and I knew he wouldn't be offended by me asking stupid questions," Addington says. (*Exempli gratia, "Troy, are you sure that fish kill in 2002 wasn't caused by meth-lab leakage somewhere down on your end of the river?"*)

For Fletcher, it was a chance to remonstrate gently about the way the farmers had framed their plight. "You're telling me how bad off you are, that you're gonna go bankrupt," he says. "My people can't *afford* to go bankrupt. If you wanna talk about the poorest of the poor, we're gonna win that one, alright? So let's just not go there."

But the thaw had begun, and it was starting to reach all the way to Fletcher and Addington's respective communities. Bob Gasser is a Klamath Basin fertilizer dealer who sits on the board of the water users' association. He helped fund the headgate protests in 2001, and to this day keeps a FEED THE FEDS TO THE FISH bumper sticker in his office. But earlier this year he acknowledged, "Everybody's tired of the fight. We've got every enviro out there beatin' on us—we're fighting people we don't even know. And we don't have the funds to do it. How long can we put millions of dollars into a fight that we just aren't winning?"

And even blunt spoken Indians like Hillman felt that the time had come to break free of the see-sawing legal wars. "That shit's been going on forever, and it's very unsatisfying," Hillman says. "[Winning] is exhilarating, for a moment: you can sit around and have a beer and say, 'Yeah! We kicked their ass.' But when you go back to work on Monday morning, you better look behind you, because the other side has already set to work figuring out how to undermine that."

The Klamath Irrigation Project is an intensively plumbed system; farmers delight in pointing out that a drop of water may get re-circulated up to seven times on its trip through the project. Addington once

remarked—alluding to the old saw "water flows uphill toward money"—
that "if water can go uphill anywhere, it's here." It's not much of an
exaggeration: at one point in the system, the farmers' water is literally
pumped through a mountain.

But it takes a lot of electricity to keep that system running. And in 2004,
as PacifiCorp's dam licenses neared expiration, the company announced
that it was going to end the super-cheap, half-cent-per-kilowatt-hour
power rate it had charged irrigators for the past fifty years. The new rate
would be about a thousand percent higher.

That "brought the farmers face to face with imminent disaster," says
Hillman. "If you can't switch on a pump and move water in the Upper
Basin from point A to point B, you don't have an irrigation project."

A year earlier, that would have seemed a heaven-sent opportunity for
the tribes to pound a stake through the farmers' collective heart. Now,
though, the Indians agreed to do something that appeared to border on
self-destruction: help keep their old adversaries in business.

"Nothing brings two people together like a common enemy," says
Troy Fletcher, and both sides realized that "we had a common opponent
through this FERC negotiation, and that was PacifiCorp."

The farmers planned an appeal to the Oregon and California Public
Utility Commissions to block the hike, and quietly made it known that
they could use all the help they could get. And, Hillman says, "Troy
Fletcher and myself stood up after they made that plea and said very
publicly, in front of God and everybody, 'We acknowledge [the farmers']
right to exist in this basin.'" The Karuk and Yurok tribes agreed to support
the farmers' quest for rate relief.

That was a turning point—and it suddenly put many of the negotiators
in an uneasy relationship with the people they represented. When they
returned home from the meeting, Hillman says, "We kept it low profile.
Our respective communities were still not very hip on this whole notion
of holding hands with our enemies."

But soon after, the Indians had to make their own "ask" of the farmers:
clearing the path for salmon to get all the way back up the river. "The
basin is basically cut in half," says Hillman. "To restore runs, we need

that untapped productivity that fish aren't able to access anymore, all that spawning habitat" beyond the dams.

For the farmers who'd been symbolically barbecuing salmon with such gusto, the prospect of having the fish back in their own backyard was disconcerting. As Addington put it, "C'mon, a fish is a fish. If you need more salmon, just make more in a hatchery."

But card trading is a curious sport. The farmers realized that, after passing junk to the Indians in 2002, it might be time to kick an ace their way.

At a February 2006 meeting in Sacramento, federal fish and wildlife managers asked Addington about the farmers' position on re-opening the upper river to salmon. When Addington said that the farmers would stand with the tribes, "they were like, '*Holy shit,*' " Fletcher says. "You could hear their jaws drop on the table."

On a bluebird afternoon six weeks ago, Scott Seus was in the cab of a tractor, planting onion seed not far from Tulelake. His tractor and another worked their way in tandem across the field while a crew of men followed, laying irrigation pipe.

"When I pull this planter out of there, and the pipe's on the ground, we are already 90 percent invested into this onion crop," he said. "All my money's laying out here on the table, and I've got no way to try to recoup any of it if they shut the water off mid-season."

That was exactly what happened to farmers in 2001. And, Seus said, many of them realized that if they didn't wind up victims the next time things got tight, someone else—whether tribes or fishermen—would. And when that happened, the rest of the world was sure to hear about it.

"It's unpredictable, and it's a dangerous game," Seus said. "Everybody's playing Russian roulette."

The challenge for Addington—and everyone else—was immense. After going back and forth with former enemies to come to incremental agreements, Addington now had to sell it to people like Scott Seus, who, along with about twelve hundred other farmers in the basin, had been footing his salary for the past three years.

Addington tried to make it clear that he hadn't succumbed to a cowboys-and-Indians version of Stockholm syndrome. "When you disappear for a week at a time and you're talking to people who have not been your friends, you better hustle back and let people know what's going on," he says. "You kind of got to a point with these guys where you just really wanted to make this thing happen. But you can only go so far out on a limb before it breaks."

In the settlement negotiations—which by this point had ranged through practically every government-rate frontage-road hotel in northern California and southern Oregon—a comprehensive package was emerging. It included the creation of a council to coordinate the agreement and day-to-day operations of the river; removal of the four PacifiCorp dams; an ambitious fisheries-restoration program that would go beyond minimum survival for the coho and suckers, and restore non-endangered fish like chinook, steelhead, and lamprey; a formal water right for the area's national wildlife refuges; reduced-rate electricity for the irrigators; and a provision enabling the Klamath Tribes to buy ninety thousand acres of their homeland.

The cornerstone of the entire deal was the question of how to divvy up the river's water. During a string of back-to-back meetings in Sacramento in December 2006, the negotiating group agonized over how to balance the competing demands. Biologists from the tribes and an engineering consultant for the farmers ran a seemingly endless series of computer models to find a workable compromise. The farmers needed enough water to continue farming—and yet the tribes and environmentalists saw removing the dams as a hollow victory if there wasn't enough water for the fish.

Ultimately, they closed in on a plan that would limit irrigators to 10 to 25 percent less than they'd used historically. The upside for the farmers was a greatly reduced threat of their water being completely shut off again to protect fish. In about half the years, farmers will have to get by on less water than they've used in the past. When there's not enough water for the river and the lake, they will either have to pump groundwater, or fallow—temporarily dry up—some farmland for the year.

The nearly $1 billion budget for the settlement includes money for a one-time upfront payment to farmers willing to fallow their land when necessary to free up water for the lake and river. That money will, in theory, cover the cost of fixed expenses like land payments, taxes, and yearly operation and maintenance costs for the irrigation system, all of which farmers have to pay whether they farm a particular piece of ground or not. With clearer rules in place, farmers like Seus can plan smarter: during years when water will be tight, they can shift their crop mix from low-value crops like alfalfa to higher-value crops to maximize their return on the reduced amounts of water.

Gasser, the fertilizer dealer, pointed out that in a drought year, "if you can farm 50 percent, you can probably hold things together. You may not make anything, but you can keep your operation alive."

Still, it was a serious thing to commit to. "A lot of [the settlement] is very important, but that was locking in less water than we knew we needed in at least 50 percent of the years," Addington says. "We knew that once we committed to that, we weren't going back."

Crossing that threshold caused so much heartburn that Addington, together with several federal and state officials in the negotiations, requisitioned a plane and flew to Klamath Falls in a snowstorm to meet with the water users' board.

"It was raining, and spittin' snow, and it was just horrible. It went all night long," says U.S. Fish and Wildlife Service regional director Steve Thompson. For several hours, the water users' board deliberated in closed session; with nowhere else to go, Thompson says, the government contingent "sat out in one of the ranchers' Suburbans, with snowflakes falling and the windshield wipers going. It was a tough, tough night."

Finally, at some point late in the night, the entourage flew back to Sacramento, and started negotiating again the next morning. "It was just painful. It was terrible," says Addington. "You're having to make a call that is gonna affect everybody up here, and you can't foresee every possibility. There's things you're just having to make a gut call on, and hope you're right."

During the first two weeks of January 2007, the pace of the negotiations peaked. Even with the linchpin of the settlement in place, at least in rough form, many other issues remained unresolved, and the pressure was rising. Then something cracked. And suddenly the Indians and farmers had yet another common enemy: two of the environmental groups in the negotiations.

The Tule Lake and Lower Klamath national wildlife refuges are important layovers for birds traveling the Pacific Flyway. And about one-tenth of the farming in the Klamath Irrigation Project takes place on the two refuges, on about twenty-two thousand acres that Scott Seus and other farmers lease from the federal government.

In recent years, the lease-land program has been retooled to be more bird-friendly, most notably by the creation of a "walking wetlands" program in which farmers flood parcels of leased land on a rotating schedule to provide habitat for waterfowl. But two environmental groups, Water Watch and Oregon Wild, have long insisted that farming has no place on the refuges. Bob Hunter, a Water Watch attorney, is fond of taking visitors to Tule Lake—which is often the scene of a veritable blizzard of snow geese in the winter—and asking, "Is this a refuge for ducks or potatoes?"

Hunter says that the only real way to reduce water demand in the basin is to take farmland out of production permanently. And, his reasoning goes, it makes sense to do away with the refuge lease-land program first.

"If you're gonna try to reduce irrigation demand, maybe the best place to start is on lands already owned by the public," he says. "There's a dozen farm families that have farms around here that are situated to do [lease-land farming] and they kind of trade 'em around. But why should a couple dozen people be holding hostage some of the most valuable refuges in the nation so they can make money off of them?"

For the farmers, though, the idea of downsizing farming was a non-starter. "What we, quite honestly, have told people at the table is: if you want to reduce the project permanently, we'd be glad to take that back and see what our people say," Addington says. "But we can tell you what they're gonna say"—he starts to mouth an "f" and then thinks better of it—" 'Hell, no!' "

The details of the negotiations remain hidden behind a confidentiality agreement, and various participants give differing versions of what ultimately happened. During the fall of 2006, in side discussions, Oregon Wild and Water Watch apparently broached the possibility of phasing out lease-land farming. But as the strands of the agreement began tightening in January 2007, the two groups insisted on a provision to phase out farming on the refuges.

The reaction from the farmers—and the Yurok and Karuk tribes—was decisive. Hillman says that he wasn't himself averse to the idea of downsizing farming, but he knew that an insistence on ending the lease-land program would break the entire deal.

"[Oregon Wild and Water Watch] foreclosed an opportunity that all of us had been looking at and working on in little incremental bits and pieces for years," he says. "But [you have to] work with your allies and be strategic about the pace you address it at, instead of going nuclear and all the rest of us having to deal with the fallout.

"There was no question from that day forward that they had to get out, or we were done," he says. "It put us in a bad position. And we led the charge to throw them out of the damn room."

On April 6, the settlement group was dissolved. Then, within a matter of hours, the farmers and the two tribes created a new one and invited back all the parties except Oregon Wild and Water Watch.

Both Hunter and Steve Pedery, the conservation director for Oregon Wild, give a different version of events: they say the politically connected Klamath farmers wanted to reach an agreement that could be put into effect in the final year of George Bush's presidency. "The Bush administration," Pedery says, "[came] in with a settlement outline and demand[ed] that everyone in the process sign on."

"This," Hunter says, "was just another settlement process that got hijacked by the Bush administration to deliver some key things to a politically connected ally."

But the participants still inside the process—including representatives of the environmental groups Trout Unlimited and American Rivers— say that simply isn't true.

"The intensity of some of our meetings and discussions was just incredible. And I think it came to a point where the deadline [arrived], and the compromise was just too much for Oregon Wild and Water Watch," says Thompson, the Fish and Wildlife Service regional manager. "It was pretty obvious that they couldn't get to a resolution with us, and that they were not going to be supportive of any resolution. They said that. So then it was a matter of, 'Well, OK: We need to move on with those parties that can.' "

"They just ran into issues that they weren't willing to go any further on," says Larry Dunsmoor, a biologist with the Klamath Tribes. "Those of us who committed to the process worked our butts off, and we worked it out with the irrigators, and they worked it out with us. It was one of the hardest things we've ever done."

In January, the agreement was finally released to the public. It was the first time that most of the people the negotiators represented got to see it for themselves, and Fletcher and Addington & Co. have since been busy campaigning to win the support of their communities.

The settlement is still far from being a done deal. The federal government has decreed that PacifiCorp must add ways for fish to get around its dams, which is usually done by adding water-filled ramps called fish ladders, so salmon, steelhead, and lamprey *will* soon be headed all the way up the Klamath. But PacifiCorp still has not agreed to take its dams out, and a separate negotiation on that issue continues. The settlement will also certainly face challenges from its opponents, who say the farmers are attempting to teleport themselves back to the good old days, before there were such things as endangered species laws.

"The Endangered Species Act flipped things to where fish come first, and you have to have some minimum survival flows for them," says Bob Hunter. "This agreement's just trying to turn things back to the way it's been for a hundred years, where project irrigators get theirs first, and the fish get what's left over. You're putting the risk back on fish."

But Fletcher says the agreement could ultimately lead the way into a new world, where fish can prosper beyond mere survival levels. "We're talking about getting away from Endangered Species Act management—which means the population is (just) maintaining—to something more," Fletcher says. "We want a boatload of fish. Because we want to catch those fish. That's what we do."

Fletcher, who started the Yuroks' fisheries department in the early 1990s, says he struggled with how to integrate the tribe's traditional view of the world with the river's complicated politics. "The tribe and tribal people have an obligation to protect the river and do what we can to restore it," he said. "And we have a challenge of expressing that in today's world, and in the complexities that are out there right now."

"I think one part of how to express the obligation is to know your stuff," he said. "It's not good enough to be good enough: You've gotta be better." That led to a big tribal investment in people and expertise for its fisheries program, and the sorts of computer modeling that makes Fletcher think the settlement agreement will get fish—and not just endangered suckers and threatened coho, but chinook and lamprey, too—the water they need.

"I think a lot of people trust environmental groups, and they trust tribes, and it's confusing when you see people who typically are on the same side start to line up on different sides," Fletcher said. But the tribe's quest to uphold its obligations has forced it to break with traditional allies and strike out on its own. "Everybody's for tribal sovereignty," Fletcher said, "until you start thinking for yourselves, and make your decision that you wanna go a different way."

The most surprising thing about the Klamath Basin is that for all the rancor here, this is, ecologically speaking, an extremely promising spot for river restoration. "It's huge and complicated and complex," Hillman says, "[but] it's probably the one single place on the continent that still has an opportunity to restore an entire river basin."

At the same time, there is no shortage of places in the West that are having their own water crises—which is to say, their own Klamath moments. It's tempting to see the Klamath settlement as a harbinger for the rest of the region: if bitter enemies can bargain their way to peace here, they can do it anywhere, right?

But Fletcher isn't so sure that's the take-home message. "I went and testified before the [California] fisheries committee last year, and they wanted me to talk a little bit about the Klamath experience," he says. "I was thinking, 'I don't know if you want to repeat the Klamath experience.' We're at a point where we can almost reach a settlement that can resolve a lot of things. But you don't even wanna go through what it takes to get there.

"Have you litigated enough? Are you beating each other up enough? You gotta reach that point where everybody's felt enough pain," he said. "You have to check off all those things, and if you haven't got 'em all, then you're not ready. You're not ready to go through it." If the Klamath experience proves anything, then, it may only be that in the end—and even in the Klamath—water politics is not warfare so much as perpetual negotiation.

The same week this spring that Troy Fletcher took delivery of his doublewide, Scott Seus was planting onions. Midway through the afternoon, Seus stopped his tractor when his wife, Sara, pulled up with their year-and-a-half-old son, Spencer, and Seus' lunch. As he ate out of the back of Sara's Suburban, Seus said, "There's a whole bunch of guys that have just learned to hate, and they can't see beyond that. This is my third year of farming on my own, and there's my young wife and my son. I'd love to see him farm, too, and I see [the agreement] as the only way to provide enough certainty that I can make this farm go forward.

"And honestly," he added, "to be able to think that far forward, you gotta let go of some of the past."

June 23, 2008

Matt Jenkins is a *High Country News* contributing editor.

The Platte River

Saving the Platte

Ray Ring

The new era for the Platte River began in a downstairs Stouffer Inn conference room in Denver in December 1993. Or maybe it began a few months later in Kearney, Nebraska.

Or maybe it began sometime around then in a meeting room at Wyoming's capitol building in Cheyenne. It's hard to pin it down, because it was the kind of turning point you don't recognize until long after you've gone through it.

Still, the Denver meeting could be described as a possible beginning. Secretary of Interior Bruce Babbitt, the nation's chief official for attempting to sort out seemingly impossible natural-resources conflicts, came from Washington, D.C., to take a seat that might have been positioned, symbolically, in the middle of the room.

Surrounding him were tables occupied by several dozen key people who compete for percentages of the Platte River: water developers representing hundreds of farms and dozens of cities, environmentalists representing endangered species and an ecosystem under stress, local officials representing the water cultures of the three very different states along the river, and the attorneys.

It was tense enough—a test of whether there was any chance that all the competing interests could agree on some reform in managing the river. It would either begin to restore aspects of the natural river or blow up in increased conflict.

The Platte is the river that defines the vast edge of the West, where the mountains slide into the Great Plains. Flowing more than a thousand miles from headwaters in the Colorado Rockies, across the plains of Colorado and Wyoming and the entire length of Nebraska to join with the Missouri River, the Platte gathers water from ninety thousand square miles.

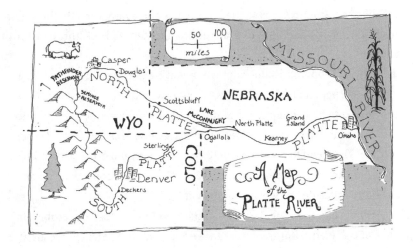

Its headwaters have the mountain personality—originating in snowpack along the Continental Divide, gathering in flashy streams that plunge down brief, narrow canyons. The plunge concludes abruptly on the flatland, where the water mellows to the other extreme, slowing and settling into the wide-bed tributaries, the North and South Platte. By the time the tributaries converge in Nebraska into a stretch called the Central Platte, the riverbed can be almost perfectly flat, dropping only seven feet per mile.

In total flow, the Platte is a trickle compared to the West's trademark rivers, averaging about 1.3 million acre-feet per year where the tributaries converge. The Colorado River's flow averages eleven times larger, and the Columbia fully one hundred and twenty times larger. Yet the Platte's water might be the most aggressively harnessed, blocked by fifteen major dams and siphoned into thousands of canals, ditches, and other projects.

More than a million city people in Colorado and one hundred thousand in Wyoming, and much of the agricultural economy in both states depend on the river.

Nebraska's development of the river has taken the form of intensively irrigated agriculture; hundreds of square miles of corn and soy fields whose harvest goes directly into local feedlots for cattle. It's estimated that in some stretches each drop of the Platte gets used eight times, as most of the diverted water returns to the river again and again, directly through treatment plants and agricultural runoffs or seeping back through the aquifer.

Not that it operates smoothly; when you treat a river like a grab bag, you get perpetual arguing about who owns which drop. The states have considered their segments as separate fiefdoms; so have the users within each state and at times the environmentalists who speak for fish and other wildlife. They tend to eye their neighbors upstream and downstream with suspicion, and they've papered the river with lawsuits, court decrees, and elaborate water-delivery plans to divvy it up.

And development of the river impacts wildlife, most noticeably on the Central Platte. But the threat to wildlife isn't immediately apparent. With the flow organized and evened out, the bed along the Central Platte never goes dry, so it might be the best-looking stretch of river, at least to the uninformed eye.

The banks are lined by woods, so that from the air, the river seems to thrive as a vein of wild vegetation amid the farms. The stretch is rich with birds, including a thousand bald eagles that winter over and millions of migrators—ducks, geese, sandhill cranes, and shorebirds that stop in for a few weeks each spring and fall, migrating between winter refuges in the Caribbean and summer nesting grounds in Canada.

Also migrating through are a significant percentage of the world's few remaining whooping cranes—charismatic, graceful wading birds that stand five feet tall with seven-foot wingspans, feathered pure white except for dabs of red around the eyes and black on the wingtips.

There are only one hundred and eighty-five whooping cranes left. They're on the federal list of endangered species. Their decline is linked to problems at both ends of the flyway, but the Central Platte figures in. Before development, the river's flow on the Central Platte averaged two-and-a-half to four times what it does today, depending on who's doing the estimating. The water that's missing evaporates from reservoirs and canals or percolates away.

The water used to come rushing down in the springtime, as the distant snowpack melted, to spread out hundreds of yards wide on the Central

Platte, creating shallows, many sandbars and islands, and seasonally wet meadows along the banks. As the runoff would subside, the bed would go dry as much as six months a year—the summer trickle from the mountains would simply vanish into the prairie. The opposite extremes of floods and summer droughts discouraged plant growth, so that instead of being wooded, many banks and islands were bare.

The whooping crane evolved to depend on that, eating the snails and worms in the wet meadows, wading around freely, nesting in the open, always with a view of any approaching predators. Other birds of the open river habitat include the least tern, also listed as endangered, and the piping plover, listed as threatened. Farther downriver, where the Platte blends into the Missouri River, the pallid sturgeon, a fish that dates back to prehistoric times, is also listed as endangered.

The rare wildlife species need more water than they're getting, or the water should be timed more naturally, to simulate the old spring floods and sweep away the invasive vegetation. That's what the federal Fish and Wildlife Service and the environmentalists' scientists believe. That's what led to the meeting six years ago in the downstairs conference room in Denver's Stouffer Inn.

Even as the meeting got under way, other attempts around the West to reform developed rivers weren't doing well. Four years of effort on a pair of rivers in Nevada—the Truckee and the Carson—were blowing up; farmers in Nevada were abandoning the negotiations there, fearing they'd have to give too much water back to wildlife. There was also a kind of stalemate on the Columbia River system, with the various federal agencies hardly able to agree on one clumsy plan (barging and trucking salmon around dams without much change in overall river management), and the states and Indian tribes holding to several more drastic plans to help the salmon.

In California, the Bay Area rivers process had gone to the top, pushing a bill through Congress calling for reform. But on the ground and riverbanks still no agreement had been reached on how to carry out that reform; in California, it was the environmentalists who feared they'd give up too much.

Regardless of all the warning signs and failures elsewhere, the Platte River consensus process took hold. No one can say exactly what the crucial breakthrough was, as meeting followed meeting. It seemed a process of subtleties, which continues today all around the river basin.

The new era on the Platte, if it is successful, will mean people along the river acknowledge the way water moves through a landscape, how all the users touch each other, and how the river connects with groundwater and the wildlife habitat. No one will ever again be able to blast out of this closed circle unilaterally with a new well field, a new dam, or a blistering regulation.

Instead, everyone will have to work together.

People talk about it the way Doug Robothom, assistant to the director of the Colorado Department of Natural Resources, does: "Some days you make progress and other days you wonder what the hell you're doing. You have some difficult people and some people emerge as leaders and some are thinking creatively and finding a middle ground. There are endless little goat paths you go down, and those frustrations. It can be very tense at times."

And the way Jay Maher, environmental resources manager for the Central Nebraska Public Power and Irrigation District, talks about it: "People have to make sure their needs are being met and the other guy isn't getting away with anything."

And Dave Sands, head of the Nebraska chapter of the Audubon Society: "There's been a lot of fighting and antagonism and nothing has been done for the river, nothing to restore flows to the endangered species. I see this as a way to stop the antagonism and start on the road to recovery."

These days, credit for the apparent progress is claimed by people in just about every camp.

When Babbitt showed up at the Stouffer Inn, he and the rest of the Clinton administration had been in power about a year, preaching consensus. Babbitt already had expertise in water; he'd overseen a reform of Arizona's groundwater management during the 1980s, when he was governor there, and his assistant secretary, Rieke, had also come from Arizona and been instrumental there.

The local situation was ready for a fresh strategy. Until then, the strategy was to attempt to reform one project at a time; occasionally some new dam was proposed, or some existing dam or diversion came up for renewal of a federal permit, and the feds and environmentalists would try to apply specific leverage.

In particular, two environmental groups—the Audubon Society and the Platte River Whooping Crane Trust, which preserves some acreage along the Central Platte—were targeting Kingsley Dam. The dam holds back McConaughy Reservoir, the largest reservoir on the river, siphoning a quarter million acre-feet per year off to farms and hydropower generators, but it was vulnerable because its license to generate power was expiring.

Studies of how the dam could be adjusted to help the wildlife downriver had bogged down. An arbitrator had failed. Opposing lawsuits had been filed by environmentalists and a group of farmers.

"It was delay after delay after delay," says Paul Currier, executive director of the Platte River Whooping Crane Trust. Even as the delay dragged on, a half-dozen projects far upriver, in the Colorado headwaters, also came up for renewal, including diversionary pipelines and reservoirs for Front Range cities such as Fort Collins, Boulder, and Greeley. Also, Wyoming was proposing some new projects for its farmers and cities.

So the federal government gained leverage at numerous points around the river basin.

With more at stake, political support for a consensus process began to materialize, from the ground up and the top down. In an expanded series of meetings around the river states, the hammer of the Endangered Species Act helped keep everyone talking. Finally a tangible milestone was reached—the first written agreement, in July 1994, a Memorandum of Understanding, signed by the feds and the governors of the three states.

The memo of agreement was only six pages, so sketchy it was hard to disagree with, saying the negotiations would continue with the stated goal of harnessing the entire river basin's development to help the wildlife, somehow. It was, says participant Dan Luecke, who works for the Environmental Defense Fund in Boulder, Coloado, "an agreement on the shape of the table."

A second series of difficult meetings began to figure out how to carry out the goal. Negotiators gathered in uninspiring motels and government offices strung along Interstate 80, in Cheyenne, Lincoln, Kearney, Omaha, and Grand Island. Whenever it was Denver's turn again, they moved from motel to motel or to the regional Fish and Wildlife Service office.

For a while they settled in the Continental Airlines frequent-flyer conference room in Denver's new airport, because it, too, was convenient. Always, as one negotiator says, "The coffee was bad."

"We'd all fly into Denver International Airport from around the country," says John Echeverria, who was the lead attorney for Audubon. "We'd go into one of the airport's conference rooms. No windows, just walls. Maybe twenty of us—two environmentalists, maybe five from the federal government, and sixteen representing the states and the development interests.

"Each time, we'd be in the room for seven hours. Meeting like that, every month or so, it's enormously demanding of your time and energy and resources."

At first, the government people were in charge, and there was a rigid order: assigned seats at the table for the states and the feds, and the rest of the people, including representatives of the irrigation districts and the environmentalists, sitting away from the table, like an audience.

The government people negotiated among themselves, with one state or another making a presentation on how no water could be spared and the feds countering. Overhead projectors hummed and blackboards were filled with charts of hundreds of months of the river's flow at dozens of checkpoints. The audience could only listen and sometimes ask questions or take potshots.

"Our irrigation district didn't even have a seat at the table, even though we were carrying the ball for Nebraska," Maher recalls.

Environmentalists were discouraged also. "We had no seats [at the table], no power in the process," Luecke says. "We'd get an opportunity from time to time to make observations, put in pleas or whine or whatever."

But on their own, the governments couldn't agree on much of anything, because they have vastly different personalities when it comes to water. One example: Colorado and Wyoming are into intensive management of both wells and surface water, while Nebraska isn't.

Nebraska, which only partly fits inside the one-hundredth meridian that traditionally marks the edge of the West, is the real cowboy state when it comes to water policy. Unlike Wyoming and Colorado, Nebraska still makes it illegal for cities and environmentalists to buy out farmers' water. Nebraska ranks behind only California in irrigated acreage, and the Nebraska farmers hold tightly to it.

The Central Nebraska irrigation district, the main Nebraska district in the Platte River negotiations, has only thirty thousand residents or oo, but they grow more than forty million bushels of corn a year, most of which goes to local feedlots that are crammed with a million cattle. The agriculture draws from more than the river. Farmers have drilled thousands of wells, inspired by the rising price of corn and advances in the technology of center pivots and pumps.

The wells now supply five times as much water to farms in the area as the river does directly. Most states have learned hard lessons about how well pumping along rivers has dried up river after river; Nebraska has tried to ignore any connection.

Only in 1996 did the state set up a cumbersome and decentralized system for regulating such wells through "natural resource districts," which until then had focused on groundwater contamination. The new law merely gives the resource districts the right to monitor and regulate wells if they choose to. No one even knows how many wells there are in Nebraska. Up to 20 percent of Nebraska's wells aren't registered, even though a law, in effect for more than forty years, requires registration.

That helps to explain why, in the Platte River negotiations, Wyoming and Colorado didn't trust Nebraska to keep its hands off any water that might be released for wildlife. For its part, Nebraska didn't trust Wyoming and Colorado to release a fair percentage of the river from upriver dams; Nebraska was even pressing a separate lawsuit based on that suspicion (ed.: the case, originally filed in 1986, was resolved in 2001).

Says Jim Cook, attorney for the Nebraska Natural Resources Commission: "There isn't really one side that aligns with another. All have individual interests."

After a while at the table with not much result, the bureaucrats realized, as Robothom says, "We needed the two main protagonists—environmentalists and water users—at the table also."

So the federal and state agencies let the process take on a life of it's own; adding more seats right at the table was a small sign of mutual respect.

The second series of meetings was supposed to last maybe a year, but dragged on for a year after that, and then another year.

Ask Robothom how it felt to be engaged hour after hour, meeting after meeting, and he laughs: "It spans the range from tedium to tenseness to breakthrough, with people employing humor."

As the adversaries spent so much time together, the respect grew. Environmentalist Luecke, for example, describes Mike Jess, Nebraska's state engineer and water resources chief: "Mike Jess was a tough negotiator, but he brought some good ideas to the table."

Glimmerings of progress created new problems. As more people learned of the negotiations, more wanted to attend. A meeting in Grand Island, Nebraska, was packed by as many as a hundred farmers. Other meetings were packed by other interest groups.

"Sometimes the tables were so big, we had fifty people at the table," says Ralph Morgenweck, regional director for the Fish and Wildlife Service. "We evolved into gigantic meetings, of seventy-five people or more." Everyone agreed: that was too large.

So the next agreement was a step in the other direction, limiting meetings to thirty people or so, and when necessary, breaking into smaller work groups, still trying to represent all the viewpoints equally.

"That became more productive, simply because we had fewer people to deal with," says Currier. "And there was less grandstanding, because people weren't saying things just to please the audience."

Little by little, people sticking with the process got used to agreeing.

Changes in personnel also had to be weathered. Halfway through, Rieke, the leading federal official at the table, resigned from the Department of Interior to take another job. Her seat was filled by Patty Beneke, another assistant secretary of Interior. Luecke, of the Environmental Defense Fund (and a member of this newspaper's board of directors), also withdrew, leaving the environmentalist viewpoint to be pushed by the Audubon Society and the Whooping Crane Trust, two groups that had more years on the river. The process continued.

It was difficult even to agree on basic facts, the most crucial being, how much water does wildlife need? Fish and Wildlife Service weighed in with what seemed like a definitive number: four hundred and seventeen thousand acre-feet per year.

That meant more than 30 percent of the flow to the Central Platte should be released when wildlife needs it. The figure stunned the water users and the states. "We were aghast," says Cook, of the Nebraska Natural Resources Commission. "Things nearly fell apart at that point."

The water users said less water is needed by wildlife. In response to the resistance, the Fish and Wildlife Service refigured and came back to the table with a number that was both lower and looser: one hundred and thirty to one hundred and fifty thousand acre-feet for wildlife. Sources for only seventy thousand acre-feet or so were identified, and the rest would have to be discovered by further research and negotiations. This concession kept water users at the table—but not environmentalists.

When their protests in the spring of 1997 failed to budge the feds back toward the higher acre-foot total for wildlife, the Audubon Society and the Whooping Crane Trust pulled out.

"We had the sense we were doing more harm than good by attending," Echeverria says. "We were present, but we weren't having an effect on the process, and by our presence, we were implicitly endorsing the process.

"It was frustration at that point." But he adds, "You can't calibrate your proposal to the strength of the opposition."

Even so, the Platte River consensus process reached its next major milestone. The feds and the states signed a roughly hundred-page "cooperative agreement," which included details of how to help the wildlife, in July 1997, with the negotiators for the water users supporting it but no environmentalists at the table.

Even among the environmentalists there was chafing about strategy and science. Luecke says he believed that "to talk about four hundred and seventeen thousand acre-feet was going to get us nowhere."

The cooperative agreement signed by the states and federal government called for a new strategy on the Platte River, called "environmental accounts."

These would be new water rights equal in priority to the most senior rights on the river. They would be managed by the Fish and Wildlife Service, which can order releases from dams and other projects according to what the wildlife needs.

The environmental account in Nebraska would be at Kingsley Dam and its reservoir, Lake McConaughy. The Fish and Wildlife Service would get 10 percent of the storable flow into the reservoir during winter, averaging fifty to seventy thousand acre-feet per year.

In Wyoming, the environmental account would be at Pathfinder Reservoir. An inflatable plastic dam would be built across the top of the dam to increase its storage capacity, and 60 percent of the additional stored water would be managed for wildlife downriver—about fifteen thousand acre-feet per year.

In Colorado, the environmental account would be an innovation called the Tamarack water bank, to be developed on state land along the Nebraska border. During winter, when the river flow is high, water would be pumped from wells along the river into nearby recharge basins. During summer, when the river needs it most, the water would seep underground back to the river. The timing of the Colorado water releases would be adjusted by about ten thousand acre-feet per year.

Overall, it's touted as a $75 million deal, with the feds chipping in about half and the rest coming from the states and water projects.

As long as the states and water users commit to it, they get a federal assurance that there will be no further Endangered Species Act challenges of individual projects or permits from here on.

So, Nebraska gets the relicensing of Kingsley Dam (recently approved for another forty years). Wyoming gets 40 percent of Pathfinder Reservoir's additional stored water, to be diverted off to cities and towns. Colorado gets its headwaters projects approved, and its Tamarack project could keep minnows there off the federal Endangered Species list.

The federal government, in return for its compromising, is supposed to get the on-the-ground aid of state and local regulators, who will work with farmers to ensure that enough water reaches the birds and fish.

The deal also calls for buying some key parcels of habitat (ten thousand acres during the first ten or fifteen years), plus conservation and water-marketing schemes to come up with the rest of the one hundred and thirty to one hundred and fifty thousand acre-feet to be managed for wildlife—or possibly more water for wildlife or possibly less.

The emphasis is on local flexibility and "adaptive management," making more changes as you go along, based on what works and what doesn't. New studies and monitoring will supposedly determine how the wildlife species are doing and what else is needed.

In effect, the negotiations continue. A governance committee, atop a hierarchy of a dozen or more new committees, oversees it and continues to try to represent all points of view. There's a new three-year stage under way now, with public hearings, preparation of an environmental impact statement, and review by the state legislatures. If the states and the federal government sign the final documents, the full program goes into effect for ten years, with possible renewal beyond that.

"Whether you applaud it or not," says former Colorado Department of Natural Resources chief Jim Lochhead, "it is a significant shift in the way people use and manage the water." The region's water industry, he believes, is beginning to shoulder "external costs' such as habitat damage.

Nebraska water resources chief Jess, who runs surface water but not groundwater, says people along the river will be asked to make "hundreds of small, incremental decisions' adding up to real change.

The deal won't stop new developments from using water along the river, but any new draw from the river must be offset by the retirement of some other water project or conservation or water buys (all in effect transferring other water back into the river).

But not much is guaranteed. That's why the Whooping Crane Trust pulled out of the negotiations almost two years ago.

"We weren't sure the water will be enough; we weren't sure it would be delivered fast enough, and there was no firm commitment from anyone," says Currier. "Anyone can pull out at any time."

There are even doubts that any change in the delivery of water will restore the lost habitat. Luecke, a hydrologist who's also a senior environmental scientist for his group, acknowledges, "The applied science of hydrologic restoration is in its infancy."

"I don't think flowing a lot of water in the springtime is going to clean out that channel like it used to," says Vernon J. Nelson, a Nebraska farmer who's on the governance committee overseeing the process now; he also co-chairs the land committee. "The only way is to dry out the bed in the summer and go in there with a defoliant or a bulldozer and clean out the vegetation." Under adaptive management, it could come to that.

The Platte River process seems stronger now, partly because the environmental groups have rejoined it. Two of the ten seats on the governance committee are reserved for environmentalists, now shared by the Audubon Society, Whooping Crane Trust, and Environmental Defense Fund.

"It didn't make sense for us to stand outside and throw stones," Currier says. "We support the program now and want to see it work."

Audubon's Sands says, "The way the cooperative agreement is structured, it would be very difficult to pursue a policy that is not environmentally sound. The governance committee has to act by virtual consensus—the committee needs nine of the ten total votes to pursue a policy." No major decision can be made unless at least one environmentalist signs on.

Some are less optimistic. Echeverria says he won't rejoin the Platte River process. He has resigned from Audubon to be director of the Environmental Policy Project at Georgetown University.

"The environmental interests were effectively outgunned," he says. "There were scores of attorneys and consultants from the water and power interests negotiating with a handful of environmentalists. This is a case of significant abdication of federal authority over a resource the federal government is uniquely qualified to address [the migration flyway and habitat that extends internationally].

"The whole process wasn't driven by what the species need, but by what the states and development interests were willing to give," Echeverria says. "I expect the program will prove to be inadequate for the wildlife.

"Going forward, it will only be more demanding, endless time and endless meetings. My sense is that the environmental organizations can't justify spending that much time and energy on it, but you know the irrigation districts and other development interests will be involved. Over time, the imbalance will only get worse."

One of the biggest chores will be containing well pumping along the river in Nebraska. Nebraska has funded a program to study its thousands of wells, searching for impacts on the river. Nebraska will probably edge closer to regulation or buy-outs of wells, or be nudged along.

"We don't hide from that," says Cook. "We know we'll have to get a handle on it, and we have to persuade the other states we do have a handle."

All along the river, the impact on the irrigators using river water will be felt mainly in drought years, when the flow through canals and ditches is crucial. As Maher says, "We're removing the drought protection."

In a sign of how the Platte River process could be derailed this far along, farmers who fear loss of irrigation water have organized.

It's similar to the Nevada rebellion that derailed the process on the Truckee and Carson rivers. The Platte rebellion has reared up in Nebraska, around a statewide group of big-acreage irrigators called Nebraskans First.

"We're trying to stop the encroachment of the federal government and the enviros into this area," says Carroll Sheldon, who's on the board of directors of Nebraskans First.

Sheldon manages or owns several thousand acres of corn and soybeans along the Central Platte. "This is probably the highest-yield land in the world," he says. "We get two hundred bushels of corn and sixty-five bushels of soybean [per acre], and if it wasn't for irrigation, we'd have almost nothing. It would just demolish us to lose our water."

Recently Sheldon and Nebraskans First have encouraged eight counties along the Central Platte to form the Coalition for Protection of Agricultural Communities. The counties have decided to spend as much as $25,000 to draw up a "custom-and-culture land-use plan," which will lay out the importance of agriculture and how the irrigation systems shouldn't be tinkered with, Sheldon says.

The law firm of Karen Budd-Falen, based in Cheyenne, Wyoming, which consults with rural counties around the West in similar anti-federal, anti-environmentalist stances, has been hired to do the plan. Another group has sprung up linking rebels in all three river states, the Platte River Basin Ag Alliance.

"We feel the cooperative agreement should be stopped right now," Sheldon says. "This [Central Platte] used to be swamps. Over time, we have drained the swamps, built up land along the river, and made it beautiful farmland. Now they want to turn it back to swampland. It blows your mind."

But Nelson, who grows corn on three thousand acres using surface and well water, speaks moderately. "I hope this doesn't turn into a range war, and I don't think it will. We have an Endangered Species Act we all have to abide by; if we don't like it, we'll have to change the law," Nelson says. His farm, Winsome Inc., has been in his family for four generations, and he looks ahead to his kids and grandkids keeping it going. "I named my farm that because I like what it means—charming, pleasant personality ... The roots go pretty deep."

Nelson believes the cooperative agreement is "achievable, as long as they stop at the one hundred and thirty to one hundred and fifty thousand acre-feet" for wildlife. "If they go up to four hundred and seventeen thousand acre-feet, it would devastate the economy here."

The people already signed onto the process—state officials, water-system managers, and environmentalists—have responded to the rebels as they have to all other opposition: by inviting the opposition into the process.

"We need to shore up our outreach efforts," says Mike Besson, director of the Wyoming Water Development Commission. "It would have been better if we'd brought these people into the process sooner. We need to identify all the adverse impacts to see which way to go."

"I think it's a very good national model for complex issues," says Fish and Wildlife's Morgenweck. "You have to be patient to see it out, and when you do, the outcome is clearly better than if you went to court with a lawsuit. A court usually doesn't come up with a comprehensive solution, a court just rules on an individual issue or two.

"And in court," Morgenweck continues, "it's a win or lose situation—everyone is trying to beat the brains out of the opposition. But in a negotiation, human nature is, 'I'm going to give a little bit here if I get a little bit over here.' ... [And] what we're hearing from the public is, 'We want face-to-face discussions, personal involvement.' That starts to rebuild people's faith in government."

Nelson is one of many who appreciate how getting acquainted has personalized the issues.

"Locking horns doesn't do anybody any good," he says. "I might not like what you're saying, but I'm going to listen and then say what I have to say. For the farming community here, my number one concern is to use the water for farming because that's my livelihood.

"Paul Currier [of the Whooping Crane Trust] tells us his number one priority is the crane. And that's okay. It doesn't make me dislike the man ... We all gave up something to make it work. I hope it holds together."

February 1, 1999

Ray Ring writes in Bozeman, Montana. *Anne MacKinnon*, who contributed to this story, is an attorney and former editor of the *Casper Star-Tribune* in Wyoming.

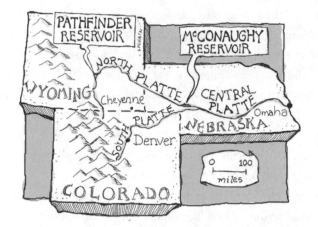

Truce Holds on the Platte River

Andrew Beck Grace

"I don't like it much," Mike Besson, Wyoming's water czar, says about the latest milestone in the difficult negotiations along the Platte River. But, he adds, it's better than all-out war.

The cautious note from Besson is understandable. With a south branch flowing through Colorado, a north branch in Wyoming, and both branches merging to cross Nebraska, the Platte is one of the West's most contested rivers. It provides drinking water to 3.5 million people and irrigates two million acres of farmland.

For at least seven years, federal and state agencies, along with environmentalists and farm interests, have been trying to address a wildlife crisis on the most degraded stretch, the Central Platte in Nebraska.

Now the U.S. Fish and Wildlife Service and the Bureau of Reclamation have an eight-hundred-page draft environmental impact statement up for public comment until September 20. It lays out four "action alternatives," any of which would shake up the river's plumbing to benefit endangered wildlife.

The proposal is a bold experiment that no one is certain will work, but the major players seem to share the tone of measured support that comes from Besson, director of the Wyoming Water Development Commission. "What I'm trying to prevent is another Klamath," says Besson, referring to the Klamath River on the Oregon-California border, where many of the same kinds of interests have fought a bitter war of lawsuits and water-shutoffs since 2001, with disastrous results for salmon.

Millions of birds, including a half-million migrating sandhill cranes, use the wetlands and islands along the Central Platte. But three bird species are in trouble, because the original wide, braided channel has been deepened by unnatural flows from dozens of upstream dams and diversions, and thick vegetation has encroached on the banks and islands. Two shorebirds adapted to nest on bare sand—the piping plover and the interior least tern—have not successfully produced young from their nests in the Central Platte for fifteen years. Only a handful of whooping cranes show up during migration. Downriver, on the Lower Platte, the pallid sturgeon is also in trouble.

The four alternatives in the draft impact statement share key elements tackling the problems. Flows devoted to wildlife would increase dramatically, likely in the range of one hundred and thirty to one hundred and fifty thousand acre-feet per year. At least ten thousand acres of habitat would be bought or protected by conservation easements, adding to about fourteen thousand acres that conservation groups have already set aside.

Dams for two big reservoirs—Pathfinder in Wyoming and McConaughy in Nebraska—would be tuned to deliver the water when wildlife needs it. In one innovative move, the river's flow through eastern Colorado would be diverted into the underground alluvial aquifer when irrigators and wildlife don't need the water, then would trickle downriver later, arriving when needed. And efforts would be made to restore vegetation-free islands and wet meadows, both important habitat.

The experiment will likely evolve for decades, as more research is done. New methods such as "island scraping" would clear existing islands for bird nesting and move sediment back into the river to create additional bare islands. The costs—estimated from $50 million to $180 million—would be paid half by the federal government and half by the states.

While a National Academy of Sciences report has generally backed up the Fish and Wildlife Service's approach, there are no guarantees that the plan will save endangered wildlife. "We decided to embrace adaptive management," says Paul Tebble of the National Audubon Society in Nebraska. "It's scary, it slows down the process, we may have to go back to the political process to ask for more water, but it beats litigation."

The draft impact statement estimates that eleven thousand acres of irrigated farmland would be taken out of production, with a $4 million loss in crops. Water and land for wildlife would be acquired only from willing sellers and lessors, but even that modest shift away from agriculture is too much for some farm interests.

Some of the Nebraska farmers who pump from thousands of wells along the river claim that the federal government is trying to shut down irrigated agriculture. But actually, the state of Nebraska is working to regulate the pumping, partly to keep the river from declining further, and partly to keep one farmer's well pumping from affecting another's. So far, agriculture interests are also holding off on lawsuits against the Platte process.

Representing many Wyoming water users, Besson wants some details adjusted or spelled out more clearly. But he says the feds are listening to his concerns. "The program is still being negotiated," he says.

The next milestone will be the Fish and Wildlife Service's draft biological opinion on the alternatives, expected any day now. The Department of the Interior will make a final decision, probably next year.

If the truce holds, and the proposed plan becomes reality, it will be a major development in western water management, says Dan Luecke, a National Wildlife Federation consultant. "We're trying to invent a way of governing ourselves on a different political basis," he says, "and that political basis is a watershed."

August 16, 2004

Andrew Beck Grace is a filmmaker and writer based in Tuscaloosa, Alabama.

The Missouri River

On the Missouri, the Middle Ground Gets Soggy

Peter Carrels

Only a decade ago, animosity between states in the Missouri River's upper and lower basins was out of control. If the states weren't suing each other over Missouri River flows, they were attacking the U.S. Army Corps of Engineers for that agency's management of the river system. South Dakota Governor William Janklow grumbled that the Corps "throws us the crumbs and operates the way downstream states want [the river] operated." South Dakotans wore baseball caps that proclaimed "The Corps Sucks," and the upper-basin states, led by Janklow, unsuccessfully sought to change the Missouri's dam-management policies in Congress and the courts.

Now, apparently, peace, if not brotherhood, unites the former combatants. An agreement between river basin states, brokered by the Missouri River Basin Association, provides the Corps of Engineers with a new approach to river management. Richard Opper, executive director of the association, applauded the agreement. "We still have issues to resolve, and we always will," he said, "but the fact remains that we have just taken a major step toward solving some of the most difficult and contentious issues we face."

However, just as the coalition of eight states and thirty Indian tribes seemingly made peace, a new antagonist entered the debate: an environmental group. It says the agreement does little to help the river's endangered species and other fish and wildlife, and provides only minimal protection to upper-basin reservoirs.

"The only consensus about this plan," said Chad Smith, a spokesman for American Rivers, "is that it will accelerate the death spiral that native fish and wildlife on the Missouri River find themselves in."

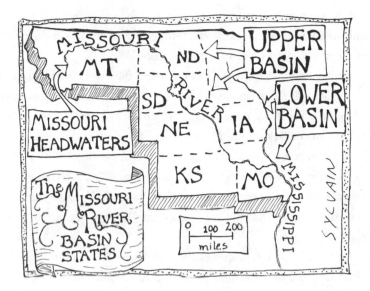

Smith and other environmentalists want to see wildlife habitat restored to a river system that has been damaged by decades of development. Dams and reservoirs in the Dakotas and Montana drowned about one million acres of the most diverse habitat on the northern plains, while channelization, straightening, and flood-control measures along the lower river eliminated seventy miles of main channel, as well as islands, wetlands, and sand bars. Once the dams and levees were in place, farmers cut down riverside forests in the former floodplain and planted crops.

But the Corps of Engineers is pleased by the compromise between river states. "The [basin association] produced some valuable recommendations that we will take very seriously as we draft our new management plan for the Missouri River," said Larry Cieslik, chief of the Reservoir Control Center for the Corps' Missouri River office, in Omaha, Nebraska.

The Missouri River Basin Association, which includes a representative from each of the eight states—both Dakotas, Montana, Wyoming, Iowa, Nebraska, Kansas, and Missouri—as well as one representative from the basin's nearly thirty Indian tribes, has existed since 1981. Not until last summer's agreement, however, was there any sign of harmony. A sticking point has been reservoir levels. Upper-basin states want to keep reservoirs high and stable to protect a thriving fishing and recreation industry. Lower-basin states want enough water flowing in their section of the river to float cargo-carrying barges.

Unlike on other major navigation rivers, there are no locks and dams on the Missouri's navigation reach. Water levels are kept deep by releases from the river's major dams, four of which are in South Dakota, with one each in North Dakota and Montana. The flows surge through the lower basin in a channel that is more ditch than river. During the dry 1980s, the Corps dramatically lowered upper-basin reservoirs, damaging stocked fisheries and recreation businesses. That led to the lawsuits launched by Governor Janklow, and the suits caused the Corps to re-examine its dam-management plan.

The compromise proposed by the basin association would halt navigation on the river and lower the reservoirs more slowly during severe drought. Although Richard Opper hailed this as a breakthrough, Chad Smith said that the protection gained by upper-basin states was slight. "The agreement translates into only about five more feet of water in the reservoirs during a drought like the 1980s," explained Smith, before adding that the agreement only deals with managing the river during drought conditions.

"Severe drought comes only twice a century to the basin," said Smith. "The rest of the time, navigation still runs the river."

American Rivers has asked the Corps to adopt a split season for navigation that would allow shippers to use the river. That, said the organization, would protect reservoirs during the busiest recreation season, and also allow river managers to simulate the river's former spring rise to help recreate pre-dam conditions on the river. Among other effects, they hope a spring rise will trigger reproduction in surviving native fish.

Some environmentalists say Missouri navigation is insignificant and should be eliminated. While barges on the Mississippi and Ohio rivers carry more than three hundred million and one hundred million tons of commercial cargo each year, respectively, Missouri River shippers haul less than five million tons per year. Only two shipping companies regularly use the Missouri.

Richard Opper acknowledged that the compromise will never completely satisfy any special interest. "Such is the price of middle ground," he said.

Opper's middle ground, however, may get soggy. The state of Missouri, an adamant defender of barges on the Missouri, is reportedly nervous about the modest concessions made to the upper-basin states in the agreement, and is considering backing out. It is also unclear if the compromise will satisfy the Endangered Species Act. Almost certainly, that question will be put before the courts when the Corps releases its plan. Already several years behind schedule, the plan might not be released for another year or two.

November 8, 1999

Peter Carrels resides in the James River valley in northern South Dakota.

Strangling the Last Best River

Hal Herring

Montana statesman Mike Mansfield, summing up the highlights of his career in the U.S. Senate, claimed to be most proud that he "had saved the Yellowstone River from the Corps of Engineers." But while the Yellowstone is still the longest undammed river in the Lower Forty-Eight, it is now a long way from "saved."

A half-dozen diversion dams interrupt its flow. Trucks have dumped rock, or riprap, along miles of river bank, locking what was once a migrating and healthy river system into a single channel that effectively moves the vast runoff from the high Rockies but performs less and less like the mighty river that meandered and eddied its way through the mountains and across the high plains. Even without dams, this last free-flowing river is beginning to resemble its tamed counterparts across the West.

Last summer, fisheries biologist Joel Tohtz studied trout species in the river near Livingston, Montana, and discovered a disturbing absence. Trout populations were down 60 percent from a previous survey, and the decline was a general one—there were simply very few fish, of any age class, in this traditionally very productive stretch of the river.

"I would have to guess that the number of stabilization projects in that area is responsible for the decline," Tohtz says. "It is an unstable and heavily populated part of the river, and we have confined it for those very reasons. In confining it, we have made it a downspout."

Back-to-back record flood years in 1996 and 1997 made the problem much worse, spurring riverfront property owners to embark on a frenzy of what the Greater Yellowstone Coalition has called "riprap anarchy."

The most common riprap method is to use heavy equipment to smooth eroding banks and then blanket them with a layer of large boulders, a process that is also referred to as "armoring." Tohtz describes the most heavily armored sections as performing "like a fire-hose" at high water, sweeping everything downstream. Where normally the river would overflow its banks and dissipate its energy into the surrounding cottonwoods, willows, and grasslands of its floodplain, a confined river can only scour its own channel down to bedrock or disperse its energy at an unconfined stretch downstream. That raises serious problems for any landowners along the river.

"Riprap begets riprap," says Missoula hydrologist and river consultant Bruce Anderson. "A river like the Yellowstone is a completely dynamic system. If you pin it down one place, the energy moves somewhere else. This fact forces a landowner downstream of a riprap project to consider a riprap project of his own."

In response, the U.S. Fish and Wildlife Agency asked the Corps for a moratorium on stabilization projects. Corps officials refused, saying that under current regulations, the Corps could not deny landowners the permits to protect their property from the river.

During a three-year period beginning in 1995, the Corps permitted seventy-eight rock barbs—walls of rock that jut into the current—and more than eleven miles of rock riprap in the portion of the Yellowstone that flows through Park County.

The river's entire, six-hundred-mile length, from its source in Yellowstone National Park to where it meets the Missouri River just across the North Dakota border, is threatened. Once the river flows north out of the park and reaches Livingston, it turns to the east and sets off across the plains of eastern Montana.

"The trend is going all the way down the river," says Rob Hazlewood of the U.S. Fish and Wildlife Service in Montana. "It's not just in Park County. We're equally concerned about the rest of the river."

In Park County, 25 percent of the river's banks are covered by blanket riprap or manipulated by large dikes, and permits were issued last summer to blanket thousands more feet of bank near Livingston. Although the Corps does weigh both the concerns of the landowner and the possible ecological effects of such projects before issuing a permit, each project is reviewed individually—cumulative effects are not considered.

In 1996 and 1997, the Fish and Wildlife Service wrote dozens of letters to the Corps protesting riprap projects. The Corps never once responded.

"We may not have replied directly to the USFWS, but we did try to address their concerns," says Allan Steinle of the Corps of Engineers. The Corps' critics disagree.

"They were turning the river into a rock-lined rain gutter simply because people wanted to live in the floodplain," says Hazlewood. "The Corps just kept on issuing the permits, in direct conflict with our interests at Fish and Wildlife."

In response, the agency asked the Corps for a moratorium on stabilization projects. The Corps refused. Afterward, Montana Governor Marc Racicot created the Upper Yellowstone Task Force to oversee a three- to five-year study of how riprap projects are affecting the health of the river ecosystem.

"Let's thank God they didn't get the moratorium," says John Bailey, chairman of the task force. Bailey spoke from his office in the back of Don Bailey's tackle shop, a longtime mecca for fly fishers from all over the world. "You've got a river here that people have been putting riprap in for a long, long, time. The repercussions of going cold turkey could be extremely radical," he says, adding that he is in no way advocating more armor for the river. "For one thing, it's ugly. But we have so much of it now that we cannot just put a halt to it. If one side of the river is confined, the other side is going to pay a price, and the moratorium says that we just write that side off. I don't think that we can do that, in all fairness."

Most people believe the task force is a step in the right direction. "It is a great idea," says Dennis Glick of the Greater Yellowstone Coalition. "I wish it represented a larger sector of the public. If you run through the list of members, you find mostly people with an economic interest in the river. There are realtors, landowners, the owners of the spring creeks where people pay to fish. There is only one person from an environmental group, only one fisheries guy."

Glick also worries that after years of study, the Task Force will confirm what officials like Rob Hazlewood already suspect—that confining the

Yellowstone River is destroying it as a functioning natural ecosystem, but that the powerful economic interests will cause the riprapping to continue.

Hazlewood of the Fish and Wildlife Service says the river must be protected from short-sighted engineering solutions now, to avoid the necessity for restoration later.

"At some point we have to understand that these things ruin rivers," Hazlewood says. "We would just like to see the river continue to do what it has done so well for thousands of years."

April 12, 1999

Hal Herring writes from Corvallis, Montana.

The Last Wild River

Alan S. Kesselheim

Right in the thick of the millennial hype, I asked myself what I most wanted to do in the new century. The first image that came to mind was paddling my sixteen-foot red canoe down the Yellowstone River near Gardiner, Montana. I would have liked nothing better, on the morning of January 1, 2000, than to set my boat in the vigorous current of that great river and paddle into the next era—if the flow hadn't been the consistency of a snow cone, punctuated by three-hundred-pound chunks of floating ice.

The Yellowstone is that sort of place. If you're a kayaker or canoeist, you want to dance down its curves.

If you're a landowner, you want to build your home close enough for a view down to the next bend, close enough to hear the chuckle of current through an open window.

If you're an angler, you want to saunter down alongside its eddies and pools, arcing flies out over the flow.

If you're a city planner, you plan a park on the riverbank. If you're a jet-boater, you'll be itching to slam full throttle through the waves above Columbus.

Like too many of the landscapes in the West, it is the Yellowstone's curse to be lovely and wild and exhilarating; to be evocative of so much we have already lost; to be another one of those places people most want to be.

As Mike Clark, executive director of the Greater Yellowstone Coalition, put it, "The Yellowstone is one of the very few landscapes left that Lewis and Clark might actually recognize."

The Yellowstone is stubbornly hanging on to its untamed qualities. Much of it feels wild and free and natural and robust, but it is also besieged and depleted and sullied and diminished. A watershed on the cusp.

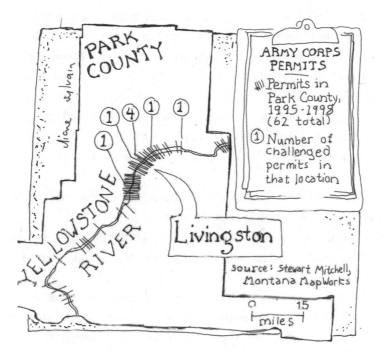

"The Yellowstone symbolizes what I see as the real spirit of Montanans," said Rob Hazelwood, who works for the U.S. Fish and Wildlife Service in Helena, "yet it's that very quality we're trying hard to control and tame."

When I paddle it—and I have paddled every one of the six hundred miles between the Yellowstone Park boundary at Gardiner, Montana, and the confluence with the Missouri River just across the border into North Dakota—I am gripped in a schizophrenic embrace, hot and cold, anger and joy, rejuvenation and despair.

Coasting around one bend, there will be white pelicans on a gravel bar and a mule deer bounding up a cliff scarp; around the next, the oil and gas refineries of Laurel will stink up the place. On one stretch I could be with William Clark, cruising downriver in hollow cottonwood trees on the way back from the Pacific in 1806, seeing the country new. Around the next bend, it's another six thousand-square-foot summer mansion going up on the bank or a steel wall slammed into the channel to protect someone's Kentucky bluegrass sod.

Back in the last century, the Yellowstone dodged the fate of a major dam, a fate that befell every other significant river in the West. As a result, it remains unique—the only big western river outside of Alaska that operates largely the way a river should, which is to say that it is unpredictable. It still builds and moves its islands, creates and abandons its channels, erodes its banks, regenerates its cottonwood groves. All things that dam-controlled rivers either don't do at all, or do in a severely handicapped way. The nearby Missouri River is a perfect example of a controlled river.

"I've traveled a lot," said Hazelwood, "and the Yellowstone is some of the best riparian habitat still left in the West."

Yet it also floods: the Yellowstone burst its banks during the summers of 1996 and 1997, when supposedly rare hundred-year floods hit twice in a row.

Suddenly, the river everyone wanted to cozy up to was eroding its channel, acre by expensive acre, toppling entire groves of mature cottonwoods and taking them downstream as battering rams. The floods captured world-renowned and big-dollar spring-creek fisheries, took out bridges, drowned houses south of Livingston to the first-floor windowsills, turned pastureland into fields you could plant rice in, and gobbled up the occasional home. The river did all this, not just once, but twice, back to back.

Two years running, late-season storms built massive snowpacks in the mountains. Cool, wet weather persisted into early summer. Then, when the heat came on, meltwater roared into the drainage in an astonishing, prolonged rush. At the gauge in Livingston, floodwaters crested at more than thirty-seven thousand cubic-feet per second (cfs). Between May 23 and June 28, 1997, 82.4 billion cubic-feet of river whistled past the gauge, a tremendous slug of water by anyone's reckoning.

The floods definitely got people's attention. Landowners along the watershed were scared silly by the power of water. Witnessing the abrupt erosive changes wrought by flooding, owners of vulnerable land felt the threat to their property on a visceral level. Given the siege mentality, to ask whether people should have built along the banks in the first place, and why building along the banks continues to go on unabated, was not a popular stance to take.

Montana's Park County offers a stunning example of landowner reaction to the flooding. The outburst of micromanagement measures taken along the river corridor, a phenomenon that environmental groups like the Greater Yellowstone Coalition (GYC) started calling "riprap anarchy," was staggering. (Riprap is stone or concrete laid along a riverbank to prevent erosion.) In the twenty years between 1975 and 1995, the Army Corps of Engineers issued thirty-eight permits for Yellowstone River projects in Park County. In the next three years, the corps approved eighty-two permits in that county alone.

Principal among them were a one-and-one-half-mile levee in the town of Livingston, at a cost of $500,000, to protect schools, a city park, and residential areas in the floodplain; and $800,000 worth of riprap, rock barbs, root wads, diking, bank stabilization, and channelization measures taken after the '96 flood to prevent the Yellowstone from capturing Armstrong Spring Creek, south of Livingston.

The '97 flood took out most of the spring-creek fortifications in a matter of days. The hastily constructed Livingston levee was almost completely dismantled by the Corps in 1999, largely because of complaints from local residents who like having access to the river.

According to Dennis Glick of the GYC, "the Corps rarely objects to a permit. They said no to fewer than five permit requests, by our estimates.

"In some instances, landowners went ahead with projects without bothering with permits in the first place, or ignored the recommendations made by the Corps," he added. "The Corps doesn't, in reality, act either as an enforcement or overseeing agency. They act as a permitting agency."

Landowner reaction to the permitting system runs the gamut. Ursula Neese, who owns a remodeled, one-hundred-year-old farmhouse on the riverbank south of Livingston, calls the permitting process "bogus." But just across the river, where Andrew Dana's family partnership has controlled a large section of riverfront property, including Nelson Spring Creek, for some thirty years, Dana said that the permitting ordeal they were put through by the Corps was "one of the most stressful times of my life.".

To complicate matters, what one landowner does upstream usually affects property owners downstream. Laying riprap along banks, for example, hardens the river channel so current speeds up and hits the next corner with greater erosive power. The upshot is a kind of domino effect rippling down the watershed as neighbors react to what upstream landowners have done. At this writing, more than eleven miles of Park County riverbank along the Yellowstone have been lined with riprap, not to mention dozens of jetties, barbs, weirs, and levees that have also gone in.

It wasn't long after the flooding that a chorus of concern began to gather. Some people wondered whether there might be worse fates than a big dam; whether the Yellowstone was well along in the process of being nibbled to death. The GYC's Glick noted that "the Yellowstone may not have a dam across it, but in some places it looks like we're working to put one in all along it!'

One federal agency was alarmed: in a letter to the U.S. Army Corps of Engineers, the U.S. Fish and Wildlife Service warned that the Corps' "bank stabilization projects could destroy cottonwood forests, deepen the streambed, threaten riparian vegetation, and adversely impact fish and wildlife." In another letter, the federal wildlife agency warned that "the Yellowstone River is moving towards [becoming] an armored channel."

And why, wondered the GYC's Mike Clark, hadn't any lessons been learned from the major flooding on the Missouri and Mississippi rivers in the early '90s? "How could the Corps reconcile spending millions dismantling riverbank structures and relocating residents after recognizing the failure of their flood-control strategies along the Missouri and Mississippi rivers," he asked, "while simultaneously granting dozens of permits for the same kinds of projects along the Yellowstone? We can't afford to make the same mistakes we've made elsewhere."

Allan Steinle, program manager for the Corps in Helena, Montana, says the Corps "isn't charged with managing the river. We apply our regulations and guidelines, on a case-by-case basis, with the information available. We work hard to modify projects to comply with our requirements."

Steinle said it is true that the agency doesn't always get out to inspect project sites. "Given the funding constraints, we have to stratify our efforts. But when landowners ask the government for help," he added, "it's not realistic to ask a government agency to tell landowners that they can't protect their property."

Park County residents, led by Livingston businessman John Bailey, convinced Governor Mark Racicot, in November 1997, to convene an Upper Yellowstone River task force to look at the proliferation of bank-stabilization projects with a fresh eye. The governor appointed twelve voting members representing constituencies including ranchers, anglers, conservationists, and other stakeholders, while another eight nonvoting members speak on behalf of state and federal agencies involved in the Yellowstone River's watershed.

The task force was given one of those inherently problematic mandates: "to ensure that upper Yellowstone River integrity remains intact, while balancing the needs of our communities and landowners."

In a recent interview, Chairman Bailey said he was optimistic, given the progress achieved by the group in its first two years. "If you had told me that we'd already have $1.5 million in watershed studies under way and a $300,000 commitment from the state legislature, I wouldn't have believed you."

The Corps' Steinle agreed that "the task force has really helped focus attention and resources in a way that couldn't have been done earlier."

Far more important than the data the group is collecting, Bailey said, is the broad-spectrum, consensus-based approach. "I believe that the educational process we're going through is more important than any specific end result.

"When the next issue comes up, I plan on being here, and I'll know where to go for data," he added. "Then we can head off problems before they happen. That's one thing you can't measure—the damage that never gets done because we were able to avoid it."

Liz Galli-Noble, who was recently hired as task force coordinator, agreed that "science has to lead the way." She has faith that patience and open-mindedness will be rewarded by good long-term management results.

Not everyone is as sanguine.

Mark Albers, director of American Rivers' Montana field office in Great Falls, echoed the sentiments of the conservation community when he cautioned, "It remains to be seen if the task force has the will to make the hard decisions required to protect and restore their portion of the Yellowstone."

While conservation groups support the efforts of the task force, some are also suing. In May 1999, the Montana Council of Trout Unlimited, along with the Greater Yellowstone Coalition and a bevy of other environmental groups, took the Corps to court, frustrated with what they saw as an out-of-control river-management process.

"Things had already gone to hell," said Glick. "Our lawsuit was a last resort. Someone had to put the brakes on."

The suit claims that in awarding scores of permits the Corps ignored its duty to carry out "cumulative impact analyses required by the National Environmental Policy Act, the Clean Water Act, and their implementing regulations." The suit also charges that "the Corps' failure to adequately consider the cumulative impacts fatally undermines the Corps' conclusions—that the projects' environmental impacts will be insignificant."

Among twenty pages of supporting evidence, the lawsuit cites warnings expressed by the Environmental Protection Agency in 1998, over the "piecemeal approach to addressing bank erosion" and the "cumulative adverse effects on the environment."

"First we need to put a moratorium on permits," said GYC lawyer Steve Mashuda. "Then we need a cumulative environmental impact statement to assess the entire drainage. Only then can we really consider our options. Our case is only the first step in addressing a very complex problem."

The lawsuit is now being considered by the U.S. District Court in Billings, with a decision expected sometime this spring.

The river's plight gained more visibility last year when American Rivers added the entire Yellowstone watershed to its list of the Ten Most Endangered Rivers. Mark Albers said American Rivers' campaign for the Yellowstone includes the ambitious hope of enrolling 50 percent of the river's meander zone in a conservation easement program by 2004; aiding fish migration past diversion dams and irrigation intakes; and increasing citizen awareness of what the river requires to remain wild.

Meantime, even some of the people who are fully committed to the less confrontational, broad-spectrum posture taken by the task force are wary about the political will to take appropriate action.

Chairman Bailey bemoaned the decision of the city of Livingston to build a new public school smack in the river's floodplain, even after the floods. "It was common knowledge that the site is actually below the level of the river!" he said.

Duncan Patten, a riparian expert and technical consultant to the task force, explained that it's "people issues, not scientific data, that drive this process."

A case in point is a wildlife study that Patten wanted the task force to fund. "The consensus process shot that study down," he said.

At the January 12 task force evening meeting in Livingston, the wildlife study was again brought up for discussion. Quickly, Jerry O'Hare, a second-generation landowner in Paradise Valley, whose property includes lucrative spring-creek fisheries, derailed any hope for the study.

"I talked to other landowners in the valley," said O'Hare. "Not one of them was for it."

For the next hour, the task force and citizens in the audience discussed the wildlife issue, all the while knowing that O'Hare's resistance had already rendered the issue moot. Fear of biologists coming onto someone's property and uncovering an endangered species was repeatedly brought up as the bogeyman in the background.

At one point in the discussion, Bailey joked, with more candor than he perhaps intended, "Our biggest problem is making a recommendation—on anything!"

Around ten o'clock, the task force moved on to wordsmithing the annual report, an excruciating process with a decided bent toward making language more general and less controversial.

I kept escaping the stultifying basement atmosphere by running mental snapshots of what the river feels like firsthand. Only a few blocks away, the river whispered through the cold night. I pictured the muscling power of current roaring through big standing waves in Gardiner; the eerie, boat-torquing upwellings at Box Car Rapid in Yankee Jim Canyon; the sheer yellow rock rising out of the flow below Columbus; the wide river feeling its way through herds of islands near Sidney.

It came to me that nowhere during the meeting had I heard the voice of that river. It was why we had all gathered on this chilly, January night, but I never once heard what the water needs to survive.

What I heard instead were the voices of landowners who spoke fervently of the great risk they faced by allowing a study of wildlife on their property, a risk, they said, with no corresponding reward.

No one suggested that the reward might be what we were all ostensibly here for in the first place—to reclaim and nourish some semblance of this river that in powerful and direct ways serves to sustain every one of us. No one said that the real risk was not that a biologist might trip over a hitherto unknown endangered species, but that we might not do what is needed on behalf of the Yellowstone.

Somewhere near midnight, the last bit of wording was massaged into paragraphs, and the meeting ended. Outside, standing by my car in the snow, I listened hard through the darkness for the river I knew was running nearby, but could only catch the late-night, midwinter sounds of a small Montana town.

March 27, 2000

Alan Kesselheim lives in Bozeman, Montana.

We Can Still Do Right by the Yellowstone

Scott Bischke

Last summer, my wife, Katie Gibson, and I traveled the length of the Yellowstone River, 678 miles from its source on Yount's Peak in Wyoming's Teton Wilderness to its confluence with the Missouri River, just inside North Dakota.

We walked through the wild headwaters country and Yellowstone Park, then paddled over five hundred miles from the park boundary across eastern Montana. We ran into grizzlies and wildfires, watched soaring eagles and pelicans, listened to the slap of beaver tails and the croaky staccato of sandhill cranes, and sat through soul-stirring sunsets.

Throughout the thirty-one-day trip, Kate and I marveled at what a special gift the Yellowstone River is, not only to those of us in south-central and eastern Montana, but also to all Americans. For here in our backyard, unbelievably, runs a river almost wild and almost free. Not undammed, because there are six irrigation weirs that cross the entire river, but flowing without interruption. This is a river still largely connected to its floodplain, with naturally braiding channels and uncontrolled spring runoffs that reshape the riverbed.

Just think of it: Elsewhere in our country wild salmon can't survive the replumbed waterworks of the Pacific Northwest. Millions are being spent to rip down or study the ripping down of ill-conceived dams. Hundreds of millions are being spent to restore the Napa River and reconnect it with its floodplain. Fish fight for their lives to survive the toxic cesspools of our polluted mining fiascos, Montana's upper Clark Fork River being a prime example. Everywhere in the West we are dewatering our streams until they look like gravel roadbeds each summer.

In the midst of these attempts to control and manipulate nature, the Yellowstone River runs on. It is a river that for much of its length William Clark might still recognize as the waterway he traveled eastward near the conclusion of his expedition with Lewis, in 1806.

That's not to say that the Yellowstone doesn't have its share of ecological challenges. Lake trout are displacing native cutthroat trout in Yellowstone Lake and threatening to destroy the food-source foundation of an entire ecosystem. Whirling disease has been found both inside and outside the park, further threatening fisheries. Septic spills from under-funded tourist facilities threaten the park's surface and subsurface waters, and by extension its major waterway, the Yellowstone River. Just outside of the park's boundary, near Gardiner, a gold mine has been proposed for an island in the middle of the river.

In Montana's Paradise Valley, the pressure to build homes in the floodplain is relentless. Developers and landowners prosper; natural riverine processes suffer. Riprap throughout the river's length protects private property but sterilizes the river. With the river disconnected from its floodplain, habitat is lost to fish and wildlife. Island formation and erosion and the great natural interplay of cottonwoods and beavers are disrupted. And when the energy of spring floods cannot dissipate naturally, they instead wreak havoc in non-armored areas.

From Paradise Valley to Sydney, the river serves as our source of industrial cooling and process water. It supplies our drinking water and accepts our municipal, industrial, and agricultural wastes. We draw life-giving agricultural irrigation waters throughout the length of the Yellowstone below Gardiner, regularly dropping water levels so low that cries for dams ring out even today. For example, operators of the Corette Power Plant proposed damming the river at Billings as recently as June 2001.

Even within the context of these challenges, the Yellowstone River remains the longest free-flowing river in the Lower Forty-Eight, providing a continuous linkage between Wyoming's rugged Teton Wilderness, Yellowstone Park, Livingston's Paradise Valley, the rimrock country around my original home town of Billings, and the agricultural lands of eastern Montana.

Yes, there are challenges, but those challenges are not yet the controlling factors of the river: we still have the opportunity to do something right with the Yellowstone. Limits to floodplain development and riprapping, maintenance of in-stream flows, protection of water quality from ill-planned mining, agricultural, or industrial practices, and more can help retain the natural character of the river.

We have opportunities still for protecting the Yellowstone River, but even more we have responsibilities to the generations yet to come. I want them to have a chance to know this magnificent river as Kate and I have come to know it, as it flows wild and free beneath the Big Sky.

June 30, 2003

Scott Bischke is a chemical and environmental engineer in Bozeman, Montana, as well as a freelance writer.

Riparian Restoration

Catch 22

Joshua Zaffos

It's a Thursday morning in October, and I count fifty-eight vehicles in the parking lot next to the "Texas Hole" of the San Juan River. A mile or so downstream of the four hundred and two-foot-high dam, this stretch of water is named for the Texans who used to fish for trout here with garlic cheese. Bait fishing is no longer allowed, and the Texas Hole has developed a near-mythic reputation among fly fishers for the finicky trout that hunker deep in the pool.

The San Juan River is home to a wriggling trout fishery that has flourished since the Navajo Dam was completed in 1962. The New Mexico Department of Game and Fish began stocking trout soon after the dam's completion, and in order to ensure the trout's success, the agency eradicated "rough fish," poisoning native species such as the Colorado pikeminnow and the razorback sucker. Since then, the river downstream of the dam has been called the "classic western tailwater trout fishery" by ESPN Outdoors, and people come from as far away as Japan to fish its waters. Biologists estimate there are two thousand trout per mile, each fish an average seventeen inches long.

That may soon change: this September, the Bureau of Reclamation released a draft environmental impact statement outlining steps to restore the native pikeminnow and sucker, both protected under the Endangered Species Act. The recovery plan aims to undo some of the damage that will be caused by the Animas-La Plata project, the last great project of the go-go dam-building era, which received final approval in 2001.

On the surface, the Bureau's intentions appear admirable. But critics say the recovery plan is just another ruse to take water from this beleaguered river for farms in the desert and homes and lawns in growing cities. In addition, the plan would likely decimate the trout fishery and the local economy that depends on it.

The Navajo Dam put the pikeminnow and sucker in a vise. Confined by Navajo Dam upstream and Lake Powell and Glen Canyon Dam downstream, the few fish that remained were restricted to one-third of their original habitat in the San Juan.

The Animas-La Plata project, first authorized in 1968, promised to tighten the screws by diverting water from the Animas and La Plata rivers, tributaries that feed the San Juan forty-five miles downstream of Navajo Dam, near the city of Farmington. The two rivers provide spring floods that create essential habitat for juvenile pikeminnows and suckers.

Over two decades, Animas-La Plata was scaled down, but in its final form, it will still divert water from the Animas River. To remedy the project's negative impacts on native fish, the Bureau called for water releases from Navajo Dam that would "mimic a natural hydrograph," releasing spring peak flows to simulate floods.

But spring releases from Navajo Dam will mean less water behind the dam during summer months, when Indian and Anglo farmers and New Mexico cities are thirsting for it. So, the Bureau reasoned, high spring flows will have to be offset; the river could be reduced to half its current size for all but a few weeks out of the year.

Ron Bliesner, an environmental consultant for several tribes with stakes in Navajo Reservoir, says the recovery plan is a trade-off: "You need to keep as much water stored [behind the dam] as possible. The [endangered] fish need a certain amount of water and the [water-development] projects need a certain amount of water." Water for other purposes, such as the trout fishery, must be restricted.

So far, the Navajo Nation has been the only water player on the San Juan to embrace the plan because it ensures water for tribal farmers. But businesses, citizens, and government officials in the local towns of Farmington and Bloomfield oppose the Bureau's plan because the low flows will negatively impact wastewater treatment, hydroelectric production, and tourism.

Perhaps most directly affected by the plan are the outfitters and guides who lead trout-fishing trips below Navajo Dam. They argue that the recovery plan could send the San Juan trout fishery into a biological and economic tailspin.

Rob DaCosta is a fishing guide with a fisheries biology degree. Across the counter of his fly shop, Float'n Fish, he tells me the low summer flows will eliminate habitat, reduce aquatic insects that fish eat, increase water temperature, promote disease, and exacerbate angling pressure upon trout.

In addition, the low flows would make it impossible to float guided boat trips on the river—trips that DaCosta and ninety other guides lead for about $300 a pop. According to the San Juan Guide Association, river outfitters could lose more than $3 million if the Bureau's plan is implemented.

My room at Abe's Motel—the oldest fishing lodge in the community of Navajo Dam—doesn't have a working smoke detector or door lock. But Abe's offers guests a wide variety of flies in its shop, a hook outside each room to hang and dry waders, and the services of fishing guides "born 'n' raised" below Navajo Dam. It's obvious what draws people here: it's not the accommodations, but the lunker trout that live downstream of the dam.

These trout mean little to some environmentalists, who favor native fish and wild rivers over tamed trout streams. Members of the Moab, Utah-based environmental group Living Rivers have turned up at public meetings dressed as Colorado pikeminnows and razorback suckers, blasting the Bureau's plan as insufficient and arguing that the only way to recover the native fish is to remove both Navajo and Glen Canyon dams.

That will obviously not happen anytime soon. But many biologists agree that the Bureau's proposal seems to hold little hope for the native fish. Spring floods will help, but the low flows will lead to only "marginal improvements" in habitat for the pikeminnow and sucker, according to Marc Wethington, San Juan River biologist for New Mexico Game and Fish.

U.S. Fish and Wildlife Service biologist Mike Buntjer adds that the Bureau's plan will meet the minimum, rather than the optimal, habitat requirements of the fish.

Still, the Bureau has offered up a brutal—and paradoxical—choice: either roll the dice on a modest recovery for native fish and destroy the trout fishery, or maintain the trout fishery to the detriment of the native fish. And the Endangered Species Act dictates that between native fish and introduced trout, the natives win out.

But the demise of the trout fishery may not be worth the price of modest native fish restoration—and it may not be necessary.

Michael Black of Taxpayers for the Animas River, a citizens' group that has fought the Animas-La Plata project, says if flows are managed judiciously—and if farmers and urbanites are willing to share—there is enough water in the San Juan for both the native fish and the trout. "The threat to the trout doesn't come from the endangered species, it comes from water development."

But the history surrounding the Animas-La Plata project has always favored humans, and, once again, people will get their water wishes granted before fish—native or introduced.

When I return to the Texas Hole late in the evening, I can still count twenty two vehicles in the huge gravel lot. I tie on a #20 Sparkle Dun, walk to the river, and find fifty feet of the San Juan between two other fishermen. My very first cast, I hook and land one of the river's finicky brown trout. It may sound like I'm bragging, but this fish story ends on a melancholy note: this is the first trout I've ever caught on the San Juan River—and it may be the last.

December 23, 2002

Josh Zaffos writes from Fort Collins, Colorado.

Reweaving the River

Hal Clifford

The San Luis Valley is a high desert that attracts waterfowl, with table-flat farmland surrounded by mountains. It's a slice of Colorado that feels like New Mexico, and almost everyone here is bilingual. Many locals trace their roots back to when this was part of Mexico's northern borderlands, before the Mexican-American War of 1848.

But this remote area entered headlines just over a decade ago, when cyanide-holding ponds at the Summitville gold mine failed spectacularly and poisoned the Alamosa River, which runs through the village of Capulin. The 1990 spill killed everything living in a seventeen-mile stretch of the river, and turned a national media spotlight on the dangers of modern mining.

Here in Conejos County, the spill also forced residents to recognize that they had mismanaged the river for a generation. Summitville was the final insult. Now, more than a hundred local people are rebuilding the Alamosa into a river that, while not pristine, will look and act much more like the river their grandparents knew. "We're farmers and ranchers," says fifth-generation farmer Alan Miller, forty-two, from beneath a sweat-stained hat. "It's not a bunch of thirty-something yuppie environmentalists."

The Alamosa River's problems began in 1970, when heavy rain blew out an upstream dam that was under repair, filling the river with a cascade of channel-clogging silt. That winter, ice dams created floods that inundated Capulin. The U.S. Army Corps of Engineers responded by doing what the Corps did best back then, and turned much of the river into a ditch.

The flooding subsided, but new problems arose. The channelized river carved into the alluvial soils, slicing ten feet down in places. The water table dropped, drying up the streamside riparian areas and adjacent fields. As the river ate into the earth, dozens of ditch companies that drew from the Alamosa found their headgates—which direct river water into irrigation ditches—perched high above the river.

In the late 1970s, Miller's uncle tried to create a coalition to restore the river. But his effort foundered, and a decade later he died. Nothing changed ... until the Summitville holding ponds, which were full of heavy metals and cyanide used in the heap-leach gold mine, failed. The mining company declared bankruptcy in 1992, and the area became a Superfund site.

"Summitville really kicked us in the pants," says Miller. While the state and the Environmental Protection Agency tackled the pollution generated by the spill (a cleanup that has cost $160 million to date), Miller and other county residents revived the effort to restore the river's channel and natural functions.

They formed the Alamosa River Watershed Foundation in 1999, a nonprofit that can apply for and accept grants. It's the outgrowth of the Alamosa River Watershed Project, which was set up in 1995 by the local office of the federal Natural Resources Conservation Service and the Alamosa-La Jara Water Conservancy District. By last spring, Miller, the foundation field coordinator, found himself in charge of a $1.1 million budget dedicated to river restoration.

Most of the funds came in the form of $759,000 in grants from the EPA, Colorado Water Conservation Board, Ducks Unlimited, the North American Wetlands Conservation Act, and the water conservancy district. Another $355,000 in in-kind contributions is coming from landowners, the Natural Resources Conservation Service, and the Conejos County government.

The foundation completed a small demonstration project near Ignacio Rodriguez's horse ranch in 2000, and this spring, tiny cottonwood seedlings were sprouting. Rodriguez, seventy-six, used to catch his limit of brown and rainbow trout in the river here. Restoration, Rodriguez says, "would very definitely give the community a sense of constructive involvement. They would have accomplished something."

In Conejos County, the second-poorest county in Colorado, that would count for a lot.

"My interest is to fix the river," says John Shawcroft, seventy-eight, who ranches on the meadows at its eastern end and heads up the Alamosa-La

Jara Water Conservancy District. Better songbird habitat isn't at the top of Shawcroft's wish list, but a river that gets farmers more water will also benefit the other creatures that depend on it.

People may not agree precisely on what they want for the river, but they know that "they don't like the way it is," says Ben Rizzi, with the La Jara field office of the Natural Resources Conservation Service.

Miller intends to place nine thousand refrigerator-sized boulders in 4.5 miles of river this year. The rocks won't be used as riprap along the banks; rather, they'll be placed in the river to direct the flow of the river upon itself, to slow and pool its waters. It is the aikido form of civil engineering.

"We plan to shorten the stream's evolution by a hundred years," says Miller, who adds that the foundation will plant grasses and trees to stabilize the river's banks. In places, the river will return to its old meanders. Sediment will pile up where there is only cobble now, and willows and cottonwoods are likely to sprout soon. The water table will rise. Ranchers will move their cattle out of the riparian zone for two years, while people see what the new river looks like and decide what happens next.

Miller's project covers less than 10 percent of the river's length. But it has taken a generation to get this far. As Miller strolls the bank near Rodriguez's ranch, he recognizes that he is building not only a river, but also a community of people who are invested in the waterway.

"This is what the river is about," he says, pointing to a headgate. "We're using it. But we can use it wisely. You've got to give the resource back to the people. They've got to manage it. Who else is going to take care of it in the future?

"If we do that," he adds, "there probably won't be another Summitville."

September 29, 2003

Hal Clifford is the executive editor of *Orion* magazine and the cofounder of the communication services firm Drift Storytelling.

"Restoration Cowboy" Goes against the Flow

Joshua Zaffos

There's a man standing on the bank of the Weminuche River in southern Colorado, telling forty-five people who just shuffled off a tour bus how to restore a river. Stop, he says, chew a toothpick, and think about what you're doing. "Sometimes you just need to sit and drink a beer."

The man is Dave Rosgen, and he's wearing a white cowboy hat and a belt buckle bigger than his fist. The outfit is authentic. When he's not teaching stream restoration to government scientists and private consultants, Rosgen drives a Cadillac or rides cutting horses. *National Geographic* has called him "the Restoration Cowboy."

A former U.S. Forest Service hydrologist, Rosgen struck out on his own and started a private firm, Wildland Hydrology, in 1985. His mission is to repair rivers that have been dammed and straightened, restore streambanks that have been armored with riprap and gabions (think of shopping carts filled with rock), and revive overgrazed floodplains and streambeds mined for gravel.

Rosgen embodies a new generation of river managers who champion "natural channel design," the art of making rivers look and function like rivers rather than canals. During the last fifteen years, over fourteen thousand hydrologists, engineers, biologists, and ecologists from around the world have taken Rosgen's courses.

But not everyone is ready to follow this brash, righteous cowboy into the sunset. Some academics and consultants believe Rosgen is misleading the masses with an oversimplified approach to a complex field of science.

"What is fluvial geomorphology?" Rosgen asks the class on the opening morning of his introductory course. "Fluvial geomorphology is the study of landforms shaped by water." The forty-five participants hail from almost every

249

western state, as well as Michigan, North Carolina, and New Jersey. They represent federal agencies, state environmental departments, tribes, and private consultants, and they've each paid $1,500 to be here.

Over the course of five days, these pupils will learn the basics of Rosgen's stream classification system, which uses a simple alphanumeric code (such as A2, C4, G1) based primarily on the river's slope and the size of the gravel and rock in its bed. The system distills geomorphology, helping people to assess the health of streams and apply restoration techniques, which Rosgen also shares with the class.

Rosgen first tried his approach on the East Fork of the San Juan River in southern Colorado, one of the stops on his course's bus tour. Back in 1986, the East Fork was an overgrazed stream with a braided channel and eroding banks. Rosgen restored the river to a single meandering channel by using bulldozers and front-end loaders to arrange massive, native cottonwood trunks and quarter-ton boulders.

Rosgen's students recognize the project's success seventeen years later: trout hide in deep pools and willows cover gravel bars. Visits to other sites like the Weminuche and scores of projects by colleagues and former students win over the class before the end of the week.

"Without question, Dave is the most outstanding practitioner of small-river restoration in the United States," says Luna Leopold, the father of modern fluvial geomorphology and son of conservation pioneer Aldo Leopold. But classification systems, by definition, simplify things—and it's easy to oversimplify them. Few of Rosgen's students have strong backgrounds in engineering and geomorphology and, on average, less than half of the class will return for additional advanced courses. So Rosgen shows photos to the class of failed projects where people misapplied his system: "That's what I call crapping your chaps in the saddle and sitting in it."

Critics say Rosgen and his classes encourage messy saddles.

"It really takes a high level of expertise to restore a river," says David Montgomery, a University of Washington geomorphology professor who has created his own stream classification system. "The thing I fear most about [Rosgen's] courses is he may be over-empowering people, making them think they know more than they do."

An example is Uvas Creek in California, where, in 1995, a river manager tried to turn a braided channel into a meandering one. Uvas Creek had never been a meandering stream, and within four months of "restoration," the creek had washed out, abandoned the single channel, and returned to its braided wanderings.

Scott Gillilan, a Bozeman, Montana-based hydrologist who runs Gillilan Associates, says such failures occur because Rosgen offers a "cookbook" approach to restoration.

Gillilan and others resent the "disciples" who question restoration projects that don't use the Rosgen system. Adding to the resentment is the fact that the Forest Service has adopted Rosgen's method as its standard classification system. Nearly a dozen states require contractors to take Rosgen's courses in order to bid on stream monitoring or restoration projects.

Rosgen says the classification is "only the start" of a successful restoration project. "There's fifty steps of analysis that I use in natural channel design," he says. "That's not a cookbook."

Many critics recognize that the Rosgen classification system is a useful communication tool and for now, at least, it's the leading one of its kind.

"The thing I don't see," says Montgomery, the Washington professor, "is anyone asking, 'Who can do anything better?' "

"People say, 'Rosgen, you make people dangerous. You teach them for one week,' " Rosgen tells his students, many of whom are already tackling stream restoration projects. "Well, after listening to your backgrounds, you're already dangerous."

November 10, 2003

Josh Zaffos writes from Fort Collins, Colorado.

Persistence Frees the Mokelumne

Tim Holt

California's Mokelumne (pronounced *ma-call-a-mi*) River flows from a high mountain lake in the Sierra Nevada, plunging down in a series of cascading waterfalls through a steep forest canyon in the foothills. Dams and diversions have reduced the once free-flowing river to a relative trickle. But that is changing, thanks in large part to the efforts of a gravel-voiced river-lover.

Pete Bell, fifty-three, is a former rock drummer who now makes his living as a sound and recording engineer. For the past twenty-four years, he's lived high up on a ridge near the tiny foothill town of Volcano, and he's passionate about restoring the river that flows near his home.

Bell spent most of the 1990s defending the Mokelumne Watershed, fighting off a proposed dam, and monitoring timber sales that threatened to send soil eroding into waterways. More recently, using an obscure 1986 law, he has helped get three dams removed from the watershed, and his efforts will lead to increased river flows from nine other dams. Yet Bell is neither a fisherman nor a recreational boater—he's simply someone who loves rivers for their own sake.

"There's something about free-flowing water that's almost magical," he says.

Early on in his river crusade, Bell found a little-known tool attached to the 1920 Federal Power Act, which gives the U.S. government control over hydroelectric dams. Under the act, dam operators are required to renew their federal licenses every thirty to fifty years.

In the early years of hydropower, relicensing agreements were usually sweetheart deals. Government biologists won some concessions for sport fisheries, but they largely gave utilities whatever water flows they needed to generate power.

Then, in 1986, Congress amended the Federal Power Act, requiring the Federal Energy Regulatory Commission (FERC) to consider the health not only of fish, but also of the entire river ecosystem. Recreational opportunities had to be considered as well. Fourteen years later, the amendment gave Bell a seat at the negotiating table, when the Mokelumne became one of the first of the new, all-inclusive relicensing efforts in the United States.

The effort brought together not only Pacific Gas and Electric, the utility company that operates the dams, but also sport boaters, sport fishers, and seven government agencies. Bell, as a representative of the local environmental group, the Foothill Conservancy, was the only volunteer at the table during thirteen months of negotiations.

Bell worked hard to convince Pacific Gas and Electric to remove three small dams on tributaries of the Mokelumne. He pointed out that these dams had become clogged with silt and hadn't been used for power generation since 1996. Even when they were operating, they generated less than one percent of the Mokelumne project's electricity.

"He just refused to let go of that issue. He was adamant about getting those dams removed," says Stafford Lehr, a state Fish and Game biologist who sat alongside Bell at the negotiating table.

Bell was persistent—and he was also passionate. Early in the negotiations, the group got sidetracked with a lengthy discussion of how improved stream flows might affect the utility company's bottom line. Bell lost his cool, arguing that the health of the river should take priority over profits.

"I could see the agency people nodding their heads in agreement," he recalls. "They were in sympathy with what I was saying, but they didn't have the luxury of expressing the kind of outrage I did. For me, it really reinforced why I needed to be at that table."

Ultimately, Pacific Gas and Electric agreed to take out the three dams, under a relicensing agreement completed in July 2001. As a result, three creeks in the watershed will flow freely for the first time in more than seventy years.

"It was a matter of achieving sustainable balance," says David Moller, chief negotiator for the utility. "The generation impacts of these three dams was modest, whereas the ecological impacts seemed to be substantial."

In order to restore the Mokelumne, the utility company also gave up some of the water that had been diverted through its power-generating turbines. Stream flows will be increased dramatically in the critical spring months, to wash sediment and debris from stream channels, distribute nutrients, and trigger fish spawning.

But Bell's work is not over yet: he is now part of the team monitoring the river's health. Every five years, the team will measure the density of vegetation, fish populations, and "all the other bugs and critters," as Bell puts it, to see if the increased flows are meeting objectives.

The Mokelumne agreement is being used as a model for relicensing negotiations throughout the United States. With some one hundred aging dams coming up for relicensing over the next fifteen years in California alone, conservationists say they have a rare window of opportunity. In Bell's region, the Stanislaus, Feather, and American rivers are currently in negotiation, as is another major river system, the Klamath, that straddles Oregon and California.

Bell is working with the California Hydropower Reform Coalition to educate citizens about the 1986 Power Act amendment.

What advice does Bell have for fellow river-lovers before they plunge into relicensing negotiations? "It comes down to persistence and building relationships and doing your homework," he says.

"And," he adds, "getting passionate at the right time can be very helpful."

March 15, 2004

Tim Holt is a freelance journalist and author who lives in the Mount Shasta region of Northern California.

Seattle Embarks on a Dramatic Experiment in Restoration

David Williams

At first glance, the forest looks like an area in the initial stages of harvesting by a timber company. A stack of logs sits by a dirt road not far from a harvester-processor, a tractor-mounted machine with a thirty-foot-long arm that cuts, de-limbs, and piles up trees. Behind the logs, stumps poke up through the understory of leathery-leaved salal. Farther down the road, a brush-covered track winds into a grove of telephone pole-sized Douglas firs, many painted with either a thin blue or thin red line.

This isn't the work of loggers, however: ecologists employed by the city of Seattle are behind it. Ironically, the goal of the so-called "45 Road Forest Restoration Project" is to start to reverse the negative impacts of a century of cutting throughout the Cedar River Watershed, the source for 70 percent of Seattle's drinking water. Seattle Public Utilities, which manages this watershed, is experimenting with a variety of techniques that should make this young forest function ecologically more like the grand old-growth stands that once grew here.

The ecologists' tools include selective thinning, tree planting, and practices that are more experimental, such as planting lichens and mosses in the forest canopy.

Jerry Franklin, professor of ecosystem science at the University of Washington, and one of the deans of restoration ecology, says the work in the Cedar River Watershed is on the cutting edge of forest restoration. "People suggest that once you walk away from [a forest] you can leave it alone and that it will take care of itself. It's not true. Nature will adjust, but you won't like the outcome. You'll lose values. You'll lose big old trees. You'll lose owls. You'll lose watershed protection."

Understanding the scene in Seattle's watershed requires a trip back to June 6, 1889, when John E. Back let his pot of glue boil over onto the stove of a downtown Seattle cabinet store. Back, described in the *Seattle Post-Intelligencer* as "a thick-set blond of mediocre intelligence," tossed water on the flames, which merely spread the fire to wood shavings on the floor, and set the building ablaze. Within the hour, flames had spread to nearby sawmills, lumberyards, and creosote-coated pilings supporting city streets and buildings.

Fire crews arrived quickly, but when a messenger ordered water pumping crews to "Give her all she'll take," they responded, "We've already given her all she'll take." There wasn't enough water. Before the fire could be contained, it burned over one hundred and fifteen acres and destroyed the downtown retail and industrial core. Thirty-two days later, Seattleites approved a $1 million bond to form a publicly owned waterworks not only for firefighting, but also for drinking.

The source of that waterworks is the Cedar River, which flows west out of the Cascades from headwaters about fifty miles east of the city. Over the century following Seattle's "Great Fire," the city acquired all of the 90,546-acre Cedar River Watershed. Because the city lacked the funds to buy the land and timber rights together, however, it allowed timber companies to clear-cut 83 percent of the forests.

Logging in the watershed only ended in 1997, four years after Seattle began work on a habitat-conservation plan to protect the threatened Puget Sound chinook salmon and eighty-two other species. Early drafts of the plan proposed paying for protection by logging even more of the watershed. This inspired Seattle Mayor Paul Schell's famous quip about a city councilwoman who supported cutting: "So she wants to pay for saving the trees by cutting them? I'd like to give [the watershed] to the next generation."

Environmentalists questioned whether cutting trees was worth the estimated annual savings per family, equivalent to the cost of one latte. The final plan, passed by the city council in 2000, banned all commercial logging in the watershed.

To meet the requirements of the fifty-year habitat-conservation plan, Seattle Public Utilities is working to create better fish habitat, remove roads, and replace culverts, while keeping the drinking water clean for its 1.3 million customers. It is also cutting trees; despite the ban on commercial logging, the plan does permit thinning for ecological reasons.

Last fall, workers cut about a quarter of the 45 Road forest, which, like much of the watershed, was dominated by a dense forest of even-aged Douglas firs. Unlike an old-growth forest, these woods lacked standing and fallen dead trees, uprooted trees, canopy gaps, and a diversity of tree species and sizes. As a result, the forest wasn't providing much habitat for imperiled species. The challenge was to get to old-growth conditions without waiting a hundred years.

"As you can see, in some areas we didn't cut any trees. In others, we cut a few, and in several patches, we removed almost everything," says Melissa Borsting, a plant ecologist for Seattle Public Utilities. Foresters call this "variable density thinning" or "skips and gaps." The uneven patterns break up the second growth, leapfrogging toward the conditions found in a more mature forest. This winter, restoration crews also planted nearly seven thousand red alder, bigleaf maple, and western red cedar seedlings.

In the next restoration project, due to begin this year, crews may attach lichens to trees and import soil and logs from old-growth forests.

"Restoration is an experimental science. We have good ideas but we don't know exactly how to make old growth," says Jim Erckmann, the utilities' watershed ecosystem manager. But, he adds, "because we don't have an economic incentive, we can be more experimental."

Franklin, at the University of Washington, also praises Seattle for taking the initiative. "[Local control] is an anathema to a lot of us. That's one of the approaches that we are going to have to think more about in this century. This isn't the twentieth century. This isn't timber vs. owls."

May 10, 2004

David B. Williams is a freelance natural history writer based in Seattle, Washington.

The Hoopa's Fight for a River Is a Lesson for Us All

Tim Holt

The Hoopa Indians of Northern California are a tenacious people. In the mid-nineteenth century, when the U.S. Army tried to drive them out of their villages along the Trinity River, the Hoopas waited them out, camping in the nearby hills until the soldiers gave up and left.

One hundred years later the government started draining their river, damming it and diverting most of its waters through mountain tunnels to farmlands to the south. For the past forty years, the Hoopas have struggled in the courts and in the halls of Congress to bring their river and its fishery back to life.

Up until now, this has involved a lopsided battle between the impoverished twenty-five-hundred-member Indian tribe and Westlands, the largest irrigation district in the United States, one whose farmers grow crops worth roughly $1 billion of crops every year. But the balance of power is beginning to tilt in favor of the Indians, a seismic shift in California water politics that has been a couple of decades in the making.

Last July, a three-judge panel of the Ninth Circuit Court of Appeals ordered the permanent restoration of nearly half the Trinity's historic flows. The increased flows are part of a broader Trinity-restoration program launched four years earlier by then-Interior Secretary Bruce Babbitt. It had been blocked by a lawsuit filed by the Westlands Water District, representing the farmers of the San Joaquin Valley, who may still make a last-ditch appeal to the Supreme Court.

The judges' decision bodes well not only for the Hoopas and their river but for the cause of restoring ravaged watersheds throughout the West. The decision, stripped down to its essentials, says that minimum standards for the health of a river take precedence over the demands of water consumers.

The Hoopas are looking out for their own interests, to be sure, but with their growing clout they're adding a new perspective to the debate over California's water supplies. They view their river as a life-sustaining force, not a commodity to be drained. The San Joaquin Valley farmers, by contrast, began siphoning off the Trinity only after they'd depleted their groundwater and tapped out the rivers in their region. In their view, a river that flows to the sea is a waste of water. In the Indians' view, a river that flows naturally to the sea produces a healthy fishery. For all but forty of the past ten thousand years, that has been the basic tenet of their survival.

The next big task facing the Hoopas is restoring their river, whose configuration was dramatically transformed by four decades of minimum flows. Heavy equipment will be needed to remove brush and sediment that filled up the old river's side pools. These quiet pools are crucial to the rearing of juvenile fish.

The seeds of the Hoopas' victory were planted back in the 1980s, when they began hiring some well-connected and highly respected advocates, including Seattle-based attorney Tom Schlosser, who specializes in tribal law, and Washington, D. C., lobbyist Joe Membrino, who helped shepherd through a series of laws that put the Congress on record in support of the Trinity's restoration. That, and countless studies by federal biologists, led to Secretary Babbitt's order to dramatically increase the river's flows to 47 percent of their historic levels, the minimum needed, the studies showed, to increase fish populations to sustainable levels.

The environmentalism of the Hoopas, like that of West Coast commercial fishermen who fight for clean, free-flowing streams, grows out of their livelihood and their way of life. But the Hoopas' commitment goes even deeper than that of the fishermen: the salmon the Hoopas fight for are a centerpiece of their culture, one that involves elaborate ceremonies celebrating the fish's return to the Trinity each year.

Native Americans' deep reverence for the natural world has given them a mythical, iconic status within the environmental movement. In the real world they often live in the shadows, struggling with poverty and alcoholism. In this context, the Hoopa effort is all the more remarkable—

an attempt, against great odds, to restore the basic values of their culture to a central role in reservation life and a refusal to allow themselves to be defined, and marginalized, by the larger society.

The Hoopas, through a combination of geography and cultural tradition, have tied their hopes and their future to the natural resources of their region; they've always been too far off the beaten track to capitalize on the casino craze sweeping other reservations. Theirs is an important contribution to the public debate over California's increasingly scarce supplies of fresh water.

Not a moment too soon, they're bringing a healthy dose of sanity to a society that sometimes seems hell-bent on exhausting what we have left.

October 4, 2004

Tim Holt is a freelance journalist and author who lives in the Mount Shasta region of Northern California.

River Redux

Matt Jenkins

Three generations ago, the San Joaquin River was home to one of the largest chinook salmon runs on the West Coast. Spawning fish returned from the ocean in such large numbers that local farmers speared them with pitchforks and fed them to their hogs. Then, in 1939, the federal Bureau of Reclamation began pouring the first of 4.3 million tons of concrete to build Friant Dam and supply water to farms from Fresno to Bakersfield.

For a couple of years after the dam was completed in 1945, the bureau still released some water downstream, and the chinook adapted and began spawning in pools below the dam. In 1948, a crew from the state Division of Fish and Game lent the fish a hand, trapping two thousand salmon from the lower reaches of the river, trucking them past a dried-up stretch, and releasing them in those pools.

By 1949, however, the Bureau was holding back the river's entire flow behind Friant Dam. Undaunted, the Fish and Game crew erected a makeshift webbing dam in an attempt to force the fish up the Merced River at its confluence with the San Joaquin. George Warner, a member of the crew, would later write: "Despite very poor water quality they pushed and probed at the webbing, trying to get up their home stream. The small San Joaquin was mostly warm return irrigation water loaded with salts and chemicals. In contrast, the Merced flow was clear, purer, and much cooler. But it was not home stream water."

A year later, San Joaquin spring-run chinook went extinct. "The damage done to the San Joaquin is some of the most extreme environmental damage caused by any water project anywhere," says Hal Candee, an attorney with the Natural Resources Defense Council, which has been trying for the past eighteen years to force the federal government to restore flows for fish in the river. Now, the fight is finally reaching a resolution that may mark a new, albeit grudging, era of compromise, one that highlights the challenges of returning fish to a river, and a world, far different from sixty years ago.

The quest to revive the San Joaquin began in 1988, when the Friant water users' forty-year contracts came up for renewal. The Natural Resources Defense Council (NRDC) sued the federal government, charging that renewing the contracts without "reallocating" some water back to the river would violate the federal Endangered Species and National Environmental Policy acts.

"We considered it a nuisance lawsuit initially," says Kole Upton, the chairman of the Friant Water Users Authority. But the NRDC borrowed a legal doctrine forged in the landmark fight to halt Los Angeles' water diversions from Mono Lake, on the eastern side of the Sierra. That battle helped establish that a long-neglected part of the California fish and game code—known as Section 5937—imposed a "public trust" responsibility on the state to protect fish populations below dams, above and beyond federal environmental law.

"What's trailblazing is the applicability of those principles to a federal project," says Phil Atkins-Patterson, an attorney representing the NRDC in the lawsuit.

As the San Joaquin case dragged on, the farmers began losing ground. In 1999, after the Ninth Circuit Court of Appeals upheld a lower court's ruling that the federal government had violated the Endangered Species Act when it allowed the contracts to simply roll over, the Friant water users began settlement negotiations.

"It was a tough call, whether to cooperate and try to make this work, or do an all-out fight and force society to make a decision to dry up this community to try to restore a river that's been dead for sixty years," Upton says.

The negotiations turned on the contentious issue of how much water the farmers would have to give up to restore the river, and in 2003 the discussions fell apart on exactly that point. The following year, however, U.S. District Judge Lawrence Karlton ruled that, under Section 5937 of state law, the federal government was required to release as much water as necessary to restore the "historic" fishery.

But as both sides exchanged evidence in preparation for trial, they discovered an opportunity for a settlement. "Our experts were indicating that [a restoration program] would take about a third of our water," says Upton. "We'd have to start fallowing land, and some farmers would just have to get out." But the NRDC's consultants projected that the restoration could be successful if the farmers gave up about 19 percent of their water, an average of 242,000 acre-feet a year. (An acre-foot is the amount of water that will cover an acre, one foot deep.)

"In this case," says Upton, "we were willing to say the enviros were right—as long as we're not held accountable if they're wrong."

On September 13, the two sides finalized the 19 percent settlement. Longtime water observer Dan Beard, who headed the Bureau of Reclamation from 1993 to 1995 and is now a private consultant, says the pact is especially important because the federal government "gave away all the water in the river and was unwilling to take the political heat to take the water back." The NRDC intervention and the resulting settlement agreement, he says, show that "when the federal government and the state government won't do their job, you can solve these problems."

The salmon-restoration program—which includes a raft of measures to return the long-dry river channel to its historic shape, to re-establish native vegetation, to protect surrounding land with levees, and to provide fish passage around obstructions below Friant Dam—could cost as much as $800 million. Much of that will come from redirecting payments that the farmers currently make—which go into a general environmental-protection pool and to pay off the cost of the dam itself—into the more specific San Joaquin-restoration program. The rest will come from state and federal funding. This November, California approved Proposition 84, a ballot initiative that could provide up to $200 million for the effort. The state's congressional delegation is also seeking some $250 million in federal funding.

Participants in the settlement say that the commitment of the state and federal governments is critical to the twenty-year restoration program. Federal funding for another ambitious program, the effort to restore the San Francisco Bay-Delta, has essentially evaporated in recent years.

Under the plan, salmon will be reintroduced to the San Joaquin in 2012. "You're talking about a relatively small amount of salmon," says Peter Moyle, a professor of fish biology at the University of California, Davis who serves as a consultant to the Natural Resources Defense Council. "In a way, it's almost a symbolic run. But you get a river out of it, and that's what's really important."

As tenacious as the San Joaquin salmon were, the Friant Dam did wipe them out, and finding a twenty-first-century replacement required some twenty-first-century thinking. Earlier this year, Moyle recommended that the San Joaquin reintroduction program use a strain of chinook salmon from Butte Creek, near Chico. Moyle's recommendation came largely because the Butte Creek strain is very plentiful. But, he says, those fish may also prove especially resilient in the face of global warming.

"There is an advantage to fish that can exist in warmer water, surviving at temperatures, it seems, that should be lethal," he says. "That's always a plus, because you never know what's going to happen."

December 11, 2006

Matt Jenkins is a *High Country News* contributing editor.

Border Restoration's Odd Couple

Morgan Heim

In the borderlands of southwestern Arizona lie the remains of Hunters Hole, a clump of tangled marshland sprawling across the lower Colorado River. This four hundred and forty-acre wetland just south of Yuma was once so full of ducks people couldn't sleep for all the quacking, and an angler could snare a fish so fat it filled a frying pan. Cocopah Indians relied on the bounty of Hunters Hole in days when the only line separating the United States from Mexico was the river itself. As new settlers moved in, the area became a cross-cultural meeting place, where German farmers fished and hunted alongside tribal members.

"It was a way of life," says Cocopah elder Colin Soto, "not just for Cocopah, but for everybody."

That life faded over the last century as the once-full flows of the Colorado turned to little more than a trickle; invasive trees overran the shores, and communities changed. Rather than a place teeming with flotillas of birds and fish, Hunters Hole became a dense thicket of tamarisk, littered with the occasional old car, discarded shoes, and bullet shells. It became a forgotten place, where bandits and illegal immigrants hid amid the brush. "That camaraderie, the social ties didn't really exist anymore," says Soto. "It all dwindled down to nothing without anyone really noticing."

Now, almost thirty groups, ranging from the Cocopah Indian Tribe to the U.S. Border Patrol, are teaming up to rescue this degraded habitat and rid it of crime. This effort entails the unlikely marriage of habitat restoration and national security. "I guess we all have the same goal in mind," says Arizona Border Patrol supervisory agent Carlos Dominguez. "Restore the area and make it safer."

That common ground has not always existed. The Border Patrol has been criticized for tearing up the desert as it pursues illegal immigrants. And while a proposed border fence could keep out border crossers who litter and trample sensitive ecosystems, it would also close important wildlife corridors.

Occasionally, the Border Patrol has helped with restoration, but mostly in a peripheral sense. Earlier this summer, Dominguez was one of several agents cleaning up trash along the California border, and recently, Arizona-based Border Patrol agents guarded workers as they cleared roughly a hundred acres of non-native vegetation from the Cocopah Tribe's western reservation.

The Hunters Hole project significantly advances the Border Patrol's role in restoring borderland habitat. Planners see the project as a possible alternative to "the fence," as well as a way to foster more environmentally friendly patrolling efforts.

The project is coming none too soon. Crime has invaded the lower Colorado as though it were a derelict urban neighborhood. At least two people a year have been murdered there since 2004, and during the last year and a half alone, there were more than two hundred and fifty armed robberies involving at least fifteen hundred victims, says Yuma County Sheriff Lieutenant David McBride, an eightfold increase from the previous year. Most of those victims, he says, are illegal immigrants.

But police officers have also fallen prey to area bandits: since 2005, twenty have been injured, and there have been more than fifty assaults on officers. Twenty-foot-high walls of tangled branches mask people standing ten feet away, says Dominguez, making bandits virtually invisible. "I wouldn't send my worst enemy down there to hunt or fish," agrees lead restoration planner Fred Phillips. "Hunters Hole is rampant with crime."

Violence and the lack of strong partnerships hindered previous restoration efforts. But now, the Border Patrol and the Yuma County sheriff have agreed to provide protection to researchers and other volunteers as they work in the field. "In order to restore Hunters Hole, we're going to have to secure it," says Dominguez.

The effort to clean up Hunters Hole is modeled on the nearby Yuma East Wetlands project, a roughly fourteen hundred-acre wetland adjacent to town. Though situated farther from the border than Hunters Hole, the Yuma East Wetlands exhibited similar problems—a degraded and trashed wetland, harboring vagrants and illegal activity.

The marsh is an important Quechan tribal area, and in late 2005, the tribe began working with Phillips and other collaborators, including the Yuma Crossing Natural Heritage Area, on restoration. In contrast to the sluggish pace of many environmental-recovery efforts, sections of East Yuma were transformed in little more than a year, with native cattail marshes and flocks of migratory birds replacing tangles of saltcedar and trash. One can now visit areas like Ibis Lake Marsh to watch great egrets tip-toeing amongst the reeds.

Hunters Hole should be a similar project, except that along with restoring the wetland, crews will also incorporate patrol routes and levees into the landscape, melding security into the natural environment.

Restoration crews will excavate five miles of existing canal swamped by invasive vegetation and replant its banks with native cattail, bulrush, and mesquite. Groundwater wells will re-supply water to the dried-out wetlands as well as to a sixty-foot-wide channel running the length of Hunters Hole. And native vegetation will blanket the entire area, opening the view to illegal activity and providing habitat for wildlife, such as the endangered southwestern willow flycatcher and Yuma clapper rail.

Phillips estimates the project's cost to be about $7 million, funded primarily through grants. He has already received almost $200,000 from sources such as the Yuma Crossing Natural Heritage Area, the U.S. Bureau of Reclamation, and the Walton Family Foundation. Restoration, says Phillips, should be under way by early 2008.

In the meantime, Cocopah elder Soto looks forward to a day when wildlife returns to Hunters Hole, and the river near his home is once again filled with fish. For him, restoration is a necessity, a treasure beyond all price: "We have a saying," he says. "If the river dies, we die."

September 3, 2007

Morgan Heim is a freelance journalist and photographer.

A River Sacrificed

Gisela Telis

Every September in south-central Washington, the gates of Tieton Dam open and the Tieton River pours through. More than a half-million gallons of water flow each minute for forty-five days. The sudden and sustained surge sends the river raging and frothing through the Yakima Basin, brimming against its banks with the kind of force that fuels whitewater-rafting businesses and earns mentions in travel guides.

This human-made flood was born from the best intentions. In 1980, the U.S. Bureau of Reclamation found itself taken to task—and to court—by the Yakama Nation for allowing culturally and religiously significant spring chinook salmon runs to decline. Forced by a federal court decision to develop a way to manage water that would help Yakima River spring chinook recover, fish biologists invented the system called "flip-flop," which alternates flows in the Yakima and Naches rivers to serve both farming and fish. And for a while, it seemed to work: farmers got their water in the key late-summer and early-fall dry periods, and the spring chinook rebounded, albeit modestly.

But the compromise was paid for by the Tieton, a tributary of the Naches. The river's artificial lows and highs make survival difficult for its native steelhead, a species now listed as threatened under the Endangered Species Act. "We did this to the Tieton so we wouldn't continue to do what we were doing to the Yakima chinook," says Dale Bambrick, the eastern Washington branch chief of the National Marine Fisheries Service. "We've turned this river into a biological desert."

And new research suggests flip-flop may also take an unexpected toll on the Yakima spring chinook, the very fish it was designed to protect. Faced with the possible failure of the system, the Yakama Nation, the irrigation districts, and the federal and state agencies that regulate Yakima water and wildlife, once fierce opponents, must now work together to decide the future of the basin's fish.

The Yakima Basin is a green blot in a rolling, rainless sagebrush landscape, its five hundred thousand irrigated acres famous for fruit, hops, and wine grapes. The basin flourishes thanks to elaborate waterworks: the Yakima and the Naches and their tributaries, plus six reservoirs, dams, irrigation channels, and the flip-flop system.

For the century before the 1980 court decision, business as usual meant fish were a "fleeting" thought for the Bureau, admits Bureau biologist Scott Kline. Rivers were run primarily for irrigation; once the irrigating season ended in October, dam gates closed and rivers dried to save water for next year.

"Every single salmon nest was killed, and any fish out there rearing was killed," says John Easterbrooks, regional fisheries program manager for the Washington Department of Fish and Wildlife, who has worked in the basin for thirty years. "They turned it on and off like a faucet."

The dams and fluctuating flows pushed the basin's seagoing, or anadromous, salmon population—which once included sockeye, coho, chinook, and steelhead—to extinction. Sockeye succumbed to dams within four years of their construction, while overfishing and development extirpated the coho by the 1970s. The changing flows destroyed chinook eggs, eliminating summer chinook and drastically reducing spring chinook numbers.

Salmon spawning in high flows sometimes made their nests, or "redds," in riverbed gravel near the shores. These redds then dried up in winter, when the water levels dropped so low that much of the riverbed was exposed. By the late 1970s, spring chinook salmon, so named for their springtime return from the ocean, had dwindled from hundreds of thousands of fish to a few hundred.

When Bob Tuck went to work for the Yakama Nation in 1979, he was the only anadromous-fish biologist in the basin. "The feds and state had given up on eastern Washington," he says. "Those were pretty desperate times."

In October of 1980, Tuck was out looking for redds on the Yakima River when he witnessed firsthand how reduced water flows expose redds and kill eggs. "The river was literally dropping out from under me," he recalls. He ran to a nearby home and used the phone to call the Bureau. "I told them, 'Stop what you're doing.' And that drew some attention."

It also spurred the Yakama to action: the tribe took the Bureau to court over its treaty-guaranteed fishing rights, and won. U.S. District Court Judge Justin L. Quackenbush ordered the Bureau to protect the redds and put a committee of local fish biologists—including Tuck and Easterbrooks—in place to advise them. The rest was up to the Bureau.

After months of contention between the tribe, the committee, the Bureau, and farmers, flip-flop began. From April to September, the Bureau would continue, as it had for decades, to release reservoir water into the Yakima River for diversion into irrigation channels downstream. But in September, when the spring chinook spawn, the agency would ramp down the Yakima's flow to force the salmon to make their redds lower in the stream, where they would remain water covered through the winter. Simultaneously, the Bureau would ramp up flows on the Tieton, creating a torrent that would then flow into the Naches and downstream for irrigation.

This meant sacrificing the Tieton, which was already damaged by highway development and the construction of Tieton Dam and its reservoir, Rimrock Lake, in the 1920s. The Tieton was smaller than the Yakima, with a steepness and a propensity to flash flood that made it inhospitable to spring chinook. Tuck, who grew up in the Yakima Basin and wrote his master's thesis on its fish, remembers it running bone-dry in winter, bereft of chinook.

"We wrote [the Tieton] off as a fish producer in exchange for lower flows in the Yakima," Easterbrooks says. "We thought we weren't losing a lot, creating flip-flop and sacrificing the Tieton."

What they were losing, however, were steelhead trout. They just didn't know it yet.

"The Tieton is a big piece of real estate—just because you don't see fish doesn't mean they're not there," Bambrick notes. "Before the dam, the Tieton had one of the most important steelhead populations," and even after the dam was completed in 1925, steelhead may have still numbered in the hundreds.

When the extreme flows of flip-flop began, they flushed out young steelhead in the Tieton and, to a lesser extent, the Naches, along with the seeds of cottonwoods and other riparian plants and the aquatic insects on which steelhead depend. What Kline likes to call "the food of the river" was gone, and the steelhead with it.

But spring chinook, not steelhead, were the basin's concern until 2000, when steelhead were listed as threatened. The listing prompted a review of flip-flop. As required by the Endangered Species Act, the Bureau submitted a new biological assessment and plan for water management in the Yakima Basin to the National Marine Fisheries Service (NMFS) in 2003. NMFS responded with a biological opinion that asked the Bureau to recognize the extent of flip-flop's impact on steelhead and to either tweak the alternating flows for their benefit or help with other recovery efforts. But persistent disagreements with the Bureau meant that the biological opinion was never signed or made public. "We concluded, 'That's bad,' " says Bambrick, "and the Bureau concluded, 'So what?' "

Its impact on steelhead aside, flip-flop may not be the best way to protect spring chinook either. Armed with nearly thirty years of data—a luxury Tuck and Easterbrooks didn't have—Steve Cramer, an independent fisheries consultant hired by the irrigators, has found that the alternating water flows on the Yakima River protect spring chinook eggs at the expense of stable habitat in which the salmon can grow once they hatch. Despite the Bureau's efforts to moderate Yakima flows, the summer's releases disrupt plant and insect life and make natural shelters for juvenile spring chinook scarce.

The Yakama Nation's most recent annual salmon count turned up 2,495 returning wild spring chinook in a river system that historically may have seen two hundred thousand. Cramer's report suggests those numbers won't increase until fish and water managers strike a better balance between protecting redds and protecting rearing habitat, which might mean modifying or doing away with flip-flop. Until then, says Yakama Nation biologist Mark Johnston, spring chinook are "just hanging on."

In Washington, as in the rest of the world, no environmental story is complete without climate change. A 2005 study by scientists at the Pacific

Northwest National Laboratory in Richland, Washington, estimates that Yakima Basin water available for irrigation will drop 20 to 40 percent by midcentury due to global warming.

The finding supports what Stan Isley, a specialist with the Washington State Department of Ecology Water Resources Program, has long suspected: no amount of water conservation or tinkering with flows can keep both farming and fish healthy in the Yakima Basin—not without water from somewhere else.

Jack Stanford, a University of Montana ecology professor with an abiding love for the basin, agrees. That's why he proposes pumping water from the nearby Columbia River directly into the region's irrigation channels, supplying farmers while bypassing the river system entirely. It's a streamlined version of another proposal, the Black Rock Project. Currently under study by the Bureau, the billion-dollar plan would store Columbia River water for both irrigation and fish in a massive reservoir just east of the basin. Although the basin's farmers have been calling for more water storage for fifty years, the project's price tag and potential impact continue to raise concerns.

For now, Bambrick, Johnston, and their colleagues are tying their hopes to more mundane developments. After a four-year stalemate, new blood in the Bureau has brought a new willingness to work with the NMFS. Representatives from the two agencies, the Washington Department of Fish and Wildlife, and the Yakama and agricultural communities plan to meet regularly in the coming year, to work on a revised biological assessment due early next summer. Bambrick and his colleagues hope the resulting plan and biological opinion will mean relief and restoration for the Tieton, and more protection for all of the basin's fish.

In the end, it may come down to the Yakama Nation. As the tribe balances the rivers' health with its own irrigation districts and plans for development, it stands to win or lose in ways that "transcend history or economy," says Stanford. For the Yakama, the whole river system matters, and their livelihood and their identity are at stake.

"This is who we are as a people," says Phil Rigdon, the deputy director of natural resources for the Yakama and a member of the tribe. "People make this into an environmental issue. But it's a people issue. Why is one economy more important than the other? Ours was the first economy."

December 24, 2007

Gisela Telis is a freelance writer and photographer based in Tucson, Arizona.

Riparian Restoration Guru

James R. Kristofic

In a two-hour conversation about rivers, Bill Zeedyk never once uses the word "water."

Instead, the stocky, soft-spoken septuagenarian speaks of a river as if it's an animal, one that migrates in seasonal floods, erodes banks to make room for itself, and struggles to evolve a level of flow that will nurture the surrounding habitat.

But that balance can be difficult to achieve in the delicate landscapes of the arid Southwest. Invasive trees can armor a stream's banks and force it to dig too deep and fast, while cattle can overgraze grasses and shrubs that prevent erosion. Mismanaged rural roads can gash a stream's channel like a knife opening a blood vessel.

Zeedyk has spent more than a decade developing "induced meandering," a technique using wood and rock structures to help damaged streams "re-evolve" a healthy flow. He's promoted his restoration methods through the Quivira Coalition—an environmental organization that works with ranchers and conservationists throughout the West—and Zeedyk Ecological Consulting, LLC, a "two-person show" he runs with his wife out of their home in Sandia Park, New Mexico.

Zeedyk has put hundreds of thousands of miles on his pickup traveling around the Southwest to give his induced meandering workshops. One of his trips takes him more than two hundred miles to Comanche Creek in northern New Mexico, where he's worked with the state environmental department to restore habitat for the nearly endangered native cutthroat trout.

White beard framing his weathered face, brimmed hat riding low over his eyes, a staff in his hand, Zeedyk resembles a wandering wizard as he watches for clues to the Comanche's problems. He examines the stream with the studied patience he developed as a teenager, fishing and canoeing in New

Jersey and Maryland, a trait later honed over thirty-five years as a Forest Service biologist.

Then he breaks out diagrams and sketches to teach a mixed crowd of ranchers, conservationists, scientists, fly-fishermen, and other volunteers how to turn the gullied waterway into a more riparian area of green trees and lush grass that supports an array of plants and animals.

But first he has to get his audience to think like a river.

"That's actually the hardest part," Zeedyk says. "It's difficult for them to understand what a healthy riparian [environment] looks like."

To demonstrate, he shows before-and-after pictures of his baby: the Pueblo Colorado Wash in Ganado, Arizona.

When Zeedyk took on that project with the Park Service and the Navajo Nation in 1997, the wash was a twelve-foot-deep incised arroyo as wide as an elevator shaft, choked with invasive tamarisk and Russian olive trees. Today, canopies of cottonwoods and tender tribes of willows populate sandbars along a channel as wide as a four-lane highway. Grasshoppers tick and fly through bulrush reeds as long as Zeedyk's forearm. Tracks of mule deer and coyote pattern along the trickling current.

But Zeedyk doesn't talk too long. It's time to build the structures.

They fit along the stream channel almost like the fixtures in a pinball machine. The volunteers set up baffles, thick wooden posts arranged like half-buried bowling pins that bounce a stream's current into an opposite bank and create a meander that will slow the flow. They install wicker-weirs, small fences of woven sticks and branches that create riffles. They build post veins that angle out into the current like paddles and capture sediment to grow sandbars that eventually host trees and grasses along the banks.

Zeedyk likes to see the crowd working with their hands.

"There seems to be a mentality that the quickest way to do something is with a bulldozer. That's not necessarily true. You can change the course of a river by hand. So I've been trying to develop techniques that empower individuals to try rather than say, 'It's not worth it to try.'"

Zeedyk's ideas might move against some human currents. He remembers a hands-on exhibit at a local museum that ran water through a sandbox and challenged visitors to prevent erosion. Zeedyk set up miniature versions of his structures in the water's path, then watched a group of people approach the exhibit.

They tore out his structures and built dams.

July 3, 2008

James R. Kristofic is a journalism and writing teacher in eastern Pennsylvannia, where he lives with his amazing wife.

Riparian Repair

Cleo Woelflie-Erskine

Brooks Priest stands next to a massive beaver dam twelve feet above the churning waters of the Blackfoot River. When workers breached the Milltown Dam on March 28 this year, falling water levels left the beavers high and dry. Armed with a mean hoedag swing and a resource conservation degree, Priest has worked to restore rivers across the West, and her latest project is here at Milltown.

"If only the beavers could teach the human engineers," the keen-eyed, wiry Priest says, looking up at the giant mound of sticks. She has a soft spot for "nature's engineers," she says. "They're the real restoration experts."

The Milltown Dam, built in 1907 at the Clark Fork-Blackfoot confluence near Missoula, once submerged about a mile of the Blackfoot's narrow floodplain and the Clark Fork's wide valley. After the dam went up, millions of tons of arsenic and toxic tailings collected behind it, washed down from copper, silver, and gold mines near the Clark Fork's Butte headwaters. In 1983, one hundred and twenty miles of the upper Clark Fork basin were designated as a Superfund site. The Milltown dam removal was a key part of the Superfund cleanup, and now that it's gone, a levee diverts the river into a straight, riprapped channel.

Behind the levee, bulldozers scrape toxic muck out of rectangular pits, and freight cars haul it one hundred and fifty miles upstream to dump. Above the diversion, the river splits and reconverges in a tangle of silver threads around sandbars littered with toppled birches and alders. High flows this year ate away huge swaths of bank and obliterated several large islands.

The Clark Fork is sick, and no one is sure how to heal it. All agree on the need "to get the poison out of the wound," says Joel Chavez, an engineer with the Montana Department of Environmental Quality's abandoned mines program. But there's scant consensus on how to turn a sterile and mutilated floodplain back into a functioning river, here at Milltown or anywhere else in the West.

The $10 million Milltown project exemplifies the re-engineering approach, where crews will bulldoze a new channel after Superfund contractors remove tailings. But some river experts say we should devote more of the $2 billion spent yearly on U.S. river restoration to understanding how rivers like the Clark Fork work. Then we can take action that may not require re-engineering.

Sometimes excluding livestock from riparian areas, or removing key levees and dams to restore flood patterns and sediment movement, is enough to permit degraded rivers to heal themselves. River experts point to Oregon's Sandy River, which quickly washed accumulated sediment downstream after Pacific Gas & Electric blew up Marmot Dam last fall. Coho salmon swam past the dam the day after it was breached, and spawning habitat has greatly improved.

Beginning this fall, bulldozers will cut a single channel across three miles of the Clark Fork and one mile of the Blackfoot floodplains. Natural-looking structures made out of logs, coconut-husk matting, and riprap will keep the river from cutting into the mine waste that remains. Black weed mat will suppress invasive tansy while one hundred and fifty thousand willow, cottonwood, and bulrush seedlings, planted by Priest's crews and others, take root. Officials from the Environmental Protection Agency and the state of Montana promise that once the plants have established, the Clark Fork at the Blackfoot confluence will once again be a "real, dynamic river."

Surveying the scene, Priest says it's not that simple, reflecting the disagreement among river restorationists about whether we can return rivers to health by constructing stable, static channels. "Restoration cowboy" Dave Rosgen, the hydrology consultant who prescribed Milltown's meandering channel, says that carving a single, sinuous channel across a river's old path jumpstarts restoration. In the 1980s, in response to seventy-five years of Army Corps of Engineers' "fixing" that straitjacketed thousands of river miles for flood control and navigation, Rosgen came up with a straightforward method for evaluating and redesigning streams. His techniques are now used by agencies from the U.S. Department of Transportation to the Forest Service.

But many geomorphologists, who study how rivers shape the landscape, fault Rosgen's method for using a simplified template instead of a detailed study of how rivers move sediment. They note that river channels evolve in a complex interplay of water flow and the bounce and skid of waterborne sand and gravel. Although the Rosgen method is based on the notion that river channels are stable, aerial surveys show they wind across landscapes unpredictably. Old meanders yield to new meanders, to oxbows, and often intermittently to braids. Season to season, year to year, few rivers stay in the same place. In fact, over-simplifying complex rivers can lead to catastrophe, scientists warn. On Cuneo and Uvas creeks in California, costly Rosgen-inspired reconstruction projects blew out during small floods in 1996 and '97.

The Clark Fork restoration plan recreates a river that never existed, says University of Montana geologist Johnnie Moore. He worries that the reconstructed Clark Fork will be "some kind of reinforced ditch," albeit a curving, natural-looking one. The Clark Fork was once "a true, multi-threaded alluvial river," says Moore. Government surveys dating back to the 1840s depict five distinct channels. Beginning in the 1870s, a mining boom spurred logging, and railroads constricted the channels. Snow melted faster on newly clear-cut slopes; log drives scraped willow-covered islands away, and the river braided even more. Then, in 1908, a massive flood swept across the poisoned wasteland around Anaconda, carrying mountains of tailings that settled in the new Milltown reservoir.

One hundred years later, the river branches across the valley like the veins in a butterfly's wing. So why build a single channel? Money—and aesthetics. Doug Martin, restoration project manager for the Montana Natural Resources Damage Program, says building a multi-thread channel at Milltown would be trickier, and not cost effective. What's more, it would mean removing all 6.6 million cubic yards of mine waste. The EPA plans to let ARCO, the company that inherited the Superfund cleanup, leave a third of the waste behind. Besides, a meandering channel fits a cultural ideal of what rivers should look like, says UC-Berkeley landscape ecologist Matt Kondolf.

The bigger issue in restoration, though, isn't single channel versus multiple threads; most rivers left alone will display sections of both. Rather, it's the question of strict human control over the intricate and gradual patterns of natural processes. Over-controlled rivers stop functioning, some scientists say, becoming what University of Colorado geomorphologist Ellen Wohl calls "virtual rivers," because floods and crucial processes like beaver damming and log jamming are thwarted.

The Clark Fork restoration plan aims for a delicate balance of control: hold the banks in place until plants grow in, about fifteen years, then allow the river to migrate slowly across the reconstructed floodplain. Moore and fellow University of Montana geologist Andrew Wilcox worry that the rigid banks will prevent spring flooding. While the reconstructed channel may look natural, Wilcox says that it won't act like a natural river. Without floods, cottonwoods won't establish and weeds could choke out native shrubs; the diverse ecosystem that nurtures trout and migratory songbirds might never appear. However, if even a minor flood strikes before plants stabilize the banks, Martin says the river could scour out thousands of tons of arsenic and copper-contaminated mud. Toxic sediment released in a 2006 reservoir drawdown caused massive fish kills.

Silver Bow Creek, the Clark Fork's most contaminated tributary, presents a study in miniature of what Milltown might look like some years down the line. In 2000, Brooks Priest helped start a twenty-five-mile, eleven-year restoration project on Silver Bow. Workers excavated mine tailings, dumped hilltop soil on the floodplain, and carved a gracefully curved channel. Pockets of tailings remain, marked by aqua or rust-orange crystals. Even so, last year's restoration reach looks pretty good. Bunchgrasses, currants, and sagebrush cover most of the soil. A few fish are back, and killdeer fly between ponds. Downstream, islands of bright green trees erupt from gray clay. State officials consider the Silver Bow Creek restoration a resounding success — "almost a miracle," according to Greg Mullen, the restoration coordinator for the state's natural resources damage program.

But other restoration experts see plenty of room for improvement in the attempt to return Silver Bow Creek to full health. Karin Boyd, a geomorphologist and consultant on the project, wants to incorporate branching sections, to mimic the way beaver dams once split the creek's flow. In the project area, actual beaver are trapped and removed to protect new trees. Along the Silver Bow, restoration leader Priest surveys this year's restoration reach, with its fabric-armored creek banks and bulldozers stuck in the mire. "This will look how most people think a river should look ... but it's not a dynamic ecosystem." Dynamic rivers, with their wandering channels and complex floodplains, seem chaotic to people, but require less long-term maintenance and support more species diversity.

With a fleet of Bobcats and ATVs at hand, Priest speaks wistfully of the humble beaver, which evolved with North American rivers and is largely responsible for their pre-European settlement flows. Beavers by instinct follow the prime directive of process-based restoration: you can't make an instant river. What you can do is provide ample detritus and room for the river to wander and recreate its own stability and health. In the late 1990s, the Zuni Fish and Wildlife Department in New Mexico relocated twenty-three beaver to a reservation stream. Within three years, the beavers built a series of dams that raised the water table, flooding out invasive tamarisk and regenerating the willow forest. On Utah's Provo River and California's Cosumnes River, flood-control levees cut off the rivers from their floodplains. Over the past decade, state agencies have purchased floodplain land, then breached the levees. On the Cosumnes, native fish populations rebounded, flood risk declined, and willow and cottonwood survival has improved. Breaches and multi-thread channel reconstruction on the Provo show similar improvements.

But despite their success, such long-term strategies are generally out of sync with government funding cycles. Finding money to buy floodplains is difficult, so single-channel reconstruction "quick fixes" predominate.

Our predecessors streamlined crooked streams with dynamite and built thousands of dams. Now, some scientists and restoration practitioners envision a new kind of stewardship wherein we modify infrastructure to survive wildfires, droughts, and floods, then let natural processes take their course. But on most western rivers, the dams, railroads, highways, and floodplain development that constrict river floodplains will remain. River-restoration design will simply have to adapt. Ecological-restoration experts wonder just how much we've learned from our earlier meddling.

"We might do a $10 million remedy at Milltown, then realize that's not where the river means to be," says Pat Munday, professor of history at Montana Tech University in Butte. "The question is, will we have the money to re-do it?"

August 25, 2008

Cleo Woelfle-Erskine has worked on river restoration projects in New Mexico, California, and Montana, where he now lives.

Acknowledgements

This volume, along with its companion, *Water in the 21st-Century West*, has as many sources as the west has rivers. Its origins spring from a conversation with Mary Braun, the wondrous editor at Oregon State University Press, who wondered whether it was time to update an earlier anthology on western water issues that also derived from *High Country News'* remarkable archive. She was right, I realized, after but a day of reading through its extensive coverage over the past decade. Paul Larmer, *High Country News'* executive director and publisher, enthusiastically agreed with the project. Strikingly, neither hesitated when several months later I suggested that we split an overly long initial volume into two, providing a broader representation of the magazine's investigations into the region's riparian systems, its lakes, seeps, and aquifers, and the biota that depend on them.

As critical as their encouragement and support has been, these books would not exist without the articles that *High Country News'* staff and contributors have written. Year after year, issue after issue, the nation's best environmental reporters dig into stories small and large; conduct countless interviews with the high and mighty, the down and out, and everyone in between; and then craft compelling narratives that help us better understand why water has been, and remains, the West's most essential and controversial subject. They write, as *High Country News'* logo puts it, "For people who care about the West," and as you leaf through these pages you will discover just how much these devoted journalists care about that population and the places they call home.

I am grateful as well to Jo Alexander, Tom Booth, and Micki Reaman at OSU Press, for keeping this project on track. At *High Country News* Art Director Cindy Wehling and Marketing Manager JoAnn Kalenak have been indispensable. And I owe many thanks to Gary Kates, Rick Hazlett, and Helena Wall at Pomona College, who brought me to this idyllic campus as a visiting professor, and then urged me to create a new class on water in the West—they were convinced students would leap at the chance to engage one another on such a profoundly important topic. They were right, and the extraordinary conversations that have flowed up, down, and across the seminar table (and out the door) are one more inspiration for these compendiums. I can think of no better way to thank my amazing students for their insights, commitment, and laughter than to dedicate *River Basins of the American West* and *Water in the 21st-Century West* to them.

Char Miller
Claremont, California

Index